D1016934

Grief Counseling and
Grief Therapy

NATIONAL UNIVERSITY LIBRARY

SACRAMENTO *e l*

J. William Worden, Ph.D., is a professor of psychology at the Harvard Medical School and at the Rosemead School of Psychology (California). His 20 years of research and clinical work has centered on issues of life-threatening illness and behavior. Currently he is the Principal Investigator for the Boston Child Bereavement Study based at the Massachusetts General Hospital. He received his undergraduate degree from Pomona College and holds graduate degrees from Eastern Seminary, Harvard University, and Boston University in the areas of theology, education, and clinical psychology. Dr. Worden has lectured and written extensively on topics related to terminal illness, cancer care, and grief. He is the author of *Personal Death Awareness* and the coauthor of *Helping Cancer Patients Cope*.

Grief Counseling
and Grief Therapy

A Handbook for the Mental Health Practitioner

Second Edition

J. William Worden, Ph.D.

NATIONAL UNIVERSITY LIBRARY
SACRAMENTO c 1

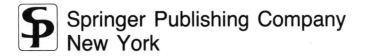 Springer Publishing Company
New York

Copyright © 1991 by Springer Publishing Company, Inc.

All rights reserved

No part of this publication may be reproduced, stored in a
retrieval system, or transmitted in any form or by any means,
electronic, mechanical, photocopying, recording, or otherwise,
without the prior permission of Springer Publishing Company, Inc.

Springer Publishing Company, Inc.
536 Broadway
New York, NY 10012-3955

90 91 92 93 94 / 5 4 3 2 1

Library of Congress Cataloging-in-Publication Data

Worden, J. William (James William), 1932–
    Grief counseling and grief therapy : a handbook for the mental
health practitioner / J. William Worden — 2nd ed.
        p.   cm.
    Includes bibliographical references.
    Includes index.
    ISBN 0–8261–4161–7
    1. Grief. 2. Bereavement—Psychological aspects. 3. Mental
health counseling. I. Title.
    [DNLM: 1. Counseling—methods. 2. Grief. 3. Psychotherapy—
methods.   WM 55 W924g]
    RC455.4.L67W67   1991
    616.89'14—dc20
    DNLM/DLC
    for Library of Congress   90-10422
                                                                    CIP

Printed in the United States of America

For information about our audio products, write us at:
Newbridge Book Clubs, 3000 Cindel Drive, Delran, NJ   08370

To My Mother and Father

Contents

Preface

It has been nine years since the first edition of *Grief Counseling and Grief Therapy* was published. In that time there has been a plethora of publications on the subject of grief and bereavement. For this second edition I have extensively reviewed the literature since 1982 and included the best of the new information along with my current thinking on bereavement from my research and clinical work.

Readers of the first edition will see some refinements in my thinking and will find several new areas of discussion. For example, there is now a section on the bereavement of AIDS survivors and there is also a section on working with the elderly. Because much bereavement counseling takes place in a group setting, I have included a section addressing factors to consider when setting up a group. In this section are suggestions to help leaders deal with difficult behaviors that often arise in group work.

An extensive and carefully selected bibliography at the end of the book should be helpful to those desiring to read more on a given topic. This can be a valuable resource for students and others planning to do research in this area, a pursuit I strongly encourage.

Special acknowledgments are due a number of people who assisted me with this project. I would like to thank Naji Abi-Hashem for his help in tracking down the vast amount of recent literature and Marilyn Weller for her encouragement and proficient editorial work. My appreciation is also extended to Karin Worden, Pam Grant, Jan Alarcon, Roy Neuner, Kevin Gilleland, and Nancy Vandevanter for their assistance. And, as always, my family and friends provided important emotional support.

JWW
Boston, Massachusetts
Laguna Niguel, California

Only people who are capable of loving strongly can also suffer great sorrow, but this same necessity of loving serves to counteract their grief and heals them.

Tolstoy

Grief Counseling and
Grief Therapy

Introduction

Over the past 20 years health care professionals have shown an increased interest in issues related to death and dying. Accompanying this has been an increased interest in the related subject of grief and bereavement. This book is aimed at helping mental health practitioners to better understand the complex phenomenon of bereavement in order to help those who mourn resolve their grieving in a healthy manner.

Why should mental health professionals be interested and involved in the area of bereavement? The answer is simple. People come for mental health treatment feeling stuck in their grieving. They come believing that they are not passing through the experience, that mourning is not coming to an end, and that they need help to get through it and get back to living. Also, grief often surfaces as the underlying cause of various physical and mental aberrations. People seek physical and mental health care without necessarily recognizing that there may be a grief issue underlying their particular physical or mental condition.

Aaron Lazare, a psychiatrist colleague, estimates that 10 to 15 percent of the people who pass through the mental health clinics at the Massachusetts General Hospital have, underneath their particular psychological condition, an unresolved grief reaction (Lazare, 1979). Zisook found that 17 percent of patients entering an outpatient psychiatric facility in California had unresolved grief, according to their own estimate (Zisook, 1985). Psychiatrist John Bowlby confirms this phenomenon when he says, "Clinical experience and a reading of the evidence leave little doubt of the truth of the main proposition—that much psychiatric illness is an expression of pathological mourning—or that such illness includes many cases of anxiety state, depressive illness, and hysteria, and also more than one kind of character disorder" (Bowlby, 1980, p. 23). The mental health practitioner needs to understand grief and to recognize the role it plays in medical and psychiatric problems.

There are a number of studies in the literature that point to the impact of grief on morbidity and mortality. Grief exacerbates not only physical morbidity but psychiatric morbidity as well; this is especially true of morbidity associated with conjugal bereavement, the loss of a spouse. Some of the most significant research relating to physical and psychological symptoms during bereavement was done by Parkes and his associates in London and in Boston (the Harvard Bereavement Study), by Clayton and her associates in St. Louis, by Weiner and associates in New York City, by Crisp and Priest in London, by Heymon and Gianturco at Duke University, and by Shuchter and his collaborators at San Diego.* These studies are significant because they are prospective studies of bereavement. There are numerous retrospective studies and many anecdotal records relating bereavement to various physical and psychiatric diseases, but the prospective studies are the most valid.

The conclusions from these various types of studies of conjugal bereavement are mixed and by no means consistent. One of the difficulties in comparing studies is that they have focused on people from varying age groups, geographical areas, and socioeconomic strata. However, most of these studies do show that the bereaved suffer from more depressive symptoms during the first year after the loss than nonbereaved controls (Parkes & Brown, 1972). In addition, certain studies suggest that young bereaved people have more physical distress and take more drugs for symptom relief than do their married, non-bereaved counterparts (Clayton, 1974). Others show that, for the most part, there are few changes among older men and women in regard to physical health, visits to physicians, and number of hospitalizations (Heymon & Gianturco, 1973). So it seems that though all widows and widowers suffer from significant depressive symptoms in the first year of bereavement, young widows and widowers may have more physical distress (Bowlby, 1980; Clayton, 1979).

In spite of these varied findings, it appears that following the death of a spouse there is an increase of symptoms such as headaches, trembling, dizziness, heart palpitations, and various gastrointestinal symptoms. But there is no increase in specific diseases such as asthma, diabetes, or cancer. It has been suggested that these symptoms of decreased well-being can be manifestations of grief itself as an individual attends to the various bodily sensations of depression (Lieberman & Jacobs, 1987). In addition, there has been increasing interest in the impact of loss on physiological functioning mediated through altered immune responses (Schleifer, 1983).

*References for these studies can be found in the Bibliography.

When looking at the health consequences of bereavement, one must consider masked grief, or what is sometimes called facsimile illness (Zisook & DeVaul, 1976). The survivor may develop symptoms like those experienced by the loved one before the death. Physicians treating grieving people who present with somatic symptoms would do well to solicit information about the deceased's symptoms and assess the possibility of the patient's disorder falling into this category. This will be discussed in greater detail in Chapter 4.

There is also interest in whether or not people who are bereaved require more psychiatric care during the period of mourning. There have been several studies investigating this phenomenon, but as yet the data are also inconclusive. Paula Clayton, in her prospective study of widowhood, concludes that "psychiatric consultation is rare following the death of a spouse. Psychiatric hospitalization is even more rare and probably occurs so infrequently that bereavement need not be considered a cause of mental illness" (Clayton, 1979, p. 1532). Colin Parkes and his colleagues in London hold another viewpoint. They believe that acute grief reactions frequently become chronic, thus making psychiatric intervention necessary (Parkes, 1964, 1965).

A third area being researched is the relationship between conjugal bereavement and mortality. Nearly everyone has heard stories of how one spouse has died a short time after the death of a partner. Men appear to be at special risk. What is the evidence to support this vulnerability to death following the loss of a spouse? Unfortunately, it is inconsistent.

Wolfgang and Margaret Stroebe in West Germany closely examined the studies of mortality and bereavement only to discover that these are inconclusive. They encourage further longitudinal studies that would include alternative explanations for a positive relationship between bereavement and mortality. Other explanations might include the following: (a) both spouses died of a common infection; (b) both spouses shared the same environment unfavorable to health; (c) the surviving spouse no longer had the care of the deceased spouse; (d) loneliness led to physical symptoms; and (e) the bereaved spouse's health was impaired through the increased use of drugs, alcohol, or tobacco (Stroebe & Stroebe, 1987).

K. J. Helsing and colleagues studied the mortality rates of those who had become widowed between 1963 and 1974 in Washington County, Maryland. When matched to a married sample, the researchers found that, after adjusting a number of demographic and behavioral variables, mortality rates based on person-years at risk were about the same for widowed as for married females, but significantly higher for male widowed than male married. Another interesting finding was that men who remarried were at lower risk than men who remained single. This was not true for the women (Helsing et al., 1981). One possible explanation for this might be that only the fittest men remarried.

Two recent studies using large samples, one from Great Britain and the other from Finland, show remarkably similar findings—mortality was higher for both men and women very early after the loss of a spouse. During subsequent years it was slightly higher only for men when compared to their nonbereaved male counterparts. This was especially true for younger men (Jones & Goldblatt, 1987; Kapiro et al., 1987). Although the final word is not in and more good prospective studies are needed, it does seem that the death of a spouse may be associated with a higher mortality for both sexes, with the excess risk much greater for men.

People have been grieving for thousands of years—long before the advent of the mental health professional. Nonetheless, the empirical reality is that people seek us out for help with their grieving. This may be in part because of the secularization of the age. Earlier, people would have looked to religious leaders and religious institutions for help with their grief, but because so many people no longer belong to formal religious organizations, they often turn to the mental health worker. Also, the excessive mobility of our society lends itself to this change of focus. In the past, extended families were close and neighborhoods provided a cohesive bonding which helped people to cope with loss. But now that sense of community may no longer exist to provide immediate support, nor is the extended family as available. Therefore, people turn to the health care system and the mental health system for support and for care that previously would have come from other sources.

Grief has been compared to physical illness. In the Old Testament, the prophet Isaiah admonishes to "bind up the broken-hearted," giving the impression that severe grief can somehow do damage to the heart. Both grief and physical illness take time for healing and, indeed, both of them include emotional and physical aspects. In comparing physical illness and grief, social worker Bertha Simos made this obervation: "Both may be self-limiting or require intervention by others. And in both, recovery can range from a complete return to the pre-existing state of health and well-being, to partial recovery, to improved growth and creativity, or both can inflict permanent damage, progressive decline and even death" (Simos, 1979, p. 30).

Bereavement is a very complex issue and people experience their grief in many and varied ways. Although the main focus in this book is on losses resulting from death, the principles here can apply to mourning various types of losses—divorce, amputation, job loss, and losses experienced by victims of violence are just a few. In this book the mental health worker is presented with the best of our knowledge on the subject in a useful and easily understandable format. Some of this material is presented in outline form, but this does not imply that grieving is a simple or uncomplicated phenomenon.

The balance of this book offers current thinking on the following:

- What people experience following a loss
- Why they experience it
- The four main tasks of mourning
- How to help people with the various grief tasks
- How to know when grief is finished
- How to identify complicated grief
- Ways to treat complicated grief
- How to help families in the resolution of a loss
- How to help people with special loss situations
- How to maximize one's effectiveness as a grief counselor

I don't believe that we need to establish a new profession of grief counselors. D. M. Reilly, a social worker, says, "We do not necessarily need a whole new profession of . . . bereavement counselors. We do need more thought, sensitivity, and activity concerning this issue on the part of the existing professional groups; that is, clergy, funeral directors, family therapists, nurses, social workers and physicians" (Reilly, 1978, p. 49). I couldn't agree more. What I want to do in this book is to address those of you in these traditional professions who are already in a position to extend care to the bereaved and who have the knowledge and skills required to do effective intervention and, in some cases, preventive mental health work.

References

Bowlby, J. (1980). *Attachment and loss: Loss, sadness, and depression* (vol III). New York: Basic Books.

Clayton, P. J. (1974). Mortality and morbidity in the first year of widowhood. *Archives of General Psychiatry, 30,* 747–750.

Clayton, P. J. (1979). The sequelae and nonsequelae of conjugal bereavement. *American Journal of Psychiatry, 136,* 1530–1534.

Helsing, K. J., & Szklo, M. (1981). Mortality after bereavement. *American Journal of Epidemiology, 114,* 41–52.

Heymon, D., & Gianturco, D. (1973). Long term adaptation by the elderly to bereavement. *Journal of Gerontology, 28,* 359–362.

Jones, D. R., & Goldblatt, P. O. (1987). Cause of death in widow(er)s and spouses. *Journal of Biosocial Science, 19,* 107–121.

Kaprio, J., Koskenvuo, M., & Rita, H. (1987). Mortality after bereavement: A prospective study of 95,647 widowed persons. *American Journal of Public Health, 77,* 283–287.

Lazare, A. (1979). Unresolved grief. In A. Lazare (Ed.), *Outpatient psychiatry: Diagnosis and treatment* (pp. 498–512). Baltimore: Williams & Wilkens.

Lieberman, P. B., & Jacobs, S. C. (1987). Bereavement and its complications in medical patients: A guide for consultation-liaison psychiatrists. *International Journal of Psychiatric Medicine, 17,* 23–39.

Parkes, C. M. (1964). Recent bereavement as a cause of mental illness. *British Journal of Psychiatry, 110,* 198–204.

Parkes, C. M. (1965). Bereavement and mental illness, part I: A clinical study of the grief of bereaved psychiatric patients. *British Journal of Medical Psychology, 38,* 1–26.

Parkes, C. M. (1965). Bereavement and mental illness, part II: A classification of bereavement reactions. *British Journal of Medical Psychology, 38,* 13–26.

Parkes, C. M., & Brown, R. J. (1972). Health after bereavement: A controlled study of young Boston widows and widowers. *Psychosomatic Medicine, 34,* 449–461.

Reilly, D. M. (1978). Death propensity, dying, and bereavement: A family systems perspective. *Family Therapy, 5,* 35–55.

Schleifer, S. J., et al. (1983). Suppression of lymphocyte stimulation following bereavement. *Journal of the American Medical Association, 250,* 374–377.

Simos, B. G. (1979). *A time to grieve.* New York: Family Service Association.

Stroebe, W., & Stroebe, M. S. (1987). *Bereavement and health: The psychological and physical consequences of partner loss.* Cambridge: Cambridge University.

Zisook, S., & DeVaul, R. A. (1976). Grief related facsimile illness. *International Journal of Psychiatric Medicine, 7,* 329–336.

Zisook, S., & DeVaul, R. A. (1985). Unresolved grief. *American Journal of Psychoanalysis, 45,* 370–379.

Chapter 1

Attachment, Loss, and the Tasks of Mourning

Attachment Theory

Before one can fully comprehend the impact of a loss and the human behavior associated with it, one must have some understanding of the meaning of attachment. There is considerable writing in the psychological and psychiatric literature as to the nature of attachments—what they are and how they develop. One of the key figures and primary thinkers in this area is British psychiatrist John Bowlby. He has devoted much of his professional career to the area of attachment and loss and has written several substantial volumes as well as a number of articles on the subject.

Bowlby's attachment theory provides a way for us to conceptualize the tendency in human beings to make strong affectional bonds with others and a way to understand the strong emotional reaction that occurs when those bonds are threatened or broken. To develop his theories, Bowlby has cast his net wide and has included data from ethology, control theory, cognitive psychology, neurophysiology, and developmental biology. He takes exception to those who believe that attachment bonds between individuals develop only in order to have certain biological drives met, such as the drive for food or the drive for sex. Reciting from Lorenz's work with animals and Harlow's work with young monkeys, Bowlby points to the·fact that attachment occurs in the absence of the reinforcement of these biogenic needs (Bowlby, 1977).

Bowlby's thesis is that these attachments come from a need for *security and safety;* they develop early in life, are usually directed toward a few specific individuals, and tend to endure throughout a large part of the life cycle. Forming attachments with significant others is considered normal behavior not only for the child but for the adult as well. Bowlby argues that attachment behavior has survival value, citing the occurrence of this behavior in the young of almost all species of mammals. But he sees attachment behavior as distinct from feeding and sexual behavior (Bowlby, 1977).

Attachment behavior is best illustrated by the young animal and the young child who, as they grow, leave the attachment figure for increasingly long periods of time to search an ever-widening radius of their environment. But they always return to the attachment figure for support and safety. When the attachment figure disappears or is threatened, the response is one of intense anxiety and strong emotional protest. Bowlby suggests that the child's parents provide the secure base of operation from which to explore. This relationship determines the child's capacity to make affectional bonds later in life. This is similar to Erik Erikson's concept of basic trust: through good parenting, the individual sees himself as being both able to help himself and worthy of being helped should difficulties arise (Erikson, 1950). Obvious pathological aberrations can develop in this pattern. Inadequate parenting can lead people either to form anxious attachments or to form very tenuous attachments, if any at all.

If it is the goal of attachment behavior to maintain an affectional bond, situations that endanger this bond give rise to certain very specific reactions. The greater the potential for loss, the more intense these reactions and the more varied. "In such circumstances, all the most powerful forms of attachment behavior become activated—clinging, crying, and perhaps angry coercion . . . when these actions are successful, the bond is restored, the activities cease and the states of stress and distress are alleviated" (Bowlby, 1977, p. 42). If the danger is not removed, withdrawal, apathy, and despair will then ensue.

Animals demonstrate this behavior as well as humans. In his book *The Expression of the Emotions in Man and Animals*, written during the latter part of the nineteenth century, Charles Darwin described the ways in which sorrow is expressed by animals as well as by children and adult human beings (Darwin, 1872). Konrad Lorenz has described this grief-like behavior in the separation of a greylag goose from its mate:

> The first response to the disappearance of the partner consists in the anxious attempt to find him again. The goose moves about restlessly by day and night, flying great distances and visiting places where the partner might be found, uttering all the time the penetrating trisyllabic long-distance call. . . . The searching expeditions are extended farther and farther and quite often the searcher itself gets lost, or succumbs to an accident. . . . All the objective observable characteristics of the goose's behavior on losing its mate are roughly identical with human grief. [Lorenz, 1963, quoted in Parkes, 1972, p. 40]

There are many other examples of grieving in the animal world. Several years ago there was an interesting account about dolphins in the Montreal zoo. After one of the dolphins died, its mate refused to eat, and the zookeepers had the difficult if not impossible task of keeping the surviving dolphin alive. By not eating, the dolphin was exhibiting manifestations of grief and depression akin to human loss behavior. Psychiatrist George Engel, speaking at the Psychiatric Grand Rounds at the Massachusetts General Hospital, described a case of bereavement in great detail. This case sounded typical of the kinds of reactions that you would find in a survivor who has lost a mate. Later in his lecture, after reading a lengthy newspaper account of this loss, Dr. Engel revealed that he was describing the behavior of an ostrich who had lost her mate!

Because of the many examples in the animal world, Bowlby concludes that there are good biological reasons for every separation to be responded to in an automatic, instinctive way with aggressive behavior. He also suggests that irretrievable loss is not taken into account; that in the course of evolution, instinctual equipment developed around the fact that losses are retrievable and the behavioral responses that make up part of the grieving process are geared toward reestablishing a relationship with the lost object (Bowlby, 1980). This "biological theory of grief" has been influential in the thinking of many, including that of British psychiatrist Colin Murray Parkes (Parkes, 1972). The mourning responses of animals show what primitive biological processes are at work in humans. However, there are features of grieving specific only to human beings, and these normal grief reactions will be described in the next chapter.

There is evidence that all humans grieve a loss to one degree or another. Anthropologists who have studied other societies, their cultures, and their reactions to the loss of loved ones report that whatever the society studied in whatever part of the world, there is an almost universal attempt to regain the lost loved object, and/or there is the belief in an afterlife where one can rejoin the loved one. In preliterate societies, however, bereavement pathology seems to be less common than it is in more civilized societies (Krupp & Kligfeld, 1962).

Is Grief a Disease?

Psychiatrist George Engel raised this interesting question in a thought-provoking essay published in *Psychosomatic Medicine*. Engel's thesis is that the loss of a loved one is psychologically traumatic to the same extent as being severely wounded or burned is physiologically traumatic. He argues that grief represents a departure from the state of health and well-being, and just as healing is necessary in the physiological realm in order to bring the body back into homeostatic balance, a period of time is likewise needed to return the mourner to a similar state of equilibrium. Therefore, Engel sees the process of mourning as similar to the process of healing. As with healing, full function, or nearly full function, can be restored, but there are also incidents of impaired function and inadequate healing. Just as the terms *healthy* and *pathological* apply to the various courses in the physiological healing process, Engel argues that these same terms may be applied to the courses taken by the mourning process. He sees mourning as a course that takes time until restoration of function can take place. How much functional impairment there is is a matter of degree (Engel, 1961).

Is Mourning Necessary?

Engel's approach makes sense and leads logically to a further question, "Is mourning necessary?" I would have to answer this question with a definite, "Yes!" After one sustains a loss, there are certain *tasks of mourning* that must be accomplished for equilibrium to be reestablished and for the process of mourning to be completed.

All of human growth and development can be seen as influenced by various tasks. These are most obvious when observing child growth and development. According to Robert Havinghurst, the renowned developmental psychologist, there are certain developmental tasks that occur as the child grows. If the child does not complete a task on a particular level, then that child's adaptation is impaired when trying to complete tasks on higher levels (Havinghurst, 1953).

Likewise, mourning—the adaptation to loss—may be seen as involving the four basic tasks outlined below. It is essential that the grieving person accomplish these tasks before mourning can be completed. Incompleted grief tasks can impair further growth and development. Although the tasks do not necessarily follow a specific order, there is some ordering suggested in the definitions. For example, you cannot handle the emotional impact of a loss until you first come to terms with the fact that the loss has happened. Since mourning is a process and not a state, the following tasks require effort, and following Freud's example, we often speak of a person as doing "grief work." Using Engel's analogy to healing, it is possible for someone to accomplish some of these tasks and not others and hence have an incomplete bereavement, just as one might have incomplete healing from a wound.

The Four Tasks of Mourning

Task I: To Accept the Reality of the Loss

When someone dies, even if the death is expected, there is always a sense that it hasn't happened. The first task of grieving is to come full face with the reality that the person is dead, that the person is gone and will not return.

Part of the acceptance of reality is to come to the belief that reunion is impossible, at least in this life. The searching behavior, of which Bowlby and Parkes have written extensively, directly relates to the accomplishment of this task. Many people who have sustained a loss find themselves calling out for the lost person and they sometimes tend to misidentify others in their environment. They may walk down the street, catch a glimpse of somebody who reminds them of the deceased and then have to remind themselves, "No, that isn't my friend. My friend is really dead."

The opposite of accepting the reality of the loss is *not believing* through some type of denial. Some people refuse to believe that the death is real and get stuck in the grieving process at the first task. Denial can be practiced on several levels and take various forms, but it most often involves either the facts of the loss, the meaning of the loss, or the irreversibility of the loss (Dorpat, 1973).

Denying *the facts of the loss* can vary in degree from a slight distortion to a full-blown delusion. Bizarre examples of denial through delusion are the rare cases in which the bereaved keeps the deceased's body in the house for a number of days before notifying anyone of the death. Gardiner and Pritchard describe six cases of this unusual behavior and I have seen two cases. The people involved were either manifestly psychotic or eccentric and reclusive (Gardiner & Pritchard, 1977).

What is more likely to happen is that a person will go through what psychiatrist Geoffrey Gorer calls "mummification," that is, retaining possessions of the deceased's in a mummified condition ready for use when he or she returns (Gorer, 1965). A classic example of this involved Queen Victoria, who after the death of her consort, Prince Albert, had his clothes and shaving gear laid out daily and often went around the palace speaking to him. Parents who lose a child often retain the child's room as it was before the death. This is not unusual in the short term but becomes denial if it goes on for years. An example of a distortion rather than a delusion would be the person who sees the deceased embodied in one of their children. This distorted thinking may buffer the intensity of the loss but is seldom satisfactory and hinders the acceptance of the reality of the death.

Another way that people protect themselves from reality is to deny the *meaning of the loss*. In this way the loss can be seen as less significant than it actually is. It is common to hear statements like, "He wasn't a good father," "We weren't close," or "I don't miss him." Some people jettison clothes and other personal items that remind them of the deceased. Removing all reminders of the deceased is the opposite of "mummification" and minimizes the loss. It is as though the survivors protect themselves through the absence of any artifacts that would bring them face to face with the reality of the loss.

Another way to deny the full meaning of the loss is to practice "selective forgetting." As an example, Gary lost his father at the age of 12. Over the years, he had blocked all the reality of his father from his mind, even including a literal visual image. When he first came for psychotherapy as a college student, he could not even bring to mind the memory of his father's face. After he went through a course of therapy, he was not only able to remember what his father looked like, but he was also able to sense his father's presence when he received awards at his graduation ceremony.

Some people hinder the completion of Task I by denying that *death is irreversible*. One good example of this was illustrated in a film piece aired by the TV series "60 Minutes" several years ago. It told of a middle-aged housewife who had lost her mother and her 12-year-old daughter in a house fire. For the first two years she went through her days saying aloud to herself, "I don't want you dead, I don't want you dead, I won't have you dead!" Part of her therapy included the necessity for facing the fact that they were dead and would never return.

Another strategy used to deny the finality of death involves spiritualism. The hope for a reunion with the dead person is a normal feeling, particularly in the early days and weeks following the loss. However, the chronic hope for such a reunion is not normal. From his research, Parkes states:

> Spiritualism claims to help bereaved persons in their search for the dead, and seven of the bereaved people who were included in my various studies described visits to seances or spiritualist churches. Their reactions were mixed: some felt that they had obtained some sort of contact with the dead and a few had been frightened by this. On the whole they did not feel satisfied by the experience and none had become a regular attender at spiritualist meetings. [Parkes, 1972, p. 52]

Coming to an acceptance of the reality of the loss takes time since it involves not only an intellectual acceptance but also an emotional one. The bereaved person may be intellectually aware of the finality of the loss long before the emotions allow full acceptance of the information as true. It is easy to believe that my loved one is still away on a trip or has gone to the hospital again. The reality hits hard when one wants to pick up the phone to share some experience only to remember that the loved one is not at the other end. Many a bereaved parent will take months to say, "My child is dead and I will never have him again." They may see children playing on the street or catch sight of a school bus and say to themselves, "How could I have forgotten that my child is dead."

Belief and disbelief are intermittent while grappling with this task. Krupp said it well when he wrote:

> At times mourners seem to be under the influence of reality and behave as though they fully accept that the deceased is gone; at other times they behave

irrationally, under the sway of the fantasy of eventual reunion. Anger directed at the lost love object, the self, others believed to have caused the loss, and even at benevolent well wishers who remind the mourner of the reality of the loss is a ubiquitous feature. [Krupp et al., 1986, p. 345]

Although fully completing this task takes time, traditional rituals such as the funeral help many bereaved people move toward acceptance. Those who are not present at the burial may need external ways to validate the reality of the death. Unreality is particularly difficult in the case of sudden death, especially if the survivor does not see the body of the deceased. In our Boston Child Bereavement Study, we found a strong relationship between the sudden loss of a spouse and the dreams of the surviving spouse in the early months after the death. It may be that dreaming the deceased is alive is not simply wish fulfillment but rather the mind's way of validating the reality of the death, through the sharp contrast that occurs when one awakens from such a dream.

Task II: To Work Through To the Pain of Grief

The German word *Schmerz* is appropriate to use when speaking of pain because its broader definition includes the literal physical pain that many people experience and the emotional and behavioral pain associated with loss. It is necessary to acknowledge and work through this pain or it will manifest itself through some symptoms or other form of aberrant behavior. Parkes affirms this when he says, "If it is necessary for the bereaved person to go through the pain of grief in order to get the grief work done, then anything that continually allows the person to avoid or suppress this pain can be expected to prolong the course of mourning" (Parkes, 1972, p. 173). Not everyone experiences the same intensity of pain or feels it in the same way, but it is impossible to lose someone you have been deeply attached to without experiencing some level of pain.

There may be a subtle interplay between society and the mourner which makes the completion of Task II more difficult. Society may be uncomfortable with the mourners' feelings and hence may give the subtle message, "You don't need to grieve, you are only feeling sorry for yourself." This interferes with the mourner's own defenses, leading to the denial of the need to grieve, expressed as "I don't need to grieve" (Pincus, 1974). Geoffrey Gorer recognizes this and says, "Giving way to grief is stigmatized as morbid, unhealthy, demoralizing. The proper action of a friend and well-wisher is felt to be distraction of a mourner from his or her grief" (Gorer, 1965, p. 130).

The negation of this second task, of working through the pain, is *not to feel*. People can short-circuit Task II in any number of ways, the most obvious being to cut off their feelings and deny the pain that is present. Sometimes people hinder the process by avoiding painful thoughts. They use thought-stopping procedures to keep themselves from feeling the dysphoria associated with the loss. Some people handle it by stimulating only pleasant thoughts of the deceased, which protect them from the discomfort of unpleasant thoughts. Idealizing the dead, avoiding reminders of the dead, and using alcohol or drugs are still other ways in which people keep themselves from accomplishing Task II.

Some people who do not understand the necessity of experiencing the pain of grief try to find a geographic cure. They travel from place to place and try to find some relief from their emotions, as opposed to allowing themselves to indulge the pain—to feel it and to know that one day it will pass.

One young woman minimized her loss by believing her brother was out of his dark place and into a better place after his suicide. This might have been true, but it kept her from feeling her intense anger at him for leaving her. In treatment, when she first allowed herself to feel anger, she said, "I'm angry with this behavior and not him!" Finally she was able to acknowledge this anger directly.

There are a few cases in which the surviving person has a euphoric response to the death, but this is usually associated with an emphatic refusal to believe the death has occurred. It is often accompanied by a vivid sense of the dead person's continuing presence. Generally, these euphoric responses are extremely fragile and short-lived (Parkes, 1972).

John Bowlby has said, "Sooner or later, some of those who avoid all conscious grieving, break down—usually with some form of depression" (Bowlby, 1980, p. 158). One of the aims of grief counseling is to help facilitate people through this difficult second task so they don't carry the pain with them throughout their life. If Task II is not adequately completed, therapy may be needed later on, at which point it can be more difficult for the person to go back and work through the pain he or she has been avoiding. This is very often a more complex and difficult experience than dealing with it at the time of the loss. Also, it can be complicated by having a less supportive social system than would have been available at the time of the original loss.

Task III: To Adjust to an Environment in Which the Deceased is Missing

Adjusting to a new environment means different things to different people, depending on what the relationship was with the deceased and the various roles the deceased played. For many widows it takes a considerable period of time to realize what it is like to live without their husbands. This realization often begins to emerge around three months after the loss and involves coming to terms with living alone, raising children alone, facing an empty house, and managing finances alone.

Parkes made an important point when he said:

> In any bereavement, it is seldom clear exactly what is lost. A loss of a husband, for instance, may or may not mean the loss of a sexual partner, companion, accountant, gardener, baby minder, audience, bed warmer, and so on, depending on the particular roles normally performed by this husband. [Parkes, 1972, p. 7]

The survivor usually is not aware of all the roles played by the deceased for some time after the loss occurs.

Many survivors resent having to develop new skills and to take on roles themselves that were formerly performed by their partners. An example of this is Margot, a young mother whose husband died. He was the type of person who was very efficient, took charge of situations, and did most things for her. After his death one of the children got into trouble in school, necessitating meetings with the guidance counselor. Previously, the husband would have made contact with the school and handled everything, but after his death Margot was forced to develop this skill. Although she developed it reluctantly and with resentment, she did come to the awareness that she liked having the skill to handle such a situation competently and that she would never have accomplished this had her husband still been alive. The coping strategy of redefining the loss in such a way that it can redound to the benefit of the survivor is often part of the successful completion of Task III.

Not only do the bereaved have to adjust to the loss of roles previously played by the deceased, but death also confronts them with the challenge of adjusting to their own sense of self. Recent studies posit that for women who define their identity through relationships and caring for others, bereavement means not only the loss of a significant other but also the sense of a loss of self (Zaiger, 1985).

Bereavement can lead to intense regression where the bereaved perceive of themselves as helpless, inadequate, incapable, childlike, or personally bankrupt (Horowitz et al., 1980). Attempts to fulfill the deceased's roles may fail and this can lead to a further sense of lowered self-esteem. When this happens, personal efficacy is challenged and people may attribute any change to chance or fate and not to their own strengths and abilities (Goalder, 1985). However, over time these negative images usually give way to more positive ones and the survivors are able to carry on their tasks and learn new ways of dealing with the world (Shuchter & Zisook, 1986).

A third area of adjustment may be to one's sense of the world. Loss through death can challenge one's fundamental life values and philosophical beliefs—beliefs that are influenced by our families, peers, education, and religion as well as life experiences. It is not unusual for the bereaved to feel that they have lost direction in life. The bereaved person searches for meaning in the loss and its attendant life changes in order to make sense of it and to regain some control of his or her life. This is especially true when there are sudden and untimely deaths. For many there is no clear answer. A mother whose young son died in the 1988 crash of Pan Am Flight 103 said, "It is not how to find an answer, but how to live without one." Over time, new beliefs may be adopted or old ones reasserted or modified to reflect the fragility of life and the limits of control (Shuchter & Zisook, 1986).

The arresting of Task III is *not adapting* to the loss. People work against themselves by promoting their own helplessness, by not developing the skills they need to cope, or by withdrawing from the world and not facing up to environmental requirements. Most people do not take this negative course, however. They usually decide that they must fill the roles to which they are unaccustomed, develop skills they never had, and move forward with a reassessed sense of the world. Bowlby sums this up when he says:

> On how he achieves this [Task III] turns the outcome of his mourning—either progress towards a recognition of his changed circumstances, a revision of his representational models, and a redefinition of his goals in life, or else a state of suspended growth in which he is held prisoner by a dilemma he cannot solve. [Bowlby, 1980, p. 139]

Task IV: To Emotionally Relocate the Deceased and Move on With Life

When I wrote the first edition of this book, I listed the Fourth Task of Mourning as "withdrawing emotional energy from the deceased and reinvesting it in another relationship." This concept was posited by Freud when he said, "Mourning has quite a precise psychical task to perform: its function is to detach the survivor's hopes and memories from the dead" (Freud, 1913, p. 65). Although I believe this to be true, the way Task IV was worded previously was easily misunderstood. It sounded too mechanical, like one could merely pull a plug and reattach it someplace else. One never loses memories of a significant relationship.

Volkan has suggested:

> a mourner never altogether forgets the dead person who was so highly valued in life and never totally withdraws his investment in his representation. We can never purge those who have been close to us from our own history except by psychic acts damaging to our own identity. [Volkan, 1985, p. 326]

Volkan goes on to say that mourning ends when the mourner no longer has a need to reactivate the representation of the dead with exaggerated intensity in the course of daily living.

Shuchter and Zisook write:

> A survivor's readiness to enter new relationships depends not on "giving up" the dead spouse but on finding a suitable place for the spouse in the psychological life of the bereaved—a place that is important but that leaves room for others. [Shuchter & Zisook, 1986, p. 117]

The counselor's task then becomes not to help the bereaved give up their relationship with the deceased, but to help them find an appropriate place for the dead in their emotional lives—a place that will enable them to go on living effectively in the world. Marris has captured this idea when he writes:

> At first, a widow cannot separate her purposes and understanding from the husband who figured so centrally in them: she has to revive the relationship, to continue it by symbols and make-believe, in order to feel alive. But as time goes by, she begins to reformulate life in terms which assimilate the fact of his death. She makes a gradual transformation from talking to him "as if he were sitting in the chair beside me," to thinking what he would have said and done, and from there to planning her own and her children's future in terms of what he would have wished. Until finally the wishes become her own, and she no longer consciously refers them to him. [Marris, 1974, pp. 37–38]

Bereaved parents often have difficulty understanding the notion of emotional withdrawal. If we think of relocation, then the task for the bereaved parent is to evolve some ongoing relationship with the thoughts and memories that they associate with their child, but to do this in a way that would allow them to continue on with their lives after such a loss.

One such parent eventually found an effective place for the thoughts and memories of her dead son so she could begin reinvesting back into life. She wrote:

> Only recently have I begun to take notice of things in life that are still open to me. You know, things that can bring me pleasure. I know that I will continue to grieve for Robbie for the rest of my life and that I will keep his loving memory alive. But life goes on, and like it or not, I am a part of it. Lately, there have been times when I notice how well I seem to be doing on some project at home or even taking part in some activity with friends. [Alexy, 1982, p. 503]

To me, this represents movement in the accomplishing of Task IV.

It is difficult to find a phrase that adequately defines the incompletion of Task IV, but I think the best description would perhaps be *not loving*. The fourth task is hindered by holding on to the past attachment rather than going on and forming new ones. Some people find loss so painful that they make a pact with themselves never to love again. The popular song market is replete with this theme, which gives it a validity it does not deserve.

For many people, Task IV is the most difficult one to accomplish. They get stuck at this point in their grieving and later realize that their life in some way stopped at the point the loss occurred. But Task IV can be accomplished. One teenaged girl had an extremely difficult time adjusting to the death of her father. Two years later, as she began to move through the issues of Task IV, she wrote a note to her mother from college that articulated what many people come to realize when they are grappling with emotional withdrawal and reinvestment: "There are other people to be loved," she wrote, "and it doesn't mean that I love Dad any less."

When Is Mourning Finished?

Asking when mourning is finished is a little like asking how high is up? There is no ready answer. Bowlby and Parkes both say that mourning is finished when a person completes the final mourning phase of restitution (Bowlby, 1980; Parkes, 1972). In my view, mourning is finished when the tasks of mourning are accomplished. It is impossible to set a definitive date for this, yet, within the bereavement literature, there are all sorts of attempts to set dates—four months, one year, two years, never. In the loss of a close relationship I would be suspicious of any full resolution that takes under a year and, for many, two years is not too long.

One benchmark of a completed grief reaction is when the person is able to think of the deceased without pain. There is always a sense of sadness when you think of someone that you have loved and lost, but it is a different kind of sadness—it lacks the wrenching quality it previously had. One can think of the deceased without physical manifestations such as intense crying or feeling a tightness in the chest. Also, mourning is finished when a person can reinvest his or her emotions back into life and in the living.

There are those, however, who never seem to accomplish a completion to their grieving. Bowlby quotes one widow in her mid-sixties as saying, "Mourning never ends. Only as time goes on, it erupts less frequently" (Bowlby, 1980, p. 101). Most studies show that of the women who lose their husbands, fewer than half are themselves again at the end of the first year. Shuchter found that the period around two years is the time when the great majority of widows and widowers have found a "modicum of stability . . . establishing a new identity and finding a direction in their lives" (Shuchter & Zisook, 1986, p. 248). Parkes' studies show that widows may take three or four years to reach stability in their lives (Parkes, 1972).

One of the basic things that education through grief counseling can do is to alert people to the fact that mourning is a long-term process, and the culmination will not be to a pre-grief state. The counselor can also let them know that even though mourning progresses, there will be bad days. Grieving does not proceed in a linear fashion; it may reappear to be reworked.

One widow, who also lost her young adult son, said to me after a prolonged and painful mourning period, "Your expectations do you in! I now realize that the pain never goes completely away. The pain returns but I can remember the in-between times better."

I have a friend who lost someone important to him and was feeling intense pain. He does not have a great tolerance for pain, particularly emotional pain, and shortly after the loss he said to me, "I'll be glad when four weeks is over and this will all be finished." Part of my job was to help him see that the pain would not go away in four weeks and probably would not go away in four months. Some people believe that it takes four full seasons of the year before grief will begin to abate. Geoffrey Gorer believes that the way people respond to spoken condolences gives some indication of where they are in the mourning process. The grateful acceptance of condolences is one of the most reliable signs that the bereaved is working through mourning satis-factorily (Gorer, 1965).

There is a sense in which mourning can be finished, when people regain an interest in life, feel more hopeful, experience gratification again, and adapt to new roles. There is also a sense in which mourning is never finished. You may find the following quote of Sigmund Freud's to be helpful. He wrote to his friend Binswanger, whose son had died:

> We find a place for what we lose. Although we know that after such a loss the acute stage of mourning will subside, we also know that we shall remain inconsolable and will never find a substitute. No matter what may fill the gap, even if it be filled completely, it nevertheless remains something else. [E. L. Freud, 1961, p. 386]

References

Alexy, W. D. (1982). Dimensions of psychological counseling that facilitate the growing process of bereaved parents. *Journal of Counseling Psychology, 29,* 498–507.

Bowlby, J. (1977). The making and breaking of affectional bonds, I and II. *British Journal of Psychiatry, 130,* 201–210; 421–431.

Bowlby, J. (1980). *Attachment and loss: Loss, sadness, and depression* (vol III). New York: Basic Books.

Darwin, C. (1872). *The expression of emotions in man and animals.* London: Murray.

Dorpat, T. L. (1973). Suicide, loss, and mourning. *Life-Threatening Behavior, 3,* 213–224.

Engel, G. L. (1961). Is grief a disease? A challenge for medical research. *Psychosomatic Medicine, 23,* 18–22.

Erikson, E. H. (1950). *Childhood and society.* New York: Norton.

Freud, E. L. (Ed.). (1961). *Letters of Sigmund Freud.* New York: Basic.

Freud, S. (1957). *Totem and taboo* (1913), standard edition, (vol. XIV). London: Hogarth.

Gardiner, A., & Pritchard, M. (1977). Mourning, mummification, and living with the dead. *British Journal of Psychiatry, 130,* 23–28.

Goalder, J. S. (1985). Morbid grief reaction: A social systems perspective. *Professional Psychology: Research and Practice, 16,* 833–842.

Gorer, G. D. (1965). *Death, grief, and mourning.* New York: Doubleday.

Havinghurst, R. (1953). *Developmental tasks and education.* New York: Longmans.

Horowitz, M. J., Wilner, N., Marmar, C., & Krupnick, J. (1980). Pathological grief and the activation of latent self images. *American Journal of Psychiatry, 137,* 1157–1162.

Krupp, G., Genovese, F., & Krupp, T. (1986). To have and have not: Multiple identifications in pathological bereavement. *Journal of the American Academy of Psychoanalysis, 14,* 337–348.

Krupp, G. R., & Kligfield, B. (1962). The bereavement reaction: A cross cultural evaluation. *Journal of Religion and Health, 1,* 222–246.

Lorenz, K (1963). *On aggression.* London: Methuen.

Marris, P. (1974). *Loss and change.* London: Routledge & Kegan Paul.

Parkes, C. M. (1972). *Bereavement: Studies of grief in adult life.* New York: International Universities Press.

Pincus, L. (1974). *Death and the family.* New York: Pantheon.

Rubin, S. S. (1984). Mourning distinct from melancholia: The resolution of bereavement. *British Journal of Medical Psychology, 57,* 339–345.

Shuchter, S. R., & Zisook, S. (1986). Treatment of spousal bereavement: A multidimensional approach. *Psychiatric Annals, 16,* 295–305.

Volkan, V. D. (1985). Complicated mourning. *Annual of Psychoanalysis, 12,* 323–348.

Zaiger, N. (1985–86). Women and bereavement. *Women and Therapy, 4,* 33–43.

Chapter 2

Normal Grief Reactions: Uncomplicated Mourning

The term normal grief,* sometimes referred to as uncomplicated grief, encompasses a broad range of feelings and behaviors that are common after a loss. One of the earliest attempts to look at normal grief reactions in any systematic way was done by Erich Lindemann when he was Chief of Psychiatry at the Massachusetts General Hospital.

In the Boston area there are two Catholic colleges well known for their football rivalry. Back in the fall of 1942, they met for one of their traditional Saturday encounters. Holy Cross beat Boston College, and after the game many people went to the local Coconut Grove Nightclub to celebrate. During the revelries, a busboy lit a match while trying to change a lightbulb and accidentally set a decorative palm tree on fire. Almost immediately, the whole nightclub, which was packed beyond its legal capacity, was engulfed in flames. Nearly 500 people lost their lives in that tragedy.

Afterwards, Lindemann and his colleagues worked with the family members who had lost loved ones in that holocaust, and from these data and others he wrote his classic paper, "The Symptomatology and Management of Acute Grief" (Lindemann, 1944). From his observations of 101 recently bereaved patients he discovered similar patterns, which he described as the pathognomic characteristics of normal or acute grief. He listed these as:

---

*I am using the word *normal* in both a clinical and a statistical sense. "Clinical" defines what the clinician calls normal mourning behavior while "statistical" refers to the frequency with which a behavior is found among a randomized bereaved population. The more frequent the behavior, the more it is defined as normal.

1. Somatic or bodily distress of some type
2. Preoccupation with the image of the deceased
3. Guilt relating to the deceased or circumstances of the death
4. Hostile reactions
5. The inability to function as one had before the loss

In addition to these five, he described a sixth characteristic exhibited by many patients: they appeared to develop traits of the deceased in their own behavior.

There are many limitations to Lindemann's study. Some of these have been outlined by Parkes, who cites the fact that Lindemann does not present figures to show the relative frequency of the syndromes described. Lindemann also neglects to mention how many interviews he had with the patients and how much time had passed between the interviews and the date of the loss (Parkes, 1972). Nevertheless, this remains an important and much-quoted study.

What is of particular interest to me is that the bereaved we see today at the Massachusetts General Hospital exhibit behavior very similar to those described by Lindemann over 40 years ago. Within a large number of people undergoing an acute grief reaction, we find some or all of the following phenomena. Because the list of normal grief behaviors is so extensive and varied, these behaviors can be described under four general categories: (1) feelings, (2) physical sensations, (3) cognitions, and (4) behaviors. Anyone counseling the bereaved needs to be familiar with the broad range of behaviors that falls under the description of normal grief.

Manifestations of Normal Grief

Feelings

Sadness.   Sadness is the most common feeling found in the bereaved and really needs little comment. This feeling is not necessarily manifested by crying behavior, but it often is. Parkes and Weiss conjecture that crying is a signal that evokes a sympathetic and protective reaction from others and establishes a social situation in which the normal laws of competitive behavior are suspended (Parkes & Weiss, 1983).

Anger.   Anger is frequently experienced after a loss. It can be one of the most confusing feelings for the survivor, and as such is at the root of many problems in the grieving process. A woman whose husband died of cancer said to me, "How can I be angry? He didn't *want* to die." The truth is that she was angry at him for dying and leaving her. If the anger is not adequately acknowledged, it can lead to a complicated bereavement.

This anger comes from two sources: (1) from a sense of frustration that there was nothing one could do to prevent the death, and (2) from a kind of regressive experience that occurs after the loss of someone close. You may have had this type of regressive experience when you were a very young child on a shopping trip with your mother. You were in a department store and suddenly you looked up to find that she had disappeared. You felt panic and anxiety until your mother returned, whereupon, rather than express a loving reaction, you hauled off and kicked her in the shins. This behavior, which Bowlby sees as part of our genetic heritage, symbolizes the message, "Don't leave me again!"

In the loss of any important person there is a tendency to regress, to feel helpless, to feel unable to exist without the person, and then to experience the anger that goes along with these feelings of anxiety. The anger that the bereaved person experiences needs to be identified and appropriately targeted toward the deceased in order to bring it to a healthy conclusion. However, it often is handled in other less effective ways, one of which is displacement, or directing it toward some other person and often blaming them for the death. The line of reasoning is that if someone can be blamed, then he is responsible and, hence, the loss could have been prevented. People blame the physician, the funeral director, family members, an insensitive friend, and often God.

One of the most risky maladaptations of anger is the posture of turning the anger inward against the self. In a severe case of retroflection an angry person who is also down on himself may develop suicidal behavior. A more psychoanalytic interpretation of this retroflected anger response was given by Melanie Klein, who suggests that the "triumph" over the dead causes the bereaved person to turn his anger against himself or direct it outward toward others at hand (Klein, 1940).

Guilt and Self-reproach.   Guilt and self-reproach are common experiences of survivors: guilt over not being kind enough, over not taking the person to the hospital sooner, and the like. Usually the guilt is manifested over something that happened or something that was neglected around the time of the death. Most often the guilt is irrational and will mitigate through reality testing.

Anxiety.   Anxiety in the survivor can range from a light sense of insecurity to a strong panic attack and the more intense and persistent the anxiety, the more it suggests a pathological grief reaction. Anxiety comes primarily from two sources. First, the survivors fear they will not be able to take care of themselves on their own and frequently make comments like, "I won't be able to survive without him." Second, anxiety relates to a heightened sense of personal death awareness—the awareness of one's own mortality heightened by the death of a loved one (Worden, 1976). Carried to extremes, this anxiety can develop into a full-blown phobia. Well-known author C. S. Lewis knew this anxiety and said after losing his wife, "No one ever told me that grief felt so like fear. I am not afraid, but the sensation is like being afraid. The same fluttering in the stomach, the same restlessness, the yawning. I keep on swallowing" (Lewis, 1961).

Loneliness.   Loneliness is a feeling frequently expressed by survivors, particularly those who have lost a spouse and who were used to a close day-by-day relationship. Even though very lonely, many widows will not go out because they feel safer in their homes. "I feel so all alone now," said one widow who had been married for 52 years. "It's been like the world has ended," she told me 10 months after her husband's death.

Fatigue.   Lindemann's patients reported fatigue, and we see this frequently in survivors. It may sometimes be experienced as apathy or listlessness. This high level of fatigue can be both surprising and distressing to the person who is usually very active.

Helplessness.   One factor that makes the event of death so stressful is the sense of helplessness it can engender. This close correlate of anxiety is frequently present in the early stage of a loss. Widows in particular often feel extremely helpless. A young widow left with a seven-week-old child said, "My family came and lived with me for the first five months. I was afraid I would freak out and not be able to care for my child."

Shock.   Shock occurs most often in the case of a sudden death. For example, someone picks up the telephone and learns that a loved one or friend is dead. But sometimes, even when the death follows a progressive, deteriorating illness and is expected, when the phone call finally comes, it can still cause the survivor to experience shock.

Yearning.   Yearning for the lost person is what the British call "pining." Parkes has noted that pining is a common experience of survivors, particularly among the widows he studied (Parkes, 1972). Yearning is a normal response to loss. When it diminishes, it may be a sign that mourning is coming to an end.

Emancipation.   Emancipation can be a positive feeling after a death. I worked with a young woman whose father was a real potentate, the heavy-handed, unbending dictator over her existence. After his sudden death from a heart attack, she went through the normal grief feelings, but she also expressed a feeling of emancipation because she no longer had to live under his tyranny. At first she was uncomfortable with this feeling but later was able to accept it as the normal response to her changed status.

Relief.   Many people feel relief after the death of a loved one, particularly if the loved one suffered a lengthy or particularly painful illness. However, a sense of guilt often accompanies this sense of relief.

Numbness. It's also important to mention that some people report a lack of feelings. After a loss, they feel numb. Again, this numbness is often experienced early in the grieving process, usually right after learning of the death. It probably occurs because there are so many feelings to deal with that to allow them all into consciousness would be overwhelming, so the person experiences numbness as a protection from this flood of feelings. In commenting on numbness, Parkes and Weiss say, "We found no evidence that it is an unhealthy reaction. Blocking of sensation as a defense against what would otherwise be overwhelming pain would seem to be extremely normal" (Parkes & Weiss, 1983, p. 55).

As you review this list, remember that all the items represent normal grief feelings and there is nothing pathological about any one of them. However, feelings that exist for abnormally long periods of time and at excessive intensity may portend a complicated grief reaction. This will be discussed in Chapter 4.

Physical Sensations

One of the interesting things about Lindemann's early paper is that he described not only the feelings that people experienced but also the physical sensations associated with their acute grief reactions. These sensations are often overlooked, but they play a significant role in the grieving process. The following is a list of the most commonly reported sensations experienced by the people we see for grief counseling:

1. Hollowness in the stomach
2. Tightness in the chest
3. Tightness in the throat
4. Oversensitivity to noise
5. A sense of depersonalization: "I walk down the street and nothing seems real, including myself."
6. Breathlessness, feeling short of breath
7. Weakness in the muscles
8. Lack of energy
9. Dry mouth

Many times these physical sensations will be of concern to the survivor and they will come to the physician for a checkup.

Cognitions

There are many different thought patterns that mark the experience of grief. Certain thoughts are common in the early stages of grieving and usually disappear after a short time. But sometimes thoughts persist and trigger feelings that can lead to depression or anxiety.

Disbelief. This is often the first thought to occur after hearing of a death, especially if the death was sudden. The person will think to himself, "It didn't happen, there must be some mistake. I can't believe it happened, I don't want to believe it happened." One young widow said to me, "I keep waiting for someone to wake me and tell me I'm dreaming."

Confusion. Many newly bereaved people say their thinking is very confused, they can't seem to order their thoughts, they have difficulty concentrating, or they forget things. I once went out for a social evening and took a cab home. I told the driver where I wanted to go and sat back while he proceeded down the road. A little later he asked me again where I wanted to go. I thought maybe he was a new driver and did not know the city, but he commented to me that he had a lot on his mind. A little later he asked again and then apologized and said that he was feeling very confused. This happened several more times and finally I decided it would not hurt to ask him what was on his mind. He told me that his son had been killed the week before in a traffic accident.

Preoccupation. This is an obsession with thoughts about the deceased. These often include obsessional thoughts about how to recover the lost person. Sometimes preoccupation takes the form of intrusive thoughts or images of the deceased suffering or dying. In our Boston Child Bereavement Study, surviving parents with the highest levels of intrusive thoughts were those who unexpectedly lost a spouse with whom they had a highly conflicted relationship.

Sense of Presence. This is the cognitive counterpart to the experience of yearning. The grieving person may think that the deceased is somehow still in the current area of time and space. This can be especially true during the time shortly after the death.

Hallucinations. Hallucinations of both the visual type and the auditory type are included in this list of normal behaviors because hallucinations are a frequent experience of the bereaved. They are usually transient illusory experiences, often occurring within a few weeks following the loss, and generally do not portend a more difficult or complicated mourning experience. Although disconcerting to some, many others find these experiences helpful. With all of the recent interest in mysticism and spirituality, it is interesting to speculate on whether these are really hallucinations or possibly some other kind of metaphysical phenomena.

There is an obvious interface between thinking and feeling, and the recent interest in cognitive psychology and cognitive therapy emphasizes this. Aaron Beck and his colleagues at the University of Pennsylvania find that the experience of depression frequently is triggered by depressive thought patterns (Beck et al., 1979). In the bereaved, certain thoughts will pass through their minds such as, "I can't live without her," or "I'll never find love again." These thoughts can then trigger off very intense but normal feelings of sadness and/or anxiety.

Behaviors

There are a number of specific behaviors frequently associated with normal grief reactions. These can range from sleep and appetite disturbances to absent-mindedness and social withdrawal. The following behaviors are commonly reported after a loss and usually correct themselves over time.

Sleep Disturbances.   It is not unusual for people who are in the early stages of loss to experience sleep disturbances. These may include difficulty going to sleep or early morning awakening. Sleep disturbances sometimes require medical intervention but in normal grief they usually correct themselves.

After Bill lost his wife suddenly, he would wake up at 5:00 each morning filled with intense sadness and review over and over again the circumstances surrounding the death and how it might have been prevented, including what he might have done differently. This happened morning after morning and soon caused problems because he could not function well at work. After about six weeks the disorder began to correct itself and eventually it disappeared. This is not an unusual experience. However, if sleep disorder persists, it may indicate a more serious depressive disorder, which should be explored. Sleep disorders can sometimes symbolize various fears, including the fear of dreaming, the fear of being in bed alone, and the fear of not awakening. After her husband died, one woman solved the fear of being alone in bed by taking her dog to bed with her. The sound of the dog's breathing comforted her, and she continued to do this for almost a year until she was able to sleep alone.

Appetite Disturbances.   Bereaved animals exhibit appetite disturbances, which are also very common in human mourning situations. Although appetite disturbances can manifest themselves in terms of both overeating and undereating, undereating is the more frequently described behavior. Significant changes in weight may result from changes in eating patterns.

Absent-minded Behavior.   The newly bereaved may find themselves acting in an absent-minded way or doing things that may ultimately cause themselves inconvenience or harm. One patient was concerned because on three separate occasions she had driven across the city in her car and, after completing her business, had forgotten that she had driven and had returned home via public transportation. This behavior occurred following an important loss and eventually corrected itself.

Social Withdrawal.   It is not unusual for people who have sustained a loss to want to withdraw from other people. Again, this is usually a short-lived phenomenon and corrects itself. I saw one young woman shortly after the death of her mother. This single woman was a very sociable person who loved to go to parties. For several months following her mother's death she declined all invitations because they seemed dissonant to the way she felt in the early stages of her grief. This may seem obvious and appropriate to the reader, but this woman saw her withdrawal as abnormal. Some people withdraw from friends perceived as being oversolicitous. "My friends tried so hard that I wanted to avoid them. How many times can you say, 'I'm sorry'?" Social withdrawal can also include a loss of interest in the outside world, such as not reading newspapers or watching television.

Dreams of the Deceased.   It's very common to dream of the dead person, both normal kinds of dreams and distressing dreams or nightmares. Often these dreams serve a number of purposes, such as giving some diagnostic clues to where the person is in their whole course of mourning.

For example, for several years after the death of her mother, Esther suffered from intense guilt over circumstances related to the death. This guilt was manifested in low self-esteem and personal recrimination and was associated with considerable anxiety. Although she had visited her mother faithfully every day, Esther had left for coffee and a bite of food. While she was out, her mother died.

Esther was filled with remorse, and although we used the usual reality testing techniques in therapy, the guilt still persisted. While in therapy she had a dream about her mother. In this dream she saw herself trying to assist her mother to walk down a slippery pathway so she would not fall. But her mother fell and nothing Esther could do in the dream would save her. It was impossible. This dream was a significant turning point in her therapy because she allowed herself to see that nothing she could have done would have kept her mother from dying. This important insight gave her permission to shed the guilt that she had been carrying for years.

Avoiding Reminders of the Deceased.   Some people will avoid places or things that trigger painful feelings of grief. They might avoid the place where the deceased died, the cemetery, or they might avoid objects that remind them of their lost loved one. One middle-aged woman came for grief counseling when her husband died after a series of coronary attacks, leaving her with two children. For a period of time she put all pictures of her husband away in the closet along with other things that reminded her of him. This obviously was only a short-term solution, and as she moved toward the end of her grief, she was able to bring out the items that she wanted to live with.

When the bereaved quickly gets rid of all the things associated with the deceased—gives them away or disposes of them in any way possible—even to the point of having a quick "disposal" of the body, it could lead to a complicated grief reaction. This is usually not healthy behavior and is often indicative of a highly ambivalent relationship with the deceased.

Searching and Calling Out.   Both Bowlby and Parkes have written much in their work about searching behavior. "Calling out" is related to this searching behavior. Not infrequently somebody may call out the name of the loved person with an associated comment: "Larry, Larry, Larry. Please come back to me!" When this is not done verbally, it can be going on subvocally.

Sighing.   Sighing is a behavior frequently noted among the bereaved. It is a close correlate of the physical sensation of breathlessness. Colleagues at the Massachusetts General Hospital tested respiration in a small group of bereaved parents and found that their oxygen and carbon dioxide levels were similar to those found in depressed patients (Jallinek et al., 1985).

Restless Overactivity.   A number of widows in both the Harvard Bereavement Study and the Harvard Omega Project Study entered into restless hyperactivity following the deaths of their husbands. The woman mentioned above, whose husband left her with two teenaged children, could not stand to stay at home. She would get into her car and drive all over town trying to find some sense of relief from her restlessness. Another widow could stay in the house during the day because she was busy, but at night she fled.

Crying.   There has been interesting speculation that tears may have potential healing value. Stress causes chemical imbalance in the body, and some researchers believe that tears remove toxic substances and help reestablish homeostasis. They hypothesize that the chemical content of tears caused by emotional stress is different from that of tears secreted as a function of eye irritation. Tests are being done to see what type of catecholamines, mood-altering chemicals produced by the brain, are present in emotional tears (Frey, 1980). Tears do relieve emotional stress, but how they do this is still a question. Further research is needed on the deleterious effects, if any, of suppressed crying.

Visting Places or Carrying Objects that Remind the Survivor of the Deceased.   This is the opposite of the behavior that avoids reminders of the lost person. Often underlying this behavior is the fear of losing memories of the deceased. "For two weeks I carried his picture with me constantly for fear I would forget his face," one widow told me.

Treasuring Objects that Belonged to the Deceased.   One young woman went through her mother's closet shortly after her mother died and took many of her clothes home. Although they wore the same size and this might seem like an example of someone being thrifty, the fact was that the daughter did not feel comfortable unless she was wearing something that had belonged to her mother. She wore these clothes for several months. As her mourning progressed, she found it less and less necessary to wear clothing that had belonged to her mother. Finally, she gave most of it away to charity.

The reason for outlining these characteristics of normal grief in such detail is to show the wide variety of behaviors and experiences associated with loss. Obviously, not all these behaviors will be experienced by one person. However, it is important for bereavement counselors to understand the wide range of behaviors covered under normal grief so they will not pathologize behavior that should be recognized as normal. Having this understanding will also enable counselors to give reassurance to people experiencing such behavior as disturbing, especially in the case of a first significant loss. However, if these experiences persist late in the bereavement process, they may be indicative of a more complicated bereavement (Demi & Miles, 1987).

Grief and Depression

Many of the normal grief behaviors may seem like manifestations of depression. To shed some light on this, let's look at the debate about the similarities and differences between grief and depression.

Freud, in his early paper on "Mourning and Melancholia," addressed this issue. He tried to point out that depression, or "melancholia" as he called it, was a pathological form of grief and was very much like mourning (normal grief) except that it had a certain characteristic feature of its own—namely, angry impulses toward the ambivalently "loved" person turned inward (Freud, 1917). It is true that grief looks very much like depression and it is also true that grieving may develop into a full-blown depression. Gerald Klerman, a prominent depression researcher, believes that "many depressions are precipitated by losses, either immediately following the loss or at some later time when the patient is reminded of the loss" (Klerman, 1981). Depression may also serve as a defense against mourning. If anger is directed against the self, it is deflected away from the deceased and this keeps the survivor from dealing with ambivalent feelings toward the deceased (Dorpat, 1973).

The main distinctions between grief and depression are these: In depression as well as grief, you may find the classic symptoms of sleep disturbance, appetite disturbance, and intense sadness. However, in a grief reaction, there is not the loss of self-esteem commonly found in most clinical depressions. That is, the people who have lost someone do not regard themselves less because of such a loss or if they do, it tends to be for only a brief time. And if the survivors of the deceased experience guilt, it is usually guilt associated with some specific aspect of the loss rather than a general, overall sense of culpability.

A section in the *Diagnostic and Statistical Manual III-R* of the American Psychiatric Association suggests:

. . . a full depressive syndrome frequently is a normal reaction to such a loss with feelings of depression and such associated symptoms as poor appetite, weight loss, and insomnia. However, morbid preoccupation with worthlessness, prolonged and marked functional impairment, and marked psychomotor retardation are uncommon. [APA, *DSM III-R*, 1987, p. 361]

In this case, the bereaved generally regard their feelings of depression as normal, although they may seek professional help for some symptom relief.

Even though grief and depression share similar objective and subjective features, they do seem to be different conditions. Freud believed that in grief, the world looks poor and empty while in depression, the person feels poor and empty. However, there are some bereaved who do develop major depressive episodes following a loss. The APA Diagnostic and Statistical Manual allows for this: "Morbid preoccupation with worthlessness, suicidal ideation, morbid functional impairment or psychomotor retardation, or prolonged duration suggest bereavement [is] complicated by major depression" (p. 223). If a major depressive episode develops during bereavement, I would consider this as exaggerated grief (see Chapter 4).

Jacobs and his colleagues at Yale have been interested in depression within the context of bereavement and have said, "Although the majority of depressions of bereavement are transient and require no professional attention, there is growing appreciation that some depressions, especially those that persist throughout the first year of bereavement, are clinically significant" (Jacobs, 1987, p. 501). He has used antidepressant medication to treat several patients whose depression persisted late in the course of bereavement and did not resolve spontaneously or respond to interpersonal interventions. These were usually people who had a history of depression or some other mental health disorder. He found improvement in sleep disorders and appetite disturbance as well as an improvement in mood and cognition. This response suggests a biologic dimension to the depression.

One of the functions of the counselor who has contact with people during the time of acute grief is to assess which patients might be undergoing the development of a major depression. These patients might then be given additional help, such as a medical evaluation, and possibly the use of antidepressant medications would be in order.

Determinants of Grief

If you assess a large number of grieving people you will see a wide range of behaviors, and although these behaviors may reflect those on the list of normal grief reactions, there are major individual differences. For some, grief is a very intense experience, whereas for others it is rather mild. For some, grief begins at the time they hear of the loss, while for others it is a delayed experience. In some cases grief goes on for a relatively brief period of time, while in others it seems to go on forever. In the Harvard Bereavement Study there was strong interest in identifying the significant parameters, or determinants, of grief (Parkes & Weiss, 1983). If you were to try and predict how a person would respond to a loss, what would you need to know? Although the experience of grief is related to the developmental level and conflict issues of the individual involved, most important determinants seem to fall into the following six categories.

1. *Who the Person Was.* To begin with the most obvious, if you want to predict how someone will respond to a loss, you need to know something about the deceased. A grandparent who dies of natural causes will probably be grieved differently than a sibling killed in a car accident. The loss of a distant cousin will be grieved differently than the loss of a child. The loss of a spouse may be grieved differently than the loss of a parent.

2. *The Nature of the Attachment.* Not only do you need to know who the person was, but you need to know something about the nature of the attachment. This would include knowing something about:

a. The strength of the attachment. It is almost axiomatic that the intensity of grief is determined by the intensity of love. The grief reaction will often increase in severity proportionate to the intensity of the love relationship.

b. The security of the attachment. How necessary was the deceased for the sense of well-being of the survivor? If the survivor needed the lost person for his or her own sense of self-esteem, for example, feeling OK about themselves, this will portend a more difficult grief reaction. For many, their security and esteem needs are met by their spouse and after their spouse dies, the needs remain the same but the resources are missing.

c. The ambivalence in the relationship. In any close relationship there is always a certain degree of ambivalence. Basically, the person is loved, but there also coexist negative feelings. Usually the positive feelings far exceed the negative feelings, but in the case of a highly ambivalent relationship in which the negative feelings coexist in almost equal proportion, there is going to be a more difficult grief reaction. Usually in a highly ambivalent relationship, there is a tremendous amount of guilt, often expressed as "Did I do enough?" along with intense anger at being left alone.

d. Conflicts with the deceased are also important determinants of a grief response. This refers not just to conflicts around the time of death, but also to a history of conflicts. Of special note are conflicts stemming from earlier physical and/or sexual abuse (Krupp, 1986).

3. *Mode of Death.* How the person died will say something about how the survivor grieves. Traditionally, deaths have been catalogued under the NASH categories: natural, accidental, suicidal, and homicidal. The accidental death of a child while still young may be grieved differently than the natural death of an older person seen as dying at a more appropriate time. The suicidal death of a father may be grieved differently than the

expected death of a young mother leaving small children. There is evidence (see Chapter 6) that survivors of suicidal deaths have unique and very difficult times handling their grief.

Other dimensions associated with the mode of death include where the death occurred geographically—whether it happened near at hand or far away—and if there was some advanced warning or was the death unexpected. A number of studies suggest that survivors of sudden deaths, especially young survivors, have a more difficult time a year or two years later than people with advanced warning (Parkes & Weiss, 1983). Sometimes the circumstances surrounding the death make it easy for survivors to express their anger and blame. This is particularly true in the case of accidental deaths even though they heighten feelings of helplessness (Bowlby, 1980). In circumstances where the survivor killed the person in an accident or a homicide, guilt will obviously be a key factor in coping with the loss.

4. *Historical Antecedents*. In order to predict how someone is going to grieve, you need to know if they had previous losses and how these were grieved. Were they grieved adequately or does the person bring to the new loss irresolution from a previous one? A person's prior mental health history is important here. This is especially true of people with a history of depressive illness, because they will often have a more difficult time grieving than those without such a history.

One area that our research group has explored is that of life-change events. The "Schedule of Recent Experience," created by Drs. Holmes and Rahe, enables one to compile a listing and weighting of change events which occurred six months and/or a year prior to the death (Holmes & Rahe, 1967). We have hypothesized that people with a large number of changes prior to bereavement will have more difficulty with their grief. However, this does not seem to hold up under evidence, probably because the mere listing of life crises is insufficient. Not only is it important to know what life crises occurred, but it is also important to be able to assess an important cognitive variable—how people see these life crises impinging on themselves.

5. *Personality Variables*. Bowlby makes a strong plea to take the mourner's personality structure into account when trying to understand an individual's response to loss (Bowlby, 1980). The variables include the age and sex of the person, how inhibited they are with their feelings, how well they handle anxiety, and how they cope with stressful situations. Also of importance is the highly dependent person and the person who has difficulty forming relationships. Persons diagnosed with certain personality disorders may have a difficult time handling a loss. This is especially true of those classified with borderline personality disorders or narcissistic personality disorders (see APA, 1987).

6. *Social Variables*. All of us belong to various social subcultures—ethnic and religious subcultures are only two of many. They provide us with guidelines and rituals for behavior. The Irish, for example, grieve differently

than the Italians and the Old Yankees grieve still differently. In the Jewish faith, sitting *shivah* is often observed—a period of seven days when the family stays home and friends and family come to help them and help facilitate their grief under the best circumstances. This is followed by other rituals such as going to the temple and unveiling the headstone a year later. Catholics have their own rituals, as do Protestants. In order to adequately predict how a person is going to grieve, you have to know something about the social, ethnic, and religious background of the survivor. How much participation in ritual affects a good adjustment to bereavement is still unknown. More research is needed here.

The degree of perceived emotional and social support from others, both inside and outside the family, is significant in the bereavement process. Several studies have shown that perceived social support alleviates the adverse effects of stress, including the stress of bereavement (Blazer, 1982; Pennebaker-O'Heeron, 1984; Levav et al., 1988; Bowling, 1988). Even pet owners showed fewer symptoms than those without companion animals (Akiyama, 1986). Most studies find that those who do less well with bereavement have inadequate or conflicted social support.

One last dimension that should be mentioned under social variables is the secondary gain that the survivor may find in grieving. A survivor might get a lot of mileage in his social network out of grieving and this would have an effect on how long it goes on. However, extended grieving can have an opposite effect and alienate the social network.

7. *Concurrent Stresses*. Other factors that affect bereavement are the concurrent changes and crises that arise following a death. Some change is inevitable, but there are those individuals and families that experience high levels of disruption following a death, including serious economic reversals. In the Boston Child Bereavement Study, surviving parents who experienced the largest number of life change events following the death of their spouse also had the highest levels of depression three months following the death.

The Mourning Process

Stages

In this book I am using the term *mourning* to indicate the process which occurs after a loss, while *grief* refers to the personal experience of the loss. Since mourning is a process, it is appropriate to view it in terms of stages, and, indeed, many people writing on the subject of grief have listed up to nine stages of grief and at least one other person lists 12. One of the difficulties with using the stage approach is that people do not pass through stages *in seriatim*. Also, there's a tendency for the novice to take the stages too literally. An example of this literalism is the way that people responded to Dr. Elisabeth Kübler-Ross's stages of dying. After her first book, *On Death and Dying* (1969), many people expected dying patients literally to go through the stages she had listed in some neat order.

Phases

An alternative approach to stages is the concept of phases used by Parkes, Bowlby, Sanders, and others. Parkes defines four phases of mourning (Parkes, 1970). Phase I is the period of numbness that occurs close to the time of the loss. This numbness, which is experienced by most survivors, helps them to disregard the fact of the loss at least for a brief period of time. Then the person goes through the second phase, the "phase of yearning," in which he or she yearns for the lost one to return and tends to deny the permanence of the loss. Anger plays an important part in this phase (Parkes, 1970).

In the third phase, the phase of disorganization and despair, the bereaved person finds it difficult to function in the environmet. Finally, he or she is able to enter Phase IV, the phase of reorganized behavior, and begin to pull life back together. Bowlby, whose work and interest has overlapped with that of Parkes, has reinforced the idea of phases and posits that the mourner must pass through a series of phases before mourning is finally resolved. As with stages, there are overlaps between the various phases and they are seldom distinct (Bowlby, 1980).

Tasks

Although I have no quarrel with Bowlby and Parkes and their schema of phasing, I think the Tasks of Mourning concept which I present in this book is as valid an understanding of the mourning process and much more *useful* for the clinician. Phases imply a certain passivity, something that the mourner must pass through. Tasks, on the other hand are much more consonant with Freud's concept of grief work and imply that the mourner needs to take action and can do something. Also, this approach implies that mourning can be influenced by intervention from the outside. In other words, the mourner sees the concept of phases as something to be passed through, while the tasks approach gives the mourner some sense of leverage and hope that there is something that he or she can actively do.

There is obvious validity to both of these approaches. Grieving is something that takes time; the oft-quoted phrase "time heals" holds true. There is also truth to the notion that grief creates tasks that need to be accomplished, and although this may seem overwhelming to the person in the throes of acute grief, it can, with the facilitation of a counselor, offer hope that something can be done and that there is an end point. This can be a powerful antidote to the feelings of helplessness that most mourners experience.

References

Diagnostic and statistical manual of mental disorders, Volume III-Revised. (1987). Washington: American Psychiatric Assn.

Akiyama, H., Holtzman, J. M., & Britz, W. E. (1986-87). Pet ownership and health status during bereavement. *Omega, 17*, 187–193.

Beck, A. T. et al. (1979). *Cognitive therapy of depression.* New York: Guilford.

Blazer, D. G. (1982). Social support and mortality in an elderly community population. *American Journal of Epidemology, 115*, 684–694.

Bowlby, J. (1980). *Attachment and loss: Loss, sadness, and depression* (vol III). New York: Basic Books.

Bowling, A. (1988-89). Who dies after widow(er)hood? A discriminant analysis. *Omega, 19*, 135–153.

Demi, A. S.,. & Miles, M. S. (1987). Parameters of normal grief; A Delphi study. *Death Studies, 11*, 397–412.

Dorpat, T. L. (1973). Suicide, loss, and mourning. *Life-Threatening Behavior, 3*, 213–224.

Freud, S. (1957). *Mourning and melancholia* (1917), standard edition, (vol. XIV) London: Hogarth.

Frey, W. H. (1980). Not-so-idle-tears. *Psychology Today, 13*, 91–92.

Holmes, R., & Rahe, R. (1967). Social readjustment rating scale. *Journal of Psychosomatic Research, 11*, 213–218.

Jacobs, S. C., et al. (1987). Treating depression of bereavement with antidepressants: A pilot study. *Psychiatric Clinics of North America, 10*, 501–510.

Jellinek, M. S., et al. (1985). The impact of grief on ventilatory control. *American Journal of Psychiatry, 142*, 121–123.

Klein, M. (1940). Mourning and its relationship to manic-depressive states. *International Journal of Psychoanalysis, 21*, 125–153.

Klerman, G. (1981). Personal Communication.

Krupp, G., Genovese, F., & Krupp, T. (1986). To have and have not: Multiple identifications in pathological bereavement. *Journal of the American Academy of Psychoanalysis, 14*, 337–348.

Kübler-Ross, E. (1969). *On death and dying.* New York: Macmillan.

Levav, I., et al. (1988). An epidemiologic study of mortality among bereaved parents. *New England Journal of Medicine, 319*, 457–461.

Lewis, C. S. (1961). *A grief observed.* London: Faber & Faber.

Lindemann, E. (1944). Symptomatolgy and management of acute grief. *American Journal of Psychiatry, 101*, 141–148.

Parkes, C. M. (1970). The first year of bereavement: A longitudinal study of the reaction of London widows to death of husbands. *Psychiatry, 33*, 444–467.

Parkes, C. M. (1972). *Bereavement: Studies of grief in adult life.* New York: International Universities Press.

Parkes, C. M., & Weiss, R. S. (1983). *Recovery from bereavement.* New York: Basic.

Pennebaker, J. W. (1984). Confiding in others and illness rates among spouses of suicide and accidental death victims. *Journal of Abnormal Psychology, 93*, 473–476.

Worden, J. W. (1976). *Personal Death Awareness.* Englewood Cliffs, NJ: Prentice-Hall.

Chapter **3**

Grief Counseling: Facilitating Uncomplicated Grief

The loss of a significant other causes a broad range of reactions which we have now seen are normal after such an experience. Most people are able to cope with these reactions and work through the four tasks of grieving on their own, thereby seeing grief to its conclusion. Some people find, however, that they have trouble resolving their feelings about the loss and this can hinder their ability to complete the grief tasks and thus to resume a normal life. In these cases, counseling will often help them bring their grief to a more effective resolution.

I make a distinction between grief counseling and grief therapy. Counseling involves helping people facilitate uncomplicated, or normal, grief to a healthy completion of the tasks of grieving within a reasonable time frame. I reserve the term *grief therapy* for those specialized techniques, described in Chapter 5, which are used to help people with abnormal or complicated grief reactions.

To some it may seem presumptuous to imply that any counseling is needed to help people manage acute grief. Indeed, Freud (1917) saw grieving as a natural process and in *Mourning and Melancholia* wrote that it should not be tampered with. However, grieving has historically been facilitated through the family, through the church, and in funeral rituals and other social customs. Today we observe that some people do not deal effectively with the tasks of grief and seek professional counseling for help with thoughts, feelings, and behaviors they cannot cope with. Others who have not sought out counseling directly will often accept an offer of help, especially when they are having difficulty resolving the loss on their own. I see grief counseling as a valid supplement to more traditional interventions, which may not be effective with or available to some people. There is always the risk of making grief seem pathological because of the formal intervention of a mental health worker, but with skilled counseling this need not be the case.

Goals of Grief Counseling

The overall goal of grief counseling is to help the survivor complete any unfinished business with the deceased and to be able to say a final good-bye. There are specific goals and these correspond to the four tasks of grieving. These specific goals are:

1. To increase the reality of the loss
2. To help the counselee deal with both expressed and latent affect
3. To help the counselee overcome various impediments to readjustment after the loss
4. To encourage the counselee to say an appropriate goodbye and to feel comfortable reinvesting back into life

Who Does Grief Counseling?

Different types of counselors are used to facilitate these goals. Parkes, in his paper "Bereavement Counseling: Does It Work?" outlines three basic types of grief counseling (Parkes, 1980). The first involves professional services by trained doctors, nurses, psychologists, or social workers who provide support to a person who has sustained a significant loss. This can be done on an individual basis or in a group setting. The second type of bereavement counseling involves those services in which volunteers are selected and trained and supported by professionals. One good example of this is the Widow-to-Widow programs, one of the earliest of which was established through the Harvard Laboratory for Community Psychiatry (Silverman, 1986). A third type of service includes self-help groups in which bereaved people offer help to other bereaved people, with or without the support of professionals. Again, these services can be provided on an individual, one-to-one basis or in a group counseling setting.

An interesting phenomenon that has occurred with the onset of the hospice movement in the United States has been the renewed attention focused on the area of bereavement. If you look at the guidelines that are set up for hospice care, you'll find that one strong recommendation for a comprehensive hospice program is that it provide counseling and support for all families whose loved ones are dying in the hospice setting (Kilburn, 1988). Although hospices vary from palliative care units and free-standing institutions to homecare programs, whatever the basic setting of the care, there is general agreement that comprehensive care includes work with the bereaved family. Most hospice programs use some combination of professionals and volunteers to do the counseling.

When to Do Grief Counseling

In most instances grief counseling begins at the earliest a week or so following the funeral. In general, the first 24 hours is too soon for a counselor to call unless there has been contact prior to the death. The bereaved person is still in a state of numbness or shock and is not ready to come to grips with his or her confusion. In some situations, where there is awareness of an impending death, the counselor can make contact with the family members in advance of the death and then recontact them briefly at the time of the loss and offer more extended contact a week or so after the funeral service. Again, there is no set rule, and this time schedule should not be taken too literally. This really depends on the circumstances of the death and the role and setting of the grief counseling.

Where Should Grief Counseling Be Done?

Grief counseling does not necessarily have to take place in a professional office, although it might. I have done grief counseling in various parts of the hospital, including the hospital garden and various other informal settings. One setting that can be utilized effectively is the home setting; counselors who make home visits may find that it is the most suitable context for their interventions. Parkes agrees with this and says, "Telephone contacts and office consultations are no substitutes for home visits" (Parkes, 1980, p. 9). Even though the counselor will want to make clear the contract with the client and the goals and objectives of their interactions, this does not necessitate that the contacts take place in a more formal office setting. Grief therapy, on the other hand, would be more appropriate in a professional setting rather than in a home environment or in an informal setting.

Who Receives Grief Counseling?

There are basically three approaches to bereavement counseling—one might call them three philosophies. The first suggests that bereavement counseling be offered to all individuals, particularly to families in which the death has taken a parent or child. The assumption behind this philosophy is that it is a very traumatic event for the people involved and counseling should be offered to them all. While this philosophy is understandable, cost and other factors may not make it possible to offer help on such a universal basis. Furthermore, it may not be needed by everyone.

The second philosophy assumes that some people will need help with their bereavement but will wait until they get into difficulty, recognize their own need for help, and reach out for assistance. This philosophy is perhaps more cost-effective than the first, but it requires that individuals experience a degree of distress before help is offered.

A third philosophy is based on a preventive model. If we can predict in advance who is likely to have difficulty a year or two following the loss, then we can do something by way of early intervention to preclude an unresolved grief reaction. This third approach was used in the Harvard Bereavement Study in which significant predictors identified high-risk widows and widowers under 45 years of age.

In this study, bereaved widows and widowers were studied descriptively at regular intervals up to a period of three years following the death of the spouse. A group of them who were not doing well 13 and 24 months later was identified, and data collected early in the bereavement were used to define significant predictors of the high-risk population. Below is a description of the high-risk widow as defined in this study. The focus here is on widows rather than widowers because there are significantly more, the ratio being 5:1 in the United States. No one woman in the study met all of the at-risk criteria. This is a composite picture but it gives an idea of the kind of woman who is at risk and who can be identified early and offered counseling, which may help her bring her grief to a more adequate conclusion.

Identifying the At-Risk Bereaved

The woman who will not handle bereavement well tends to be young, with children living at home and no close relatives living nearby to help form a support network. She is timid and clinging and was overly dependent on her husband, or had ambivalent feelings about their relationship, and her cultural and familial background prevents her from expressing her feelings. In the past she reacted badly to separation and she may have a previous history of depressive illness. Her husband's death causes additional stress in her life—loss of income, a possible move, and difficulties with the children, who are also trying to adjust to the loss. At first she seems to be coping well, but that slowly gives way to intensive pining and feelings of self-reproach and/or anger. Instead of declining, these feelings persist as time goes on (Parkes, 1972).

The approach of identifying the high-risk widow or widower by those who do preventive mental health was also attempted by Beverley Raphael in another landmark study. While observing widows and widowers in Australia, Raphael discovered that the following variables were significant predictors of the person who was not going to do well one and two years later:

1. A high level of perceived nonsupportiveness in the bereaved's social network response during the crisis
2. A moderate level of perceived nonsupportiveness in social network response to the bereavement crisis occurring together with particularly "traumatic" circumstances of the death
3. A previously highly ambivalent marital relationship with the deceased, traumatic circumstances of the death, and any unmet needs
4. The presence of a concurrent life crisis (Raphael, 1977)

Sheldon and colleagues at the Clark Institute in Toronto found that four main groups of predictors were important in explaining adjustment to bereavement in 80 widows. These four groups were sociodemographic variables, personality factors, social support variables, and the meaning of the death event. Of all of these, the sociodemographic factors—being younger and coming from a lower socioeconomic background—were among the strongest predictors of later distress (Sheldon et al., 1981).

In our Boston Child Bereavement Study we looked at predictors of high distress in men and women whose spouses had died leaving them with school-aged children. Those experiencing the highest levels of distress around the first anniversary of the loss were women who had not anticipated the death and who had also experienced high levels of stress and distress four months after the death. These were women who had more children under the age of 12 living at home, and who also were experiencing a larger number of life change events and stressors in the early months following the loss (Worden & Silverman, 1989).

A predictive approach can also be applied to family members other than spouses. Parkes and his colleagues at St. Christopher's Hospice in England use an eight-variable Bereavement Risk Index to identify family members in special need of support. If several of these dimensions are present in the four-week post-death assessment, that person is identified as in need of intervention:

1. More young children at home
2. Lower social class
3. Employment—little if any
4. Anger—high
5. Pining—high
6. Self-reproach—high
7. Lacking current relationships
8. Coping assessment by rater—requiring help (Parkes & Weiss, 1983)

It would be good if we had one set of predictors that would apply to all bereaved populations. Such, however, is not the case. Although there may be overlap, what predicts difficult bereavement in one population may differ from that which predicts difficulty in another group. Clinicians wanting to use a predictive approach need to do careful descriptive studies gathering measures early in the bereavement and then do systematic follow-ups with subjects not receiving intervention at selected time intervals in order to see which of the early measures are the best predictors of later difficulty. Predictors should be selected with reference to the important determinants of grief listed in Chapter 2.

Counseling Principles and Procedures

Whatever one's philosophy of grief counseling and whatever the setting, there are certain principles and procedures that help make grief counseling effective. The following will serve as guidelines for the counselor so that he or she can help the client work through an acute grief situation and come to a resolution.

Principle One: Help the Survivor Actualize the Loss

When one loses a significant other, even though there may have been some advanced warning of the death, there is always a certain sense of unreality—a sense that it did not really happen. Therefore, the first grief task is to come to a more complete awareness that the loss actually has occurred—the person is dead and will not return. Survivors must accept this reality so they can deal with the emotional impact of the loss.

How do you help someone actualize the loss? One of the best ways is to help survivors talk about the loss. This can be encouraged by the counselor. Where did the death occur? How did it happen? Who told you about it? Where were you when you heard? What was the funeral like? What was said at the service? All of these questions are geared to help the person talk specifically about the circumstances surrounding the death. Many people need to go over and over it in their minds, reviewing the events of the loss, before they can actually come to the full awareness that it has happened. This may take some time. Many of the widows we have studied said that it took up to three months before they could really begin to believe and understand that their spouse was dead and not going to return. The importance of talking about a loss was recognized by Shakespeare, who, through Macbeth, admonished, "Give Sorrow words; the grief that does not speak knits up the o'erwrought heart and bids it break."

Visiting the gravesite, or the place where the remains reside or are scattered, can also bring home the reality of the loss. Explore with the client whether they ever visit the grave and what it is like for them. If they don't visit the grave, ask what is their fantasy about going. Gravesite visits have their roots in cultural expectations and practices but they can also give some clue as to where a person is with regard to Task I issues. Some people need to be encouraged to visit the grave as part of their grief work. This can be done with care, sensitivity, and an eye to the timing of the suggestion.

The counselor can be a patient listener and can continue encouraging the person to talk about the loss. In many families, when the widow talks about the death, the response is, "Don't tell me what happened. I know what happened. Why are you torturing yourself by talking about it?" The family members do not realize that she needs to talk about it—that talking helps her to come to grips with the reality of the death. The counselor is not subject to the same impatience shown by the family and can facilitate the growing awareness of the loss and its impact by encouraging the patient to verbalize. The verbalizing can include memories of the deceased, both current and past.

Principle Two: Help the Survivor to Identify and Express Feelings

In the last chapter I outlined a number of feelings that people experience during grief, most of which are labeled dysphoric. Because of their pain and unpleasantness, many feelings may not be recognized by the survivor or they might not be felt to the degree they need to be in order to bring about an effective resolution. Many clients come to see us because they want immediate relief from their pain. They want a pill that will help them attenuate the pain. Helping them to accept and work through their pain is a major part of our intervention. Some feelings that are most problematic to survivors are anger, guilt, anxiety, and helplessness.

Anger. When someone you love dies, it's very common to feel angry. "What helped me was people who cared and who listened to me rant and rave," said one man in his twenties whose wife had died. I've suggested earlier that anger probably comes from two sources. One, from frustration, and two, from a sense of regressive helplessness. Whatever the source, it is true that many people experience intense anger, but they don't always associate it as anger toward the deceased. This anger is real and it must go somewhere, so if it is not directed toward the deceased, the real target, it may be deflected onto other people such as the physician, the hospital staff, the funeral director, the clergyperson, or a family member.

If the anger is not directed toward the deceased or displaced onto someone else, it may be retroflected—turned inward and experienced as depression, guilt, or lowered self-esteem. In extreme cases, retroflected anger may result in suicidal behavior, either in thought or in action. The competent grief counselor will always inquire about suicidal ideation. A simple question like, "Has it been so bad that you've thought of hurting yourself?" is more apt to have positive results than to prompt someone to take self-destructive action. Suicidal thoughts do not always represent retroflected anger. They can also come from a desire to rejoin the deceased.

Some of the angry feelings stem from the intense pain experienced during bereavement, and the counselor can help the client get in touch with this. Most of the time, however, it is not productive to attack the anger issue directly. For example, in many cases if you ask, "Are you angry that he died?" the person will say, "How can I be angry he died? He didn't want to die. He had a heart attack." Or people will respond like a widow I worked with recently: "How can I be angry? He was an active Christian layman. He had a strong belief in an afterlife and he's much better off." The fact is that *she* was much worse off. He left her with many worries, cares, and concerns, and we did not have to scratch very far beneath the surface to find an intense well of anger—anger that he had died and left her with all these problems.

Many people will not admit to angry feelings if you inquire directly about anger. Either they are not consciously aware of the feeling or they are adhering to the cultural admonition not to speak ill of the dead. One indirect technique that I have found beneficial is to use the low-key word "miss." I sometimes ask a survivor, "What do you miss about him?" and the person will respond with a list that often brings on sadness and tears. After a short while, I will ask, "What *don't* you miss about him?" There is usually a pause and a startled look and then the person says something like, "Well, I never thought about it that way, but now that you mention it, I don't miss the clothes on the floor, not coming home for dinner on time," and many more things. Then the person begins to acknowledge some of her more negative feelings. It is important not to leave clients with these negative feelings, but to help them find a better *balance* between the negative and the positive feelings they have for the deceased—to see that the negative feelings do not preclude the positive feelings and vice versa. The therapist plays an active role in achieving this.

In some cases, all the person has is negative feelings and it is important to help him or her get in contact with the corresponding positive feelings that exist, even though these may be few in number. Holding only negative feelings may be a way of avoiding sadness that would become conscious upon admission of any significant loss. Admitting positive feelings is a necessary part of the process of achieving an adequate and healthy resolution to one's grief. Here the problem is not the repression of a dysphoric feeling such as anger, but repressed feelings of affection.

Mike was 23 when his alcoholic father died. Over the years he had felt mistreated by him. "He created in me a dependency and I kept coming back to him for something I never got. After he died I wanted to resent him." Three years after the death, Mike was befriended by an older man. One evening as he was preparing to retire, the man touched him in a way that his father had years earlier when putting him to bed. This touch triggered off a very vivid image of his father's funeral and of his father lying in the casket. Accompanying this image was an intense feeling of sadness, and an awareness of how much he missed his father's love. He tried to counter this feeling by telling himself that it was *not* his father lying in the casket in his mind's eye, but this didn't work. The sadness prevailed. "How can I explain that I miss my father's love?" he asked me when he came for therapy, "when I never had it?" Through our work he was able to get a more balanced sense of his feelings. Gradually he found resolution and relief in the thought, "I loved him, but he was unable, because of his own upbringing, to express his love to me."

Guilt.   There a number of things that can cause guilt feelings after a loss. For example, survivors can feel guilt because they did not provide better medical care, they should not have allowed an operation, they did not consult a doctor sooner, or they did not choose the right hospital. Parents whose children die are highly vulnerable to feelings of guilt that are focused on the fact they could not help the child stop hurting or prevent the child from dying. Some feel guilty that they are not experiencing what they believe to be the appropriate amount of sadness. Whatever the reasons, most of this guilt is irrational and centers around the circumstances of the death. The counselor can help here because irrational guilt yields itself up to *reality testing*. If someone says, "I didn't do enough," I'll ask, "What did you do?" and they'll answer, "I did that." And then I'll say, "What else did you do?" "Well, I did this." "What else?" "Well, I did that." And then more things will occur to them and they will say, "I did this, and this, and this." After a while they will come to the conclusion, "Maybe I did all I could do under the circumstances."

However, there is such a thing as real guilt, real culpability, and this is much more difficult to work with. On some occasions I have used psychodrama techniques in a group therapy situation in order to help the person work through this kind of guilt. In one of these groups, Vickie, a young woman, confessed that on the night her father died, she had decided to stay with her boyfriend and was not at home with her family. She felt she had wronged her father, her mother, her brother, and herself. In the psychodrama, I had her choose different group members to be the individual family members, including herself. Then I had her interact with each of these people, confessing her sense of wrongness and in turn hearing the response from each of the principals in the drama. The session was very moving, but perhaps the most moving moment came at the end when Vickie embraced the person who portrayed herself. At that point she experienced a kind of reconciliation and healing within her own being.

Anxiety and helplessness.   People left behind after a death often feel very anxious and fearful. Much of this anxiety stems from feelings of helplessness, feelings that they cannot get along by themselves or survive alone. This is a regressive experience that usually eases with time and the realization that, even though it is difficult, they can manage. The counselor's role is to help them recognize, through cognitive restructuring, the ways they managed on their own before the loss, and this helps to throw these feelings of anxiety and helplessness into some sort of perspective.

A second source for anxiety comes from increased personal death awareness (Worden, 1976). Personal death awareness is the awareness not of death in general, or someone else's death, but of *one's own* death. This is something all of us have, something that lingers in the background of our consciousness. From time to time it comes forward to be more figural—for example when we lose a contemporary or have a near accident on the highway.

For most of us, our own personal death awareness exists at a very low level. However, with the loss of a significant other, whether it be a close friend or a family member, there is usually a heightened awareness of our own mortality, which results in existential anxiety. The counselor can take several directions, depending on the client. For some it is better not to address this issue directly but to let it go and assume that the death awareness will mitigate and fade. With others, it is helpful to address the issue directly and get them to talk about their fears and apprehensions regarding their own death. Articulating this to the counselor may help clients feel a sense of relief as they unburden their concerns and explore options. In any case, the counselor should use his or her best judgment to decide which choice is most appropriate.

Sadness.   There are some occasions when sadness and crying need to be encouraged by the counselor. Frequently people refuse to cry in front of friends for fear of taxing the friendship or losing the friendship and sustaining yet another loss. Crying in a social situation can also be suppressed in order to avoid criticism from others. One widow overheard an acquaintance say, "It's been three months. Surely she should be pulling herself together and get out of that self-pitying mood." Needless to say, this did not help her with her sadness nor did it give her the support she needed.

Some people fear that open crying will not look dignified or that it will embarrass others. Stella lost her four-year-old daughter suddenly and the funeral was held in the home of her Old Yankee in-laws some distance from where the death occurred. Stella was used to open expressions of grief but her mother-in-law so intimidated her with her stoic presence at the funeral that Stella not only suppressed her own sadness, she also ordered her aged mother to do the same, lest she embarrass her husband's family. Counseling helped her put this into perspective and to give herself permission to cry, which she needed and was denying herself.

Crying alone may be useful but it may not be as efficacious as crying with someone and receiving support. "Merely crying, however, is not enough. The bereaved need help in identifying the meaning of the tears, and this meaning will change . . . as the grief work progresses" (Simos, 1979 p. 89).

It is important that the counselor not be satisfied simply with the expression of vehement emotions. Focus is essential. Sadness must be accompanied by an awareness of what one has lost; anger needs to be properly and effectively targeted; guilt needs to be evaluated and resolved; and anxiety needs to be identified and managed. Without this focus, the counselor is not being effective, regardless of the amount or degree of feeling that is being evoked (van der Hart, 1988):

> Along with the need for focus comes the need for balance. The bereaved must achieve some balance that allows them to experience their pain, sense of loss, loneliness, fear, anger, guilt, and sadness; to let in their anguish and let out their expressions of such anguish; to know and feel in the very core of their souls what has happened to them; and yet to do all this in doses, so they will not be overwhelmed by such feelings. [Schwartz-Borden, 1986, p. 299]

Principle Three: Assist Living Without the Deceased

This principle involves helping people accommodate to a loss by facilitating their ability to live without the deceased and to make decisions independently. To do this the counselor may use a problem-solving approach—that is, what are the problems the survivor faces and how can they be solved? As mentioned earlier, the deceased played varying roles in the survivor's life and that ability to adjust to the loss is in part determined by these various roles. One role that is important in families is the decision-making role, and this role often causes problems after the loss of a spouse. In many relationships one spouse is the primary decision maker, often the man in the relationship. When he dies, the wife may feel at sixes and sevens when it comes to making the decisions independently of her husband. The counselor can help her learn effective coping and decision-making skills so she will be able to take over the role formerly filled by her husband and, in doing so, reduce her emotional distress.

Another important role that needs to be addressed when dealing with loss of a partner is that of the loss of a sexual partner. Some counselors are hesitant to address this important issue; or, it can be overemphasized to the point of discomfort in the survivor. Rita, a 50-year-old housewife, was asked to join a widows group after the sudden death of her husband. A well-meaning but inept counselor told her the group would help her find new relationships and would help her with her sexual needs. This was not what this rather repressed, middle-aged woman wanted to hear and she turned down what could have been a supportive group experience had the issue been presented in a different way. Being able to discuss emerging sexual feelings, including the need to be touched and to be held, is important. The counselor can suggest ways to meet these needs that are commensurate with the client's personality and value system. There are those whose only sexual experiences have been with their deceased spouse, so the counselor may need to address any anxiety concerning new sexual experiences.

As a general principle, the recently bereaved should be discouraged from making major life-changing decisions, such as to sell property, change jobs or careers, or adopt children, too soon after a death. Good judgment is difficult to exercise during acute grief when there is higher risk of a maladaptive response. "Don't move or sell things, for you may be running away. Work through grief where things are familiar," advised one widow in our widows group.

Another widow moved to Boston from New York right after her husband's suicide. "I thought it would make me miss him less," she told me. After a year in Boston she found it did not work and she sought out therapy. One area she had not adequately assessed was her support system—large in New York and very meager in Boston. In discouraging the bereaved from making major life-changing decisions too soon, be careful that you are not promoting a sense of helplessness. Rather, communicate that they *will* be quite capable of making decisions and taking actions when they are ready and not to make decisions just to reduce the pain.

Principle Four: Facilitate Emotional Relocation of the Deceased

By facilitating emotional relocation the counselor can help survivors find a new place in their life for the lost loved one—a place that will allow the survivor to move forward with life and form new relationships. Reminiscing is one way to gradually divest the emotional energy tied up with the deceased. Some people do not need any encouragement, but there are many who do, and this is particularly true with the loss of a spouse. Some people are hesitant to form these new relationships because they believe this will dishonor the memory of their departed spouse. Others hesitate because they feel that no one can ever fill the place of the lost person. To a certain extent this is true, but the counselor can help them realize that although the lost person can never be replaced, it is all right to help fill the void with a new relationship.

There are those who, rather than hesitating, quickly jump into new relationships, and the counselor can help interpret how appropriate this is. "If I can just get remarried everything will be okay," said one widow shortly after the death. Many times this action is not appropriate, because it can hinder adequate resolution of grief, and possibly lead to a divorce, which would be an additional loss. I once met a man who, at his wife's funeral, picked out his next wife. He successfully pursued this person and very soon had replaced his wife. It was my sense that this was a bit bizarre and inappropriate. If people rush in for a quick replacement, this may make them feel better for a time, but it may also preclude experiencing the intensity and the depth of the loss. This intensity needs to be experienced before the grieving can be completed. Also, for the relationship to work, the new person must be recognized and appreciated for himself or herself.

Principle Five: Provide Time to Grieve

Grieving requires time. It is the process of cutting cords, and such a process is gradual. "Each birthday and anniversary cuts one more strand of the cord," said a mother whose daughter was killed by an ex-boyfriend. One impediment can come in the form of family members who are eager to get over the loss and its pain and to move back into a normal routine. Children sometimes say to their mothers, "Come on, you've got to get back to living. Dad wouldn't want you to mope around all the time." They don't realize that it takes time for her to accommodate to the loss and all its ramifications. In grief counseling, the counselor can help interpret this to the family, something which may seem obvious, but surprisingly is not always obvious to family members.

I have found that certain points in time are particularly difficult and I encourage those who are doing grief counseling to recognize these critical time periods and get in touch with the person if there is no regular ongoing contact. Three months is one such time point. I worked with one family for a number of months during their father's struggle with cancer. After his death I attended the funeral. The father was a minister and there could not have been any more support for the widow and her three children than there was at the funeral and afterward. However, when I recontacted the widow at the three-month period, she was incredibly angry because no one was calling anymore, people were avoiding her, and she was displacing her anger onto her husband's successor, the new minister of the church.

Another critical time is around the first anniversary of the death. If the counselor does not have regular contact with the survivor, I would encourage recontacting her or him around that first anniversary. All kinds of thoughts and feelings come to the fore during that time and often a person will need extra support. Counselors are encouraged to make a note on their calendar as to when the death occurred and then to make arrangements to recontact by looking ahead to these critical points. For many, the holidays are toughest. One effective intervention is to help the client anticipate this and prepare in advance. "Thinking through Christmas before it occurred definitely helped me," said one young widowed mother.

Again, how often you contact the survivor depends on the relationship you have with him and on the counseling contract, be it formal or informal. However, the point I am making is that grieving takes time and the counselor needs to see the intervention role as one that may of necessity stretch over some time, though the actual contacts may not be frequent.

Principle Six: Interpret "Normal" Behavior

The sixth principle on this list is the understanding and interpreting of normal grief behaviors. After a significant loss many people have the sense that they are going crazy. This can be heightened because they often are distracted and experience things that are not normally part of their lives. If the counselor has a clear understanding of what normal grief behavior is, then he or she can give the bereaved some reassurance about the normality of these new experiences. It is rare that someone decompensates and becomes psychotic as the result of a loss, but there are exceptions. They sometimes occur when the people have had previous psychotic episodes or among those who have a diagnosis of borderline personality disorder. However, it is quite common for people to feel they are going crazy, particularly people who have not sustained a major loss before. And if a counselor understands, for example, that hallucinations, a heightened sense of distractability, or a preoccupation with the deceased are normal behaviors, then the person can be quite reassured by that counselor (Parkes, 1972).

Principle Seven: Allow for Individual Differences

There is a wide range of behavioral responses to grieving. Just as it is important not to expect everyone who is dying to die in a similar manner, likewise it is important not to expect all people who are grieving to grieve in the same way. However, this is sometimes difficult for families to understand. They are uncomfortable when one family member deviates from the behavior of the rest, or an individual who is experiencing something different from the rest of the family may be uneasy about his or her own behavior.

Once, when lecturing in the Midwest, I was approached by a young woman after the meeting wanting to talk about her family. Her parents had recently lost an infant and the mother was grieving this loss, as was the sister who was speaking to me, but she was afraid that her father was not grieving. She was concerned that he might not adequately grieve and as a result, have an arrested grief reaction. As I spoke with her, I learned that the father had asked to carry the tiny casket on his shoulders, all the way from the funeral service at the church. I pictured this lone figure walking through the town out to the cemetery. His daughter said that ever since the death, her father, a farmer, had spent long hours out on his tractor alone in the fields. It was my sense that her father was doing his grieving, but he was doing it in his own way, and my hunch was later confirmed in a letter from her.

Principle Eight: Provide Continuing Support

The eighth principle is that good grief counseling requires continuing support. Unlike grief therapy, which is more focused on a specific time period, with grief counseling, the counselors can make themselves available to the survivor and family over the most critical periods at least for the first year following death. Some of these critical time periods have already been mentioned. The counselor's role here is to provide hope and a long-range perspective. One good way continuing support can be offered is through group participation. There are special groups for those who have lost spouses, children, parents, etc. Counselors can refer to or lead such support groups and encourage their use. Developing effective bereavement groups will be discussed later in this chapter.

Principle Nine: Examine Defenses and Coping Styles

The ninth principle involves helping clients examine their particular defenses and coping styles because they will be heightened by a significant loss. This is most easily accomplished after a trust develops between the client and the counselor, when clients are more willing to discuss their behavior. Some of these defenses and coping styles portend competent behavior, others do not. For example, a person who copes by using alcohol or drugs excessively is probably not making an effective adjustment to the loss:

> The utility of small amounts of alcohol for sleep, diminishing anxiety, and obliterating ruminative thinking predispose the grieving survivor to find comfort in drinking, at times leading to gradual escalation and eventually to degrees of uncontrolled or obligatory consumption. At greatest risk are those bereaved who are recovering alcoholics or who have strong family histories of alcoholism. [Shuchter & Zisook, 1987, p. 184]

The counselor needs to be alert to this and to inquire about alcohol or other drug use and/or abuse. Heavy use of drugs or alcohol can intensify the experience of grief and depression and impair the bereavement process. If a problem exists or is suspected, the counselor would do well to pursue aggressive treatment that might include the resources of groups like Alcoholics Anonymous or Narcotics Anonymous.

Someone who withdraws and refuses to look at pictures of the deceased or keep anything around that is a reminder of the deceased may have a coping style that is not healthy. The counselor can highlight these coping styles and help the client to evaluate their effectiveness. Then together client and counselor can explore other possible coping avenues that may be more effective in lowering distress and resolving problems.

Principle Ten: Identify Pathology and Refer

The tenth and final principle on this list is to identify trouble and know when to refer. A person doing grief counseling may be able to identify the existence of pathology which has been triggered by the loss and the subsequent grieving and, having spotted such difficulty, may find it necessary to make a professional referral. This particular role is often called the "gatekeeper" role. For some people, grief counseling or the facilitation of grief is not sufficient and the loss or the way that they are handling the loss may give rise to more difficult problems. Some of these problems may require special interventions; they are discussed in Chapter 5, "Grief Therapy." Because these difficulties require special techniques and interventions and an understanding of psychodynamics, dealing with them may not be within the purview and skill of the grief counselor. And even if it is, the strategies, techniques, and goals of intervention may change. It is important for grief counselors to recognize their limitations and to know when to refer a person for grief therapy or other psychotherapy.

Before I leave the principles and practices of grief counseling, platitudes should be mentioned. These are still dispensed by well-meaning friends and occasionally by a counselor. Platitudes, for the most part, are not helpful. Many of the women in our studies said, "When somebody came up to me and said, 'I know how you feel,' this comment made me want to scream and shout back at them, 'You don't know how I feel, you couldn't possibly know how I feel, you've never lost a husband.' " Comments like, "Be a brave little boy," "Life is for the living," "This will soon end," "You're standing up well," "It will be over in a year," "You'll be fine," "Keep a stiff upper lip," are generally not at all helpful. Even "I'm sorry" can be a close-off comment to further discussion. And there are those who, in an attempt to make somebody feel better, start spouting out about the losses and tragedies they have had in their own life, perhaps unaware that comparing tragedies is not a helpful procedure. People in pain make us feel helpless. This helplessness can be acknowledged in a simple statement like, "I don't know what to say to you."

Useful Techniques

Any counseling or therapy should be based on a solid theoretical understanding of human personality and behavior and not be merely a set of techniques. However, there are several techniques I have found useful in doing grief counseling, and I want to mention them here.

(a) *Evocative language*. The counselor can use tough words that evoke feelings, for example, "Your son died" versus "You lost your son." This language helps people with reality issues surrounding the loss and can stimulate some of the painful feelings that need to be felt. Also, speaking of the deceased in the past tense can be helpful: "Your husband was . . ."

(b) *Use of symbols*. Have the mourner bring photos of the deceased to the counseling sessions. This not only helps the counselor get a clearer sense of who the person was, but it also creates a sense of immediacy of the deceased and a concrete focus for talking *to* the deceased rather than talking *about* him or her. Other symbols I have found helpful are letters written by the deceased, audio or video tapes of the deceased, and articles of clothing and jewelry.

(c) *Writing*. Have the survivor write a letter or letters to the deceased expressing thoughts and feelings. This can help them to take care of unfinished business by expressing the things that they need to say to the deceased. Keeping a journal of one's grief experience or writing poetry can also facilitate the expression of feelings and lend personal meaning to the experience of loss. Lattanzi and Hale have written a good article on the various uses of writing with the bereaved (Lattanzi & Hale, 1984).

(d) *Drawing*. Like writing, drawing pictures that reflect one's feelings as well as experiences with the deceased can also be helpful. This is a very good technique to use with bereaved children, but it works with adults as well.

(e) *Role playing*. Helping the bereaved to role play various situations that they fear or feel awkward about is one way to build skills—something that is very useful in working with Task III issues. The counselor can enter into the role playing, either as a facilitator or to model possible new behaviors for the client.

(f) *Cognitive restructuring*. Here the underlying assumption is that our thoughts influence our feelings, particularly the covert thoughts and self-talk that constantly goes on in our minds. By helping the client to identify these thoughts and reality test them for accuracy or overgeneralization, the counselor can help to lessen the dysphoric feelings triggered by certain irrational thoughts such as, "No one will ever love me again," a thought that is certainly not provable in the present. For a further discussion of this approach see *Feeling Good* by David Burns, 1980.

(g) *Memory book*. One activity a bereaved family can do together is to make a memory book of the lost family member. This book can include stories about family events, memorabilia such as snapshots and other photographs, and poems and drawings made by various family members, including the children. This activity can help the family to reminisce and eventually to mourn a more realistic image of the dead person. In addition, children can go back and revisit this memory book in order to reintegrate the loss into their growing and changing lives.

(h) *Directed imagery*. Helping the person to imagine the deceased, either with eyes closed or visualizing their presence in an empty chair, and then encouraging them to say what they need to say to the deceased can be a very powerful technique. The power comes not from the imagery, but from being in the present and again, talking *to* the person rather than talking *about* the person.

The purpose of all these techniques is to encourage the fullest expression of thoughts and feelings regarding the loss, including regrets and disappointments.

The Use of Medication

There has been much discussion about the use of medication in the management of acute, normal grief. The general consensus is that medication ought to be used sparingly and focused on giving relief from anxiety or from insomnia as opposed to providing relief from depressive symptoms. The late Thomas P. Hackett, Chief of Psychiatry at the Massachusetts General Hospital, had considerable experience treating bereaved people. He used antianxiety agents to treat both anxiety and insomnia (Hackett, 1974). However, in administering any pharmaceuticals to patients undergoing an acute grief reaction, it is particularly important to keep any potentially lethal quantities of such drugs out of their hands.

It is usually inadvisable to give antidepressant medications to people undergoing an acute grief reaction. These antidepressants take a long time to work, they rarely relieve normal grief symptoms, and they could pave the way for an abnormal grief response, though this has yet to be proven through controlled studies. The exception would be in cases of major depressive episodes. I believe that drugs might be beneficial at the time of the loss when some sedation or help managing anxiety is useful. However, such administrations are usually of short duration and unnecessary in most cases.

Grief Counseling in Groups

Bereavement counseling can be done within the context of a group. This is not only very efficient, but can also be an effective way to offer the emotional support the bereaved person is seeking. The following are guidelines for setting up a group and for making the group work effectively:

1. *Choose a Group Format.* There are several decisions that need to be made about purpose and structure when establishing a group.

(a) Purpose. Bereavement groups usually exist for one or more of the following: emotional support, education, or for social purposes. Sometimes groups begin for one purpose which then evolves into another. Groups that begin for emotional support may continue with the same people for a period of time and become more social in their purpose, even though emotional support is still offered. Although each of these purposes can be valuable, I am a strong advocate for groups that are set up for emotional support.

(b) Structure. Some groups are closed-ended, meaning they exist for a limited time period and people enter and leave the group at the same time. Other groups are open-ended with no definite ending. People come and go as the group fulfills their individual needs. There are pros and cons for each type of group structure. In open-ended groups it is more difficult to bring new members up to speed since they do not know the history of important actions and breakthroughs that have occurred prior to their arrival. Also, as people are added, a sense of trust must be developed anew among the members.

(c) Logistics. The number of meetings, length of meetings, size of the group, and location and cost of meetings are all important decisions that need to be made before the sessions begin. In our Hospice of Pasadena we have closed-ended groups of eight to ten people who meet for purposes of education and emotional support. The groups are facilitated by co-leaders and they meet weekly, for eight sessions, 90 minutes in length. Members are asked to contribute financially in the belief that this will encourage attendance and motivate people to get more out of the group.

2. *Pre-screen Participants.* A key factor in making a group work is the selection of its members. There is much to say for homogeneity—putting people together who have had similar losses, for example, a group for bereaved spouses or one for bereaved parents. However, some bereavement programs are not large enough or serve areas where there are not sufficient people sharing similar losses to have a homogeneous group. If so, try to have at least two people in a group with similar types of losses. If there is one widower in a group of widows, it is helpful to have a second widower so that the first doesn't feel like the group deviant or the odd person out. The same holds true for including at least two people with other types of losses.

Another factor in selection is the recency of the loss. It is important not to include people whose loss was six weeks earlier or less. Most people this recent in their bereavement are not ready for a group experience. Some bereavement groups have potential members wait until six months after the loss to join. However, some time spread can be useful. A newly widowed woman can learn something from one who is further along in her bereavement, and who can model how one might move forward in terms of adaptation to loss.

It is essential to rule out serious pathology when selecting people for membership in bereavement groups. Those who have serious pathological and emotional problems are much better served by individual counseling or therapy.

In selection there are two kinds of losses that may present particular problems and these potential group members ought to be carefully considered before inclusion. One type is multiple losses. People who have lost a number of loved ones over a short period of time often are so overwhelmed by their grief that they can't participate effectively in a bereavement group. These might be people who have lost many family members suddenly in an accident or a house fire, or they could be people who have sustained a number of losses in a short period of time.

The other type of losses that may present problems in bereavement groups are losses that are difficult to talk about, such as suicide. Including one person whose loved one died by suicide can make other people in the group very anxious and this should be taken into account during the selection process. It would be better to include at least two people who are survivors of a suicide death. The same consideration applies to losses by AIDS. Specific groups for suicide survivors and survivors of AIDS can be very effective.

3. *Define Expectations*. People come to the group with various expectations, and if the group does not meet these expectations, these people will be disappointed and may not return. This is not only unfortunate for the individual, but also demoralizing to the group when someone doesn't return. Before the first group meeting the intake worker who is interviewing people for group selection can shape a person's expectations and deal with any misconceptions or unrealistic fears about group membership. Recently a woman approached us about joining our hospice bereavement group and we referred her to another group because she clearly wanted anonymity. In our group everyone is encouraged to share as much as they want, and the nonsharing person would clearly not fit into the group. We referred her to a larger group that had more of an educational focus than a support focus, and where she could find the anonymity she wanted. When selecting people for a bereavement group, be sure to deal with their expectations up front.

4. *Establish Ground Rules*. Ground rules are rules that are laid out by the group leader right at the start and they serve several purposes. They provide structure, which can help members to feel safe. Knowing that there are certain rules of behavior and deportment can add to a sense of support. Ground rules also help leaders with control. For example, if a ground rule states that everybody gets a fair share of time to talk about their personal experience, and one group member is taking up an inordinate amount of

time, the leader can cite the ground rule to make the sharing more equitable. Or, if someone in the group has broken the ground rule of confidentiality, the leader can address that issue openly. Always explain the ground rules in the first session and reiterate them in the first couple of group sessions.

Examples of ground rules we use in our bereavement support groups are:

(a) Members are expected to attend each of the sessions and to be on time.

(b) Information shared in the group stays in the group. When outside the group, members are not free to talk about another group member's experience.

(c) People are free to share as much or as little about their loss as they choose.

(d) Everybody gets equal time to share their experience. This rule helps avoid the problem of one person monopolizing the group's attention.

(e) We do not give advice unless it's asked for. It's very easy, in group situations, particularly in bereavement groups, for people to give advice. Generally, the advice is *not* solicited, and is not appreciated.

By having ground rules and by shaping expectations during the screening interview, people arrive at the group knowing that it will be a safe environment, that no one's experience is more or less important or valuable than someone else's, that each person will have their own time to share as much or as little as they choose, and that they will not be told what they should be feeling or given unwanted advice.

5. *Determine Leadership Approach*. A fifth factor that makes groups work is effective leadership and there are different formats to choose from. Some groups are run only by bereaved individuals; for example, in the Society of Compassionate Friends, bereaved parents lead groups for other bereaved parents. Other groups are led by mental health care professionals, and a third model of leadership encompasses groups led by laypeople, but with professional back-up. Professional back-up gives the lay leader someone to consult with if questions arise about individuals or group interactions. At the Hospice in Pasadena our groups are led by trained mental health professionals with co-leaders who are students in training for one of the mental health professions.

Among the various styles of leadership, some may be more effective than others, depending on the purpose of the group. Some leaders are more active, while others are more passive. I believe that the most effective style for an emotional support bereavement group leader is to be active early in the life of the group, and then, as the group forms and indigenous leadership emerges from within the group, the stated leader can retreat and become less active. A passive leader can encourage feelings of anxiety on the part of group members, especially when the group is new. The style of leadership depends, of course, on the goals of the group. If the goal is educational, then the designated leader may serve as more of a lecturer or informant. If the purpose is emotional support, the leader's role is to facilitate its development by making sure that people share their stories and find support and encouragement from the others. A group set up for the purpose of social interaction would again require a different kind of leader.

The issue of co-leadership is important in any discussion of leadership. Should there be one leader, or more than one? When groups are large, co-leadership is essential. If a group uses the co-leadership model, it's important for the leaders to maintain clear and open communication with each other. I suggest they meet shortly after the group sessions and de-brief. Tensions that may be subtle and disruptive to the group can arise between leaders. This is one way to prevent this from happening.

It is important that the leader avoid choosing favorites in a group. A group replicates family dynamics and people bring in whatever experiences they've had with their own siblings and parents. These feelings and experiences emerge in group life. It's not unusual for someone to want to be the special person in the leader's life and this can create difficulties in a group if it's allowed to happen. The leader needs to be aware of this and to turn down special invitations or favors offered by individual members of the group. The leader also needs to be aware of his or her own issues that would make special deals personally desirable. It's also important that any private meetings between the leader and individuals in the group are discussed openly at the next group meeting.

6. *Understand Interpersonal Dynamics*. What do people want when they come together in any kind of a group, whether it be a bereavement, political, or a therapy group? I believe there are three needs that, at some level of awareness, are on the minds of people when they participate in groups (Shutz, 1972).

(a) Inclusion. Most people coming in new to a group will look around and ask themselves, "Do I fit?" and "Are these my kind of people?" Unless they can answer in the affirmative, they probably won't come back for a second session. Even if they do come back, this concern will still be present in the early sessions in any group experience.

(b) Control. A second concern has to do with control. "Am I important?" "Do I matter in this group?" "Does what I say make a difference?" "To what degree can I influence this group," or "To what degree will I be influenced by other members in this group?" Just as it is important for people to feel that they fit into a group situation, it's important for people to feel that they have some degree of influence over other members of the group. If they don't, they're likely not to complete the course of group counseling.

(c) Affection. A third thing people are looking for in group participation is affection. I'm using the word affection broadly. "Am I cared for?" "Do people really care what happens to me?" Affection needs tend to be met only as a group develops a sense of identity and cohesiveness and the degree of caring varies. In some groups a strong sense of affection develops among the various members. People really do care and feel cared for. In other groups this sense of affection is much less.

To summarize: People want to feel safe and people want to feel important. If problem behaviors arise that are disruptive, it is important to raise the question, "Is this person not feeling safe? Is this person not feeling important?" Addressing these issues may help to attenuate problem behavior.

7. *Handle Disruptive Behaviors Effectively.* There are several behaviors that are disruptive to groups and that give leaders difficulty. I have summarized them here, along with suggestions for handling them.

(a) My loss is bigger than your loss. This attitude occurs from time to time in bereavement groups. I recently led a group in which two women had lost young adult daughters. One of the women still had a husband, while the other didn't. The woman without the husband told the group that her loss was bigger than the other woman's because the other woman had a husband, and she didn't. One way to handle this is for the leader to say, "Everyone's loss is important in this group," and "We're not here to compare losses."

(b) The advice giver. Camille Wortman and colleagues, at the University of Michigan, interviewed bereaved people as to what was helpful and what was not helpful to them in their bereavement. Among the least helpful things reported by these people was being given advice. Managing the advice giver is rather easy, if there is a ground rule in your group that states, "We do not give advice unless it's asked for" (Lehman et al., 1986).

(c) The moralist. Another kind of difficult person is the moralist. This is the person who is giving moralistic advice couched as "musts," "shoulds," and "have tos." We recently had a member in our bereavement group who had come out of the Twelve Step tradition and, though well-meaning, was quite preachy to other people in the group. Several members of the group resented this. We encouraged him to say, "This is what *I* would do" rather than saying, "This is what *you* should do."

(d) The nonparticipant. Another difficulty comes from the nonparticipating person. People who participate very little or not at all are often mistaken by others in the group as being critical. The easiest way to avoid nonparticipation is for the leader to help everyone share something about their own loss at the very first session. Allowing someone to remain silent at the first session will only encourage that person to continue this behavior during later sessions.

(e) The person who brings up something important at the end of the group. Two minutes before the end of the group, this person says, "By the way, my son was in an accident last week." People who do this should be encouraged to bring the issue up first thing at the next session, rather than allowing the group to go overtime and get into various control struggles.

(f) The person who shares with the therapist after the group. This person doesn't share with the group, but shares something important with the leader after the meeting. It's easy for the leader to say to the person, "I think it's important for everyone here to hear this; let's begin the next session by talking about this. Could you?"

(g) The interrupter. Frequently in groups somebody will interrupt another person. A strong leader can fend off the interrupter and then, at a more appropriate time, allow the interrupter to speak the issue that's on his or her mind.

(h) The person who shows inappropriate affect. For example, a person who laughs when everyone else is sad. An appropriate intervention is for the leader to say, "I wonder what you are experiencing when these things are happening in our group. I see you laughing and I wonder what you're feeling inside." People are often experiencing anxiety and it finds its expression in laughter.

(i) The person who makes irrelevant comments. If this happens, the leader can inquire, "I don't understand how this relates to the issues we are discussing. Could you tell me how this is relevant to what we're doing right now?"

(j) The person who shares too much. Sometimes a group member shares too much early in the life of the group and then backs off and doesn't share later on or doesn't return to the group. A leader can sometimes see this coming and gently caution the person who might share too much too soon.

(k) The group member who challenges or criticizes the leader. This is perhaps more of a problem for the leader than for the group itself, but it can make group members feel uncomfortable. In one of our meetings, a member accused a colleague of mine of being homophobic. Rather than being defensive, the challenged leader inquired, "What have I just done that you perceive I might be homophobic?" This facilitated a clarifying discussion rather than the leader jumping on the defensive and escalating the problem.

Although bereavement groups are an important vehicle for grief counseling, some people will choose not to participate in a group. In other cases, people may not be willing at one point in time, but will want to participate later. A woman I know was approached by a member of the Society for Compassionate Friends shortly after the sudden death of her 19-year-old son. She attended one meeting and left saying that she didn't ever want to attend another group. However, over a year later she reconsidered and told me she was ready to attend a group and to find some benefit in that experience.

In many psychotherapy groups a ground rule states that group members will not see each other socially between sessions. This stipulation is, in my judgment, not needed in bereavement groups. One would hope that friendships would develop among the members and that these friendships might continue beyond the life of the group. One of the tasks of mourning is being able to allow new people into one's life and to allow oneself to form new relationships. Friendships that form among members of bereavement support groups, and that continue beyond the life of the group, are small but important steps forward in the overall healing process that we're trying to facilitate through our counseling efforts.

Facilitating Grief Through Funeral Ritual

The funeral service has come in for considerable criticism, especially after the 1984 report of the Federal Trade Commission. But the funeral service, if it is done well, can be an important adjunct in aiding and abetting the healthy resolution of grief. Let me outline some of the things I think a funeral can do.

1. It can help make real the fact of the loss. Seeing the body of the deceased person helps to bring home the reality and finality of death. Whether one has a wake, an open casket, or closed casket is subject to regional, ethnic, and religious differences. However, there is a strong advantage to having the family members see the body of the deceased loved one, whether it be at the funeral home or at the hospital. Even in the case of cremation (and there seems to be growing interest in cremation as an option for disposal) the body can still be present at the funeral service in either an open or closed casket and then the cremation done after the service. In this way, the funeral service can be a strong asset in helping the survivors work through the first task of grief.

2. The funeral service can give people an opportunity to express thoughts and feelings about the deceased. Earlier we saw how important it was to verbalize one's thoughts and feelings about the dead person. In its best tradition, the funeral can provide this opportunity. However, there is a greater tendency to overidealize and overeulogize a person at a funeral. The best situation is one in which people can express both the things that they are going to miss about the lost loved one and things that they are not going to miss, even though some may consider this inappropriate. The funeral service can help the grief process as it allows people to talk about the deceased.

3. The service can also be a reflection of the life of the person who is gone. It is possible to have some accoutrements of the deceased woven into the overall service so this can affirm what was important to the deceased. In one

funeral service of a minister, people stood up from various parts of the congregation and read brief statements that had been extracted from his various writings.

4. The funeral service has the effect of drawing a social support network close to the bereaved family shortly after the loss has occurred, and this kind of social support can be extremely helpful in the facilitation of grief.

One fact that dilutes the effect of funerals is that they happen too soon. Often the immediate family members are in a dazed or numb condition and the service does not have the positive psychological impact that it might have.

Funeral directors might consider their own role in grief counseling. In addition to their role of advising people and helping them cope with the arrangements that need to be made around the time of death, some type of ongoing contact with these families might be considered for the purpose of grief counseling. Although some might feel awkward about continuing contact with the funeral director after the immediate funeral, other families would not be offended and would appreciate such continued interest.

Funeral directors might also consider sponsoring Widow-to-Widow groups and other such bereavement support groups in the community* (Steele, 1975). This is already being done in many areas. Here is an ideal opportunity for the funeral director to be involved in an important aspect of grief counseling. Funeral directors can also provide the service of teaching people about grief and healthy grieving by sponsoring educational programs in the community.

Effectiveness of Grief Counseling

Does grief counseling work? Colin Parkes reviewed a number of research studies in an attempt to answer this particular question. He looked at professional services offering support to the bereaved as well as volunteer peer group support. At the end of his examination of these studies, Parkes concluded:

> The evidence presented here suggests that professional services and professionally-supported voluntary and self-help services are capable of reducing the risk of psychiatric and psychosomatic disorder resulting from bereavement. Services are most beneficial among bereaved people who perceive their families as unsupportive or who, for other reasons, are thought to be at special risk. [Parkes, 1980, p. 9]

My own clinical experience validates this conclusion.

*A directory of services for the widowed in the United States and Canada is available through the Widowed Persons Service of the AARP, 1909 K St. N.W., Washington, D.C. 20049.

References

Burns, D. (1980). *Feeling good: The new mood therapy*. New York: Signet.

Freud, S. (1917). *Mourning and melancholia*, standard edition (vol. XIV). London: Hogarth.

Hackett, T. P. (1974). Recognizing and treating abnormal grief. *Hospital Physician, 10*, 49–50, 56.

Kilburn, L. H. (1988). *Hospice Operations Manual*. Arlington, VA: National Hospice Organization.

Lattanzi, M., & Hale, M. E. (1984–1985). Giving grief words: Writing during bereavement. *Omega, 15*, 45–52.

Lehman, D. R., Ellard, J. H., & Wortman, C. B. (1986). Social support for the bereaved: Recipients' and providers' perspectives on what is helpful. *Journal of Consulting and Clinical Psychology, 54*, 438–446.

Parkes, C. M. (1972). *Bereavement: Studies of grief in adult life*. New York: International Universities Press.

Parkes, C. M. (1975). Determinants of outcome following bereavement. *Omega, 6*, 303–323.

Parkes, C. M. (1980). Bereavement counseling: Does it work? *British Medical Journal, 281*. 3–6.

Parkes, C. M., & Weiss, R. S. (1983). *Recovery from bereavement*. New York: Basic.

Raphael, B. (1977). Preventive intervention with the recently bereaved. *Archives of General Psychiatry, 34*, 1450–1454.

Schwartz-Borden, G. (1986). Grief work: Prevention and intervention. *Social Case Work*, 499–505.

Sheldon, A. R., et al. (1981). A psychosocial analysis of risk of psychological impairment following bereavement. *Journal of Nervous and Mental Disease, 169*, 253–255.

Shuchter, S. & Zisook, S. (1987). The therapeutic tasks of grief. In S. Zisook (Ed). *Biopsychosocial aspects of bereavement*. Washington: American Psychiatric Assn.

Shutz, W. (1967). *Joy: Expanding human awareness*. New York: Grove.

Silverman, P. R. (1986). *Widow to widow*. New York: Springer Publishing Company.

Simos, B. G. (1979). *A time to grieve*. New York: Family Service Association.

Steele, D. W. (1975). The funeral director's guide to designing and implementing programs for the widowed. Milwaukee: National Funeral Directors Association.

van der Hart, O. (1988). An imaginary leave-taking ritual in mourning therapy: A brief communication. *International Journal of Clinical and Experimental Hypnosis, 36*, 63–69.

Worden, J. W. (1976). *Personal death awareness*. Englewood Cliffs, NJ: Prentice-Hall.

Worden, J. W., & Silverman, P. R. (1989). Predicting grief responses. Paper presented at the NHO Conference on Hospice Bereavement Care. Denver, August.

Chapter 4

Abnormal Grief Reactions: Complicated Mourning

Before considering specific abnormal grief reactions, it is important to understand why people fail to grieve. Later we will examine types of abnormal or complicated grief and see how the clinician can diagnose and determine these cases.

Why People Fail to Grieve

When we looked at normal grief in Chapter 2, we saw a wide spectrum of behaviors that make up a normal grief reaction and identified seven major areas that can influence the type, intensity, and duration of grief. Most of these areas are important when we consider why people fail to grieve.

Relational Factors

Relational variables define the type of relationship the person had with the deceased. The most frequent type of relationship that hinders people from adequately grieving is the highly ambivalent one with unexpressed hostility. Here an inability to face up to and deal with a high titre of ambivalence in one's relationship with the deceased inhibits grief and usually portends excessive amounts of anger and guilt which cause the survivor difficulty. Another type of relationship that causes difficulty is a highly narcissistic one, whereby the deceased represents an extension of oneself. To admit to the loss would then necessitate confronting a loss of part of oneself, so the loss is denied.

In some cases, the death may reopen old wounds. The death of a parent, step-parent, or other person who has been sexually abusive to the mourner may reopen residual feelings from this situation. Research on abuse has shown that victims often suffer from low self-esteem and self-blaming attributional styles. This sense of self-blame can rearise around and after a death and can move a person into more complicated forms of grief. This is less likely to happen if the feelings surrounding the abuse have been worked out prior to the death event. However, even in cases where one has "dealt" with the abuse issues earlier, the death can bring up thoughts and feelings that stem from this type of complicated and conflicted relationship with the abuser.

In some relationships we grieve for what we wished for and never had or will never have. I recently worked with a woman whose mother suffered from Alzheimer's disease and needed nursing home care. As she watched her mother's progressive deterioration, she became acutely aware that she was losing the opportunity for her abusive mother to ever love her and care for her. After her mother died, she came for treatment of her depression. Grief work involved helping her to grieve her mother and to grieve the dissolution of her dream of ever receiving the kind of love and acceptance she craved from her mother.

Highly dependent relationships are also difficult to grieve. Mardi Horowitz and colleagues at the University of California Medical School in San Francisco believe that dependency and orality play an important part in predisposing a person to a pathological grief reaction. A person who has a highly dependent relationship and then loses the source of that dependency experiences a change in self-image from that of a strong person, well sustained by the relationship with a strong other, to the preexistent structure of a weak, helpless waif supplicating in vain for rescue by a lost or abandoning person (Horowitz, 1980).

Most people who lose a significant other will feel somewhat helpless and see themselves in a helpless position, but this sense of helplessness does not have the desperate quality that it does in the life of a person coming from an overly dependent relationship, nor in the more healthy person does the sense of helplessness preclude other, more positive self-images. In a normal, healthy personality there is a balance of self-image percepts between the positive and the negative. For the person who loses an excessively dependent relationship, feelings of helplessness and the self-concept of being a helpless person tend to overwhelm any other feelings or any ability to modulate this negative self-concept with a more positive one.

Circumstantial Factors

Earlier, we saw that the circumstances surrounding a loss are important to the determination of the strength and the outcome of the grief reaction. There are certain specific circumstances that may preclude a person's grieving or make it difficult for him or her to bring grief to a satisfactory conclusion. The first of these is when the loss is uncertain (Lazare, 1979). One example of this would be a soldier missing in action. His wife does not know whether he is alive or dead and consequently is unable to go through an adequate grieving process. After the Vietnam War some women finally came to believe that their missing husbands were actually dead. They went through the grieving process and dealt with their loss only to have their husbands, who had been prisoners of war, released and returned to them. This may sound like a good plot for a Hollywood romance, but in reality this situation caused great difficulties for these couples and some of the marriages ended in divorce.

There is the opposite situation, which also causes inconclusive grieving. There are women who still believe that their husbands are alive somewhere in Vietnam and they will hold onto this belief and be unable to resolve their grief until they know for sure their husbands are dead.

Another circumstantial difficulty arises when there are multiple losses such as occur in earthquakes, fires, or airplane crashes or when an accident kills many members of a family (Lazare, 1979). One example of multiple losses was the mass suicide in Jonestown, Guyana, in which several hundred people died. The circumstances and extent of this loss made it very difficult for the surviving families to go through an adequate grieving period. The sheer volume of people to be grieved was overwhelming, and in a case like this, it can seem easier to close down the mourning process altogether. Multiple losses also occur in less dramatic ways. I treated a woman who lost four close family members in three years. She was so overwhelmed that she did not openly grieve, but experienced her grief as disabling anxiety, the symptom that brought her in for treatment. This could be seen as bereavement overload (Kastenbaum, 1969).

Historical Factors

People who have had complicated grief reactions in the past will have a higher probability of having a complicated reaction in the present. "Past losses and separations have an impact on current losses and separations and attachments and all these factors bear on fear of future loss and separations and capacity to make future attachments" (Simos, 1979, p. 27). Those people who have had a history of depressive illness also run a higher risk of developing a complicated reaction.

One area that is of particular interest is the influence of early parental loss on the development of subsequent complicated grief reactions in other losses. There have been a number of studies of this as it relates to the development of later mental health problems, but to date the evidence is not conclusive. Early parental loss may be important, but so is early parenting. In his longitudinal studies of men, Vaillant found "orality and dependence that made grieving difficult stemmed more from having lived with inconsistent, immature, and incompatible parents rather than having lost good parents" (Vaillant, 1985, p. 62). There is some evidence that persons experiencing complicated grief reactions felt insecure in their childhood attachments and were ambivalent toward mothers—their first love objects (Pincus, 1974).

Personality Factors

Personality factors are related to the person's character and how this affects his ability to cope with emotional distress. There are some people who are unable to tolerate extremes of emotional distress so they withdraw in order to defend themselves against such strong feelings. Because of this inability to tolerate emotional distress, however, they short-circuit the process and often develop a complicated grief reaction.

Those whose personalities do not tolerate dependency feelings well will have difficulty grieving:

> Because the resolution of grief demands the experiencing of universal feelings of helplessness in the face of existential loss, those individuals whose major defenses are built around avoidance of feelings of helplessness may be among those likely to have dysfunctional reactions of grief. Thus the individuals who normally function most competently on the surface may be the very ones thrown more heavily by a major loss as it strikes at the core of their defensive system. [Simos, 1979, p. 170]

Another personality dimension that may hinder grief is one's self-concept. Each of us has ideas about who we are and generally we try to live within our definition of ourselves. If part of a person's self-concept includes being the strong one in the family, he or she may need to play that role to his or her own detriment. "Strong" people, and usually this self-concept is socially reinforced, often do not allow themselves to experience the feelings required for an adequate resolution of a loss (Lazare, 1979).

June is a middle-aged woman whose father died when she was very young. Her mother assumed the role of the strong one in the family. Circumstances necessitated putting June in a religious orphanage where they spoke only French, and though she found it difficult to cope, she identified with her mother's strength, took on the role of the strong person, and survived. Years later, when she had married and her husband died, leaving her with young children, she needed to draw on that same strength. But two years after the loss she found she was unable to resolve it and came for treatment. One of the things that was standing in her way was her need to be strong for her children, even though that strength had served her well in other difficult situations. In therapy she was able to set this need aside and explore her deeper feelings about the loss.

Social Factors

The final determinant of grief that can play an extremely important part in the development of complicated grief reactions involves social factors. Grief is really a social process and is best dealt with in a social setting in which people can support and reinforce each other in their reactions to the loss. Lazare outlines three social conditions which may portend or give rise to complicated grief reactions (Lazare, 1979). The first is a case in which *the loss is socially unspeakable,* which often happens in the case of suicidal death. When someone dies in this manner, particularly if the circumstances are somewhat ambiguous and no one wants to say whether it was suicide or an accident, there is a tendency for the family and friends to keep quiet about the circumstances surrounding the death. This conspiracy of silence causes great harm to the surviving person, who may need to communicate with others to resolve his or her own grief.

Rusty, an only child, lost his mother when he was five years old. She went into the garage, hooked up a hose to the car, and killed herself. His father was so distraught that he immediately left for the West Coast, leaving the child in the care of relatives some distance from his hometown in the Midwest. No one ever spoke to him about his mother's death and particularly about how it happened. But the problems caused by this early loss, and his father's subsequent abandonment, resurfaced when he reached his late twenties. He was having problems in his marriage and his wife was threatening to leave him. In therapy Rusty was finally allowed to examine his childhood and the effects his loss and unresolved grief had on his adult life.

In reaction to the silence surrounding suicide, there are support groups set up specifically for the families and friends of those who kill themselves. This kind of support group plays a particularly important role for those people who are not allowed the comfort derived from open communication among their family and friends.

A second social factor that complicates a grief reaction happens when *the loss is socially negated;* in other words, when the person and those around him act as if the loss did not happen. I think a good example of this is the way some people deal with abortion. Many single young women who get pregnant choose to terminate the pregnancy. One problem here is that the decision is often made in isolation—the man often is not told about the pregnancy and the woman's family is not involved, often because of fear. So the woman has the abortion and then buries the incident deep in her mind, as if it did not happen. But the loss still needs to be grieved and if it is not, it may surface later in some other situation. Grieving an abortion will be discussed in more detail in Chapter 6.

A third social dimension that may cause complications is *the absence of a social support network.* The kind of support matrix here includes people who knew the deceased and who can then give each other support. In our society, people frequently move far away from friends and family members. When someone living in Boston experiences the death of a significant loved one in California, that person may receive some support from his or her peer group in the Boston area, but it does not have the same impact if no one in that group knew the deceased. This particular absence of a social support network is due to geography, but social support can be missing for other reasons. It may be absent because of social isolation.

In Parkes' study of London widows, he found that those who were the most angry following the loss of their husbands also experienced the highest degree of social isolation (Parkes, 1972). This relationship between anger and social isolation has been noted in our research. A woman who loses her husband and who is very angry may also experience isolation, even though there are family and friends around her. This not only makes her grieving more difficult but probably serves to increase the amount of anger she is feeling. One young widow was left with three children. She experienced much support from her friends. However, six months later, she was very, very angry because no one was approaching or calling her anymore. My sense was that her anger only served to push people into the background and in turn to isolate her further.

How Grief Goes Wrong

Abnormal grief appears in several forms and has been given different labels. It is sometimes called pathological grief, unresolved grief, complicated grief, chronic grief, delayed grief, or exaggerated grief. In the most recent volume of the *Diagnostic and Statistical Manual* of the American Psychiatric Association, abnormal grief reactions have been referred to as "complicated bereavement." But whatever you choose to call it, whether it is abnormal grief or pathological grief, it is:

> the intensification of grief to the level where the person is overwhelmed, resorts to maladaptive behavior, or remains interminably in the state of grief without progression of the mourning process towards completion . . . [It] involves processes that do not move progressively toward assimilation or accommodation but, instead, lead to stereotyped repetitions or extensive interruptions of healing. [Horowitz, 1980, p. 1157]

Early in the century, Freud and Abraham wrote papers which differentiated normal from pathological grief (Abraham, 1927; Freud, 1917). However, their approach was basically to describe certain characteristics as being common to normal grief while other characteristics were common to pathological grief reactions. This descriptive approach is generally not sufficient or satisfactory. Subsequent field studies indicate that some of the characteristics which Freud and Abraham described as characteristics of pathological grief are found in typical normal grief reactions found in random populations. An example of this would be episodes of pain following a loss. Freud and Abraham thought that these episodes were indicative of a pathological reaction, whereas now we see it as a fairly common experience. Today we find that there is more of a continuous relationship between normal and abnormal grief reactions, between the complicated and uncomplicated, and that pathology is more related to the intensity of a reaction or the duration of a reaction rather than to the simple presence or absence of a specific behavior (Horowitz, 1980).

There are several ways to outline complicated grief reactions. One of the more useful paradigms describes them under four headings: (1) chronic grief reactions, (2) delayed grief reactions, (3) exaggerated grief reactions, and (4) masked grief reactions. Let's examine each one of these individually.

Chronic Grief Reactions

A chronic grief reaction is one that is excessive in duration and never comes to a satisfactory conclusion. Anniversary reactions are common for ten years or longer, but these in themselves do not indicate chronic grief. This type of grief reaction is fairly easy to diagnose because the person undergoing the reaction is very much aware that he or she is not getting through the period of mourning. Even though the person is aware of the condition, chronic grief does not necessarily resolve on its own. This awareness is particularly strong when the grieving has gone on for several years and the person is feeling unfinished. People coming for help will say things like, "I'm not getting back to living," "This thing is not ending for me," "I need help to be myself again."

For some, treatment will require facing the fact that the person is gone and will never return. For others it may be assistance to sort out and deal with confusing and ambivalent feelings toward the deceased. Some with chronic grief reactions may yearn for a relationship that never was but might have been (Paterson, 1987). I have seen this in some individuals whose background included alcoholism, as well as physical and sexual abuse. For those who had a highly dependent relationship with the deceased, help to adapt to the absence of the loved one and skill building may be a part of the intervention. For still others with high attachment needs, loss leaves them feeling unsafe and unable to make it on their own. These may need help and encouragement in forming new relationships that can help fill some of that need. A chronic or prolonged grief reaction requires that the therapist and client assess which of the tasks of grieving are not being resolved and why. Then intervention is focused on the resolution of these tasks.

Delayed Grief Reactions

Delayed grief reactions are sometimes called inhibited, suppressed, or postponed grief reactions. In this case the person may have had an emotional reaction at the time of the loss, but it is not sufficient to the loss. At a future date the person may experience the symptoms of grief over some subsequent and immediate loss, but the intensity of his or her grieving seems excessive. What is happening here is that some of the grieving, particularly as it is related to Grief Task II, which was not adequately done at the time of the original loss, is carried forward and is being experienced at the time of the current loss. The person generally has the distinct impression that the response they are experiencing is exaggerated vis-à-vis the current situation.

An interesting example of delayed grief occurred in a case where a woman lost several of her children in an accident. She was pregnant at the time and was advised not to get too upset because intense feelings could jeopardize her pregnancy. She heeded this advice, only to have intense grief appear when her last child left home (Geller, 1985).

Overwhelming feelings at the time of the loss may cause the person to delay their grief. This is often true in the case of a death by suicide. Although some grieving is done at the time, it is not sufficient for the loss and grief may surface later. Delayed grief can also be stimulated by other types of losses. I have seen several people whose grief for an earlier loss by death has been triggered by an impending or recent divorce. Delayed grief can also arise years after a spontaneous abortion.

Such delayed reactions can occur not only to a subsequent loss, which is directly related to the individual undergoing the experience, but also when watching someone else go through a loss or when watching a film, television, or some other media event in which loss is the main theme. When you see a sad play, it is normal to have sad feelings. But what earmarks the characteristics of a delayed grief reaction is the intensity of these feelings which, on further examination, often turn out to be unresolved grief for a former loss. Bowlby suggests a probable explanation of the tendency for a recent loss to activate or reactivate grieving for a loss sustained earlier. When a person loses the figure to whom he is currently attached, it is natural for him to turn for comfort to an earlier attachment figure. If, however, the latter, for example a parent, is dead, the pain of the earlier loss will be felt afresh, or possibly for the first time (Bowlby, 1980).

Exaggerated Grief Reactions

This third diagnostic category has to do with exaggerated grief responses in which the person experiencing the intensification of a normal grief reaction feels overwhelmed and resorts to maladaptive behavior. Unlike masked grief, where the person is unaware that their symptoms are related to a loss, the person with an exaggerated grief response is aware that the symptoms and behaviors they are experiencing are related to the loss and they seek therapy because their experience is excessive and disabling. Exaggerated grief responses include major psychiatric disorders that develop following a loss.

Clinical depression that develops following a loss is one example. Feeling depressed and hopeless after the loss of a significant other is a common and usually transient phenomenon for many bereaved. But most are not clinically depressed. However, if these feelings of hopelessness blossom into irrational despair, and are accompanied by other depressive features, a diagnosis of clinical depression may result.

Anxiety is another common response following loss. If the anxiety is experienced as panic attacks or by the development of phobic behavior, then I would include these disorders under exaggerated grief. Phobias that arise in the context of loss are often centered around death. One patient, who had a previous history of psychiatric care, lost her father, and then, within a three-month period, began to develop serious thanatobia and returned for treatment to get relief from the symptoms. Often underlying this type of phobia is unconscious guilt and the thought, "I deserve to die too," usually stemming from an ambivalent relationship with the deceased.

Serious alcoholism or other substance abuse that develops or is exacerbated by a death would be included here under exaggerated grief reactions. Those who treat alcoholism should explore the possibility of unresolved grief as part of the recovery process.

There are some who suffer loss, usually of a catastrophic nature, who develop signs and symptoms of Post-Traumatic Stress Disorder (PTSD). I have worked with Vietnam veterans as well as survivors of serious automobile accidents who exhibited the classic symptoms of PTSD. There are specific approaches to working with this disorder which are beyond our discussion of grief therapy. However, this disorder precipitated by a death would fall under exaggerated grief.

Several cases of mania occurring after loss have been reported in the literature. Usually this occurs in a person with a history of affective disorder. Should this occur, I would consider it a form of complicated bereavement (Rosenman & Tayler, 1986).

Masked Grief Reactions

Masked grief reactions are interesting in that patients experience symptoms and behaviors which cause them difficulty but do not see or recognize the fact that these are related to the loss. They develop nonaffective symptoms or, as Parkes says, symptoms which are seen as affective equivalents of grief.

Helene Deutsch, in her classic paper on the absence of grief, comments on this phenomenon. She says that the death of a beloved person must produce some kind of reactive expression of feeling and that the omission of such is just as much a variation of normal grief as grief which is excessive in time and intensity. She further states that if a person does not express feelings in an overt manner, this unmanifested grief will be found expressed to the full in some other way. Her suggestion is that people may have absent grief reactions because their ego is not sufficiently developed to bear the strain of this work of mourning and that the person uses some mechanisms of narcissistic self-protection to circumvent the process (Deutsch, 1937).

Masked or repressed grief generally turns up in one of two ways: either it is masked as a physical symptom or it is masked through some type of aberrant or maladaptive behavior. Persons who do not allow themselves to experience grief directly may develop medical symptoms similar to those which the deceased displayed or they may develop some other kind of psychosomatic complaint. For example, pain can often be a symbol for suppressed grief, or patients being treated for various somatoform disorders may have an underlying grief issue.

Zisook and DeVaul report on several cases where the physical symptoms experienced by the survivor were similar to those suffered by the deceased during their last illness. They call these "facsimile illnesses." One case involved a woman who presented with chest pains identical to those suffered by her husband before he died of a heart attack. The symptoms first appeared around the anniversary of his death. In another case a woman presented with stomach pain. Her mother had died seven years earlier and the first episode of pain occurred on the first anniversary of the loss. In both cases there was no organic pathology and the symptoms abated after the grief issues were dealt with in therapy (Zisook & DeVaul, 1976).

On the other hand, physical symptoms may not be the only manifestation of repressed grief—it may also be masked as a psychiatric symptom, such as unexplained depression, or as some type of acting out or other maladaptive behavior. There have been some studies which suggest that delinquent behavior can be seen as an adaptive equivalent in the case of a masked grief reaction (Shoor & Speed, 1963).

Diagnosing Complicated Grief

How does a therapist go about diagnosing a complicated grief reaction? There are generally two ways. Either a patient will come with a self-diagnosis or the patient will come for some kind of medical or psychiatric problem quite unaware that unresolved grief is at the heart of the distress. In the latter case it requires the skill of the clinician to determine that unresolved grief is the underlying problem, while in the first case, diagnosis is a rather easy matter. I have yet to see a case in which a person came for therapy because he believed that his condition related to his loss where this has not been true. May is a good example. When she was in her early fifties, her son was killed in a midair collision over Florida. There were a number of factors that made it difficult for her to grieve her son: it was a sudden death; it happened far away from their home; because of the circumstances surrounding the death, there was no body at the funeral. Approximately two years later, May approached her minister and said that she was not getting through her grief. She was not back doing the kinds of things that she had done prior to the loss. She had a definite feeling of being stuck in the grieving process and requested his help. This type of self-diagnosis is very typical.

However, many times people come for medical or psychiatric care unaware of the dynamics of grief, and this requires that the clinician help make the diagnosis. Most intake procedures require a fairly detailed history from the client or patient, but deaths and losses can be overlooked, and these can have a direct relationship to the current problems. It is very important to take a loss history when doing a formal intake procedure.

There are a number of clues to an unresolved grief reaction. Lazare has given us an excellent taxonomy of these (Lazare, 1979). Any one of these clues in and of itself may not be sufficient for a diagnostic conclusion. However, any of these clues should be taken seriously and the diagnosis of complicated grief be considered when they appear.

Clue One. The person being interviewed cannot speak of the deceased without experiencing intense and fresh grief. A man in his early thirties came to my office, not for grief therapy, but with a sexual dysfunction problem. In doing the intake, I inquired about deaths and losses and he told me his father had died. As he spoke of the loss, there was a great freshness to his sadness, which made me think that the loss might have been quite recent. However, on inquiry, he told me that his father had died some 13 years earlier. Later on in therapy we explored this irresolution to his loss and its relationship to his sexual dysfunction. So when a person is unable to speak about a previous loss without losing equanimity, one should consider the possibility of unresolved grief. Again, what you look for here is a fresh, intense sadness which occurs many years after the loss.

Clue Two. Some relatively minor event triggers off an intense grief reaction. In Chapter 6 I present the case of a young woman whose friend lost a baby *in utero* and her continuous overreaction to her friend's trouble, which led us to discover an ungrieved abortion of her own some years earlier.

Clue Three. Themes of loss come up in a clinical interview. In any good counseling or therapy, it is important to listen to themes, and when they concern loss, watch for the possibility of unresolved grief.

Clue Four. The person who has sustained the loss is unwilling to move material possessions belonging to the deceased. Someone who preserves the environment of the deceased just as it was when the death occurred may be harboring an unresolved grief reaction.

Clue Five. An examination of a person's medical record reveals that they have developed physical symptoms like those the deceased experienced before death. Often these physical symptoms will occur annually, either around the time of the anniversary of the death or around holiday seasons. These symptoms can also surface when the client reaches the same age as the deceased was at the time of death. This particular phenomenon can also happen when the client reaches the age at which the parent of the same sex died. One young man began an affair on the anniversary of his mother's death. In group therapy he confessed this, only to experience cardiovascular symptoms. Later we discovered the symptoms were similar to those his mother had had before her death.

Physicians who see patients presenting with vague somatic complaints, increased susceptibility to illness, or chronic illness behavior, may want to consider the possibility of grief-related issues. A simple inquiry into recent or past losses, how they feel they have adjusted to the loss, and if they still cry or feel the need to cry, can give the doctor important clues for deciding if there is a possible grief component.

Clue Six. Those who make radical changes in their lifestyle following a death or who exclude from their life friends, family members, and/or activities associated with the deceased may be revealing unresolved grief.

Clue Seven. A patient presents a long history of subclinical depression, often earmarked by persistent guilt and lowered self-esteem. The opposite of this can also be a clue. The person who experiences a false euphoria subsequent to a death may be experiencing unresolved grief.

Clue Eight. A compulsion to imitate the dead person, particularly if the client has no conscious desire nor competence for the same behavior, comes from the need to compensate for the loss by identifying oneself with the deceased. "Just as the frightened child has to set up a permanent mother inside himself, the adult mourner has to internalize, take into himself, his loved object so he will never lose it" (Pincus, 1974, p. 128). This can even include taking on personality characteristics of the deceased which previously were rejected by the survivor. Through imitation, the survivor may attempt to repair the rejection and gain restitution.

Clue Nine. Although self-destructive impulses can be stimulated by a number of situations, unresolved grief can be one of these and should be considered.

Clue Ten. Unaccountable sadness occurring at a certain time each year can also be a clue to unresolved grief. This feeling may occur around times that were shared with the deceased such as holidays and anniversaries.

Clue Eleven. A phobia about illness or about death is often related to the specific illness that took the deceased. For example, if the death was of cancer, the person may develop cancer phobia, or if the person died of heart disease, the client may have an abnormal fear of heart attack.

Clue Twelve. A knowledge of the circumstances surrounding the death can help the therapist determine the possibility of unresolved grief. If clients have suffered significant loss, always ask them what it was like for them at the time of that loss. If they avoided visiting the gravesite or participating in death-related rituals or activities, they may be harboring unresolved grief. This can also be true if they did not have family or other social support during the bereavement period.

With an understanding of diagnostic clues to unresolved grief, we can now move on to a consideration of grief therapy itself. However, a caveat is important. I agree with Belitsky and Jacobs who advocate a cautious approach:

> . . . diagnostic decisions ought to be conservative in the circumstances of bereavement to avoid interference in a normal human process and iatrogenic complications with the associated introduction of professional interventions and their accompanying side effects. [Belitsky & Jacobs, 1986, p. 280]

In Chapter 5, we will look at specific techniques that the therapist can use to help people with complicated mourning to resolve their grief and move through to a completion of the four tasks of grieving.

References

Abraham, K. (1927). *Selected papers on psychoanalysis.* London: Hogarth.

American Psychiatric Association (1987). *Diagnostic and statistical manual of mental disorders,* Volume III-Revised. Washington: American Psychiatric Assn.

Belitsky, R., & Jacobs, S. (1986). Bereavement, attachment theory, and mental disorder. *Psychiatric Annals, 16,* 276–280.

Bowlby, J. (1980). *Attachment and loss: Loss, sadness, and depression* (vol III). New York: Basic Books.

Deutsch, H. (1937). Absence of grief. *Psychoanalytic Quarterly, 6,* 12–22.

Freud, S. (1917). *Mourning and melancholia,* standard edition (vol. XIV). London: Hogarth.

Geller, J. L. (1985). The long-term outcome of unresolved grief: An example. *Psychiatric Quarterly, 57,* 142–146.

Horowitz, M. J., Wilner, N., Marmar, C., & Krupnick, J. (1980). Pathological grief and the activation of latent self images. *American Journal of Psychiatry, 137,* 1157–1162.

Kastenbaum, R. (1969). Death and bereavement in later life. In A. H. Kutscher (Ed.), *Death and bereavement.* Springfield, Ill: Thomas.

Lazare, A. (1979). Unresolved grief. IN: A. Lazare (Ed.), *Outpatient psychiatry: Diagnosis and treatment.* Baltimore: Williams & Wilkens.

Parkes, C. M. (1972). *Bereavement: Studies of grief in adult life.* New York: International Universities Press.

Paterson, G. W. (1987). Managing grief and bereavement. *Primary Care, 14,* 403–415.

Pincus, L. (1974). *Death and the family.* New York: Pantheon.

Rosenman, S. J., & Tayler, H. (1986). Mania following bereavement: A case report. *British Journal of Psychiatry, 148,* 468–470.

Shorr, M., & Speed, M. N. (1963). Delinquency as a manifestation of the mourning process. *Psychiatric Quarterly, 37,* 540–558.

Simos, B. G. (1979). *A time to grieve.* New York: Family Service Association.

Vaillant, G. (1985). Loss as a metaphor for attachment. *American Journal of Psychoanalysis, 45,* 59–67.

Zisook, S., & DeVaul, R. A. (1976). Grief related facsimile illness. *International Journal of Psychiatric Medicine, 7,* 329–336.

Chapter 5

Grief Therapy:
Resolving Pathological Grief

The goal of grief therapy is somewhat different from the goal of grief counseling. The goal in grief counseling is to facilitate the tasks of mourning in the recently bereaved in order that the bereavement process will come to a successful termination. In grief therapy the goal is to identify and resolve the conflicts of separation which preclude the completion of mourning tasks in persons whose grief is absent, delayed, excessive, or prolonged.

Grief therapy is most appropriate in situations that fall into these three categories: (1) the complicated grief reaction is manifested as prolonged grief; (2) the grief reaction manifests itself through some masked somatic or behavioral symptom; (3) the reaction is manifested by an exaggerated grief response. Let's briefly look at these individually.

Prolonged Grief. Persons who experience this difficulty are consciously aware that they are not coming to an adequate resolution of their grief, because the loss has occurred many months, sometimes years, earlier. Often the reason behind this type of complicated grief reaction is a separation conflict leading to the incompletion of one of the tasks of grieving. Because these people are aware that there is a problem, they are generally self-referred. Much of the therapy involves ascertaining which of the grief tasks has yet to be completed and what the impediments to this completion are, then moving forward with that issue.

Masked as Somatic or Behavioral Symptoms. Here the patients are usually unaware that unresolved grief is the reason behind their symptoms. However, a peripheral diagnosis, such as the one described in Chapter 4, reveals unresolved grief of a much earlier loss as the culprit. People usually experience this kind of complicated grief reaction because, at the time of the loss, the grief was absent or its expression was inhibited. Consequently, their grieving was never completed and this caused complications that surfaced later as somatic or behavioral symptoms.

Exaggerated Grief.   A precise definition of exaggeration is difficult because of the wide variety of manifestations that normal grief can take, but persons falling into this category would be those with excessive depression, excessive anxiety, or some other feature usually associated with normal grief behavior manifested in an exaggerated way so that the person is dysfunctional and a psychiatric disorder diagnosis could apply.

Goals and Setting for Grief Therapy

The goal of grief therapy is to resolve the conflicts of separation and to facilitate the completion of the grief tasks. The resolution of these conflicts necessitates experiencing thoughts and feelings that the patient has been avoiding. The therapist provides the social support system necessary for all successful grief work and essentially gives the patient permission to grieve, permission which the patient, in his or her previous social environment, was not granted. Obviously, such permission or support implies an adequate therapeutic alliance. One way to enhance this alliance is to recognize and acknowledge the difficulty some people may experience when they resurrect the past loss or, if you will, agree to "open up the case." The greater the underlying conflict, the more resistance there will be to exploring thoughts and feelings previously too painful. As in any good psychotherapy, resistances are constantly monitored and worked with as a part of the therapy process.

Grief therapy is usually conducted in an office setting and frequently on a one-to-one basis. This does not mean, however, that it cannot be done in other settings such as group therapy, particularly if an unresolved grief issue arises while the person is participating in a course of group therapy.

The first step is to set up the contract with the patient. Usually grief therapy is set up on a time-limited basis; that is, the therapist will contract with the patient for eight to 10 visits during which they will explore the loss and its relationship to the present pain or distress. In my experience, someone presenting with a focused unresolved grief reaction, without unusual complications, can usually effect a resolution of his or her problem within this eight to 10 session time frame. Patients are usually seen once a week, but more frequent meetings are sometimes more effective. Hodgkinson writes, clients can be seen:

> two or three times a week, frequently enough to ensure continued emotional facilitation but with gaps sufficiently long to allow some working through

between sessions. One session per week . . . ran more danger of the process of emotional catharsis becoming disjointed. [Hodgkinson, 1982, p. 32]

Occasionally, during a contracted sequence of grief therapy sessions, more serious underlying pathology emerges which is of such substantial nature that it may require a prolonged period of non-grief treatment for the same patient. "With people who are neurotically dependent personality types expert psychotherapeutic intervention is needed to deal with both the legitimate grief reaction as well as the underlying personality disorder" (Simos, 1979, p. 178). The therapist may also encounter an unresolved grief issue while doing a routine sequence of psychotherapy, and in this case, grief therapy may take place within the context of a longer therapy.

It is important to remember that in this type of treatment, as in any short-term treatment, the therapist must be knowledgeable and the sessions must be kept focused. One way the patient will express resistance is not to keep the focus and to go off on distracting issues that are unrelated to grief. In such cases, the therapist needs to remind the patient of the task at hand and to explore this resistance and what is being avoided.

Procedures for Grief Therapy

One can no more do good therapy by numbers than paint by numbers. However, listing therapeutic procedures may help one to remember them. The assumption underlying these procedures is that they will be applied within each therapist's own theoretical framework and level of professional competence.

1. *Rule out Physical Disease*. If the patient presents with a physical symptom, it is important to rule out physical disease. Although some symptoms do appear as grief equivalents, this is not true of all symptoms and one should never enter a course of grief therapy in which a physical symptom is the major presentation unless there is conclusive exclusion of physical disease behind the symptom. This would also be important during grief counseling if the person is manifesting physical complaints.

2. *Set up the Contract and Establish an Alliance*. Here the patient agrees to re-explore his or her relationship with the person or persons involved in the previous loss. The patient's belief that this will be beneficial is reinforced by the therapist, who agrees that this is a worthy area to explore. The focus is specific:

Past relationships are explored only if they directly affect the response to the immediate bereavement. Temporarily the therapist becomes the substitute for the lost person, whether parent, child, spouse, or lover, and aims to give hope and comfort. The therapist must remain aware of the mourner's feelings of guilt and destructiveness and must let him see that this awareness does not diminish his compassion and concern for him. [Pincus, 1974, p. 266]

3. *Revive Memories of the Deceased.* Talk about the person who has died—who he was, what he was like, what the client remembers about him, what they enjoyed doing together, and so on. It is very important to begin to build a groundwork of positive memories that will help the patient later on if he or she is resisting experienceing some of the more negative affects. This will provide balance and will enable the patient to get in touch with some of these negative areas. So considerable time is spent in the early sessions talking about the deceased, particularly about positive characteristics, quali-ties, and pleasant activities that the survivor enjoyed with the deceased. Gradually talk about some of the more "mixed" memories. Finally, lead the person into a discussion of memories filled with hurt, anger, and disappoint-ment. If the patient comes to treatment aware of only negative feelings, the process is reversed and positive memories and affects need to be revived, if only few in number.

If there are multiple losses you will need to deal with each one separately. In general, it is best to explore the loss that you believe has the fewest complicating factors first. One woman in her late twenties lost two brothers by suicide and she came for therapy. While exploring both of these losses, it became clear that the first brother to take his own life was the one with whom she had the most unfinished business and the greatest attachment. Although we dealt with each loss, she reported the greatest sense of relief when she was able to deal with her anger and guilt about the first loss.

4. *Assess Which Four Grief Tasks Are Not Completed.* If the incompletion is at the point of Task I, and the patient is saying to himself, "I won't have you dead," or "You're not dead but just away," the therapy focuses on the fact that the person *is* dead and that the survivor is going to have to accept the reality and let the person go. If the difficulty lies in Task II, where the patient accepts the reality without the affect, then the therapy focuses on the fact that it is safe to feel both positive and negative emotions with regard to the deceased, and that one can come to a balance of these feelings. One of the key interventions needed to come to the completion of Task II is the redefinition of the patient's relationship with the deceased. If the difficulty lies around Task III, then problem-solving is a major part of grief therapy—the patient is taught to overcome his or her helplessness by trying out new skills, developing new roles and, in general, is encouraged to get back to living. This was particularly true in the case of Margaret, a young widow who, prior to her husband's death, enjoyed going out to a club where people sat around a piano bar and sang show tunes. She and her husband had

enjoyed this together, but three years after his death she still would not go there, not because she did not want to be reminded of him, but because she felt she lacked the social skills to go there alone. Part of the therapy involved helping Margaret to relearn these social skills, and I remember how pleased she was the day she came in and said she had, after many failed attempts, gone to the club alone.

Finally, if the incompleted task is Task IV, then the therapist helps the patient to be emancipated from a crippling attachment to the deceased and thus be free to cultivate new relationships and go on with life. This involves giving the patient permission to stop grieving, helping sanction new relationships, and helping the patient explore the difficulties involved in saying a final goodbye.

5. *Deal with Affect or Lack of Affect Stimulated by Memories*. Often, when a patient is undergoing grief therapy and begins talking about the person who had died, the description of the deceased comes off bigger than life, e.g., "the best husband who ever lived," and it is important for the therapist to allow the patient to describe the deceased in this way early in therapy. When there is this type of description, however, there is often considerable unexpressed anger beneath the surface, and this anger can be worked through gradually by exploring the more ambivalent feelings about the deceased and, finally, by helping the patient to be in touch with his or her angry feelings. Once angry feelings are identified, the patient needs to be helped to see that these do not obliterate the positive feelings and indeed are there because he or she did care for the deceased.

The woman mentioned earlier, whose son was killed in a midair collision, described her son in this bigger-than-life way—he was a top cadet in the military, he was a graduate of an Ivy League school, he was the most wonderful son who had ever lived. As we worked together in therapy, she began to get in touch with the fact that she did have some ambivalent feelings about him. Finally, she was able to allow into consciousness and to share with me the fact that shortly before he died, he had done something which had severely displeased her and then he was gone and all of her anger was suppressed. It was very important for her, as part of her therapy, to re-experience this anger and to see that the angry feelings did not preclude the positive ones, and vice versa, and to be able to express them to her son.

In a similar situation is Laura, a woman in her late twenties, who came in for psychotherapy. During the course of the treatment, it seemed as though there were some unresolved issues concerning her father. He had died when she was 12 years old and, as she described him, he came off bigger than life, the greatest Dad that ever lived. It was important for her to hold these positive feelings because underneath there was an incredible amount of anger that she was not in touch with. During therapy she went back to the old family homestead in the Midwest to visit the place where they had lived while he was alive. Then one day during one of our regular sessions, which just happened to fall on the anniversary of her father's death, the anger and rage erupted. She said that he had ruined her life by his death, she had to move out of her pleasant suburban home into a large city and share a room with her brother. Her anger had gone underground and she was not aware of it, but it was the stimulus that lay behind the aberrant behavior that brought her into psychotherapy. Again, it was important to leave her with a balance between positive and negative feelings.

Another affect which may come up frequently when stimulated by memories of the deceased is *guilt*. (Keep in mind we are talking about memories of someone who may have died a number of years earlier; this is grief therapy, not grief counseling.) As the patient begins to talk about the deceased, he becomes aware of some of the guilt associated with the former relationship. Again, once this guilt is identified, it is important to help the person reality test the guilt. As in acute grief, much guilt is irrational and doesn't hold up under reality testing.

Some guilt is real. Karen, a young mother whose six-year-old son died of a long and complicated illness, felt very guilty about the fact that she had not stood between him and the physicians during his final and difficult hospitalization. She had carried this guilt with her for nearly seven years. Part of her treatment involved reality testing this guilt, which she determined was real. She was then able, through psychodrama, to seek her son's forgiveness and understanding for her limitations. It is important when dealing with real guilt to include the seeking and granting of forgiveness between the deceased and the patient. In facilitating this, certain role-playing and imaging techniques may be useful.

6. *Explore and Defuse Linking Objects*. In grief therapy, you may encounter cases in which linking objects play a role in the irresolution of mourning. These are symbolic objects that the survivor keeps to provide a means through which the relationship with the deceased can be maintained externally. This concept was developed by Vamik Volkan, a psychiatrist at the University of Virginia Medical Center, who has written widely on the issue of pathological grief (Volkan, 1972, 1973).

It is important to be aware of and to understand the concept behind this phenomenon because these objects can hinder satisfactory completion of the grieving process. After the death the mourner may invest some inanimate object with symbolism that establishes it as a link between themselves and the dead individual. Most mourners are aware that they have invested the object with symbolism and most are aware of some aspects of the symbolism without perhaps comprehending all that is symbolized. Generally, linking objects are chosen from one of four areas: (1) some belonging of the deceased's, such as something they wore like a watch or a piece of jewelry; (2) something with which the dead person extended his senses, like a camera, which would represent a visual extension; (3) a representation of the deceased, such as a photograph; (4) something that was at hand when news of the death was received or when the mourner saw the dead body (Volkan, 1972).

As an example, Donna, a young woman, was at her mother's bedside as she lay dying of cancer. When it was obvious that the death was very near, she began compulsively rummaging through her mother's jewelry box, picking out the pieces that she wanted to have as mementos. After her mother died, Donna wore the jewelry on a regular basis and, indeed, she found that she felt somewhat uncomfortable when she was not wearing it. Later on, as her grieving progressed, she found less and less need to wear her mother's jewelry. Volkan believes that these types of linking objects are used to handle separation anxiety and that they provide a "token of triumph" over the loss. He believes that linking objects mark a blurring of psychic boundaries between the patient and the one mourned, as if representations of the two persons or parts of them merge externally through their use (Volkan, 1972).

It is important for the person who possesses a linking object to know where it is at all times. One patient kept a tiny stuffed animal with him always. He and his deceased wife had given a name to this particular animal and he carried it with him in his pocket, especially when he was going away on trips. One time, as he was flying home from a business trip, he felt in his pocket and discovered that the animal was missing. He was seized with panic and in desperation he pulled the seat and carpeting up in an effort to find the missing linking object. He never found it, and his anxiety was the focus of many therapy sessions following that incident. Volkan believes that the need for such an object comes from the conflicting wish to annihilate the deceased and at the same time to keep him or her alive. Both of these wishes are condensed in the linking object (Volkan, 1972).

Linking objects are similar to *transitional objects* such as children hold onto as they grow away from their parents. As they grow older, they may hold onto a blanket, stuffed animal, or some other object that makes them feel safer and more secure during the transition between the safety and security associated with their parents and their own need to grow and detach from the family and become their own person. In most cases transitional objects are dropped as children grow up. However, when they are needed and not available, it can cause a tremendous amount of anxiety and uproar.

One patient disposed of all her husband's clothing except for two or three items which she had given him. These items represented positive and happy times that they had had together. By holding onto them, she kept herself from being fully in touch with her negative feelings about the many unhappy times that they had had together. In therapy she developed the awareness that this was one of the functions that her linking objects served.

Incidentally, linking objects are different from keepsakes. Most people keep something as a memento or token of remembrance when someone dies. Linking objects, however, are invested with much more meaning and cause a great deal more anxiety when they are lost. Volkan talks about one of his cases in which the person holding the linking object was in an automobile crash. He made a desperate attempt to go back and retrieve this object and it ended up being the only thing that was retrieved from the wreckage of this very serious accident (Volkan, 1973).

It is important to ask patients about what items they have saved after the death and, if you determine that they are using something as a linking object, this should be discussed in therapy. Like Volkan, I encourage people to bring these objects to the therapy session. Doing this can be extremely helpful in facilitating the mourning and also helpful in pointing up the main conflicts causing people to get stuck in the grieving process. It is interesting to see what happens when people complete the course of grief therapy. Without external suggestion, they often put away or give away these objects in which they had previously invested extreme amounts of meaning. One patient would not leave home without carrying letters she had received from her husband while he was alive. As therapy progressed, she left the letters at home through her own initiative.

The survivor keeping the clothing that the deceased wore at the time of death is another type of transitional object behavior that I see from time to time. This particularly true in the case of sudden-death experiences. One woman whose husband died very unexpectedly found it important to keep the jacket he was wearing; she held onto it until she was able to work through her grief. Another patient and her husband had bought a small toy lobster together and had given this toy a name. Since they had no children, the lobster became a kind of pet or mascot for them. After the husband killed himself, she found it was important to sleep with this stuffed toy under her pillow and was very anxious when she did not have it. After we worked through a series of grief therapy, she was able to put the animal away in a drawer. She wanted to keep it because of the happy memories that it represented, but she no longer felt the need to have it as a source of comfort. Again, here was a person who had a very ambivalent relationship with her husband and an important part of the therapy revolved around focusing on this ambivalence and her need to understand it better and to deal with it.

7. *Acknowledge the Finality of the Loss*. Although most people accomplish this during the early months after a loss, there are those who maintain long after that it is not final—that somehow the person is coming back in some form or another. Volkan calls this a chronic hope for reunion (Volkan, 1972). Again, it is important to help these patients assess why they can not acknowledge the finality of their loss. Carol was a young woman who came from a very puritanical, restrictive family background, and although she was a

young adult at the time her father died, she would not allow herself, even after five years, to acknowledge the finality of her loss. To do so would mean that she would have to make her own choices and be subject to her own needs and impulses, something that scared her. She avoided personal choices maintaining, on one level of consciousness, the fantasy that her father was not gone and that somehow he was still there, pulling the strings and providing the external restraints on her behavior.

8. *Deal with the Fantasy of Ending Grieving.* One helpful procedure in doing grief therapy is to have the patients explore their fantasies of what it would be like to complete the grieving or what would be in it for them. What would they lose in giving up their grief? Although this is a rather simple procedure, it often yields very fruitful results.

9. *Help the Patient Say a Final Goodbye.* Just what saying goodbye to a deceased loved one is can be confusing to some. People may assume that saying goodbye will mean forgetting the person who is gone, but this is not so. Earlier, when discussing Task IV, I commented on the repositioning of the deceased in one's life so that the survivor can get on with the business of living. I view saying goodbye as saying goodbye to the desire for the deceased to be alive, to be here with me, and goodbye to the fantasy that I can ever recover the lost person. This process of goodbye places the deceased in a less central place in the survivor's life so that he or she can go on with living. And, as with each of these tasks, some never do accomplish this.

Saying goodbye may be done gradually during the course of therapy. At each session the patient is encouraged to say a temporary goodbye—"goodbye for now"—to the deceased, which eventually leads up to the point of saying a final goodbye as the therapy moves to conclusion. Usually this comes out in a statement like, "I have to let you go," "I have to say goodbye," "You're causing me too much pain and I have to let you go." After a patient has been able to say this final goodbye, there is often a tremendous sense of relief that is obvious when you see him or her at the following session. It is important for the therapist to let the patient take the lead in this process by asking if the patient is ready to say goodbye. When the unfinished business is completed the patient will know he is ready. Readiness is an oft-overlooked concept by many doing grief counseling and grief therapy.

Special Considerations for Grief Therapy

There are several special considerations that one needs to be aware of when doing grief therapy. The first is the importance of completing the grief work so that the patient is not worse off than before he or she came to you for treatment. If the problem underlying the unresolved grief has been unexpressed anger, it is critical that once this anger has been identified and felt, adequately explained during the introduction to the procedure. Even the most hesitant patient has complied, with a little encouragement. This is a very powerful technique and, as with any other psychotherapeutic technique, should not be used unless the therapist is adequately trained. Such a technique is obviously counterindicated with schizophrenic or borderline patients.

A related technique described by F. T. Megles and D. R. DeMaso involves having patients sit in chairs, close their eyes, and imagine they are talking to the deceased (Megles & DeMaso, 1980). This is an acceptable alternative to the empty chair, but what makes the technique important is not whether the person's eyes are opened or closed, but the fact that they are able to address the deceased directly in the first person and in the present time mode. I was explaining this technique to a colleague of mine who is a prominent biological researcher trained in psychoanalytic psychiatry. I wondered how he would respond when I explained these gestalt-oriented procedures, but he laughed and shared a personal experience with me. He said that his father had died two years earlier and from time to time he imagines that his father is there and holds conversations with him.

Another technique is the use of role-playing psychodrama. On occasion I have had patients play both themselves and the role of the deceased person, talking back and forth until the particular conflict is resolved. Using pictures of the deceased can often facilitate the goals of therapy. The patient will bring to the session a favorite photograph, which will then be used to stimulate memories and affects and on occasion be used as the focus for discussions with the deceased in the present tense.

With any technique, timing is essential! It is crucial that the therapist know how to time the interventions. Affect encouraged before a patient is ready will not be forthcoming. Ill-timed interpretations will fall on the floor. Training people to time psychotherapeutic interventions is always difficult. The best I can do is to reiterate that timing is extremely important because of the sensitive nature of the material and the time-limited nature of the contract.

Evaluating Results

There are usually three types of change that help one to evaluate the results of grief therapy. These are changes in: (1) subjective experience, (2) behavior, and (3) symptom relief.

Subjective Experience

People who complete a course of grief therapy report subjectively that they are different. They talk of increased feelings of self-esteem and less guilt. They make comments like, "The pain, which has been tearing me to pieces, is now gone," "I feel like this time I have really buried my mother," or "I can speak of my father without getting choked up with watery eyes."

Another subjective experience that patients report is an increase in positive feelings about the deceased. They are able to think about the deceased and to relate their positive feelings to positive experiences (Lazare, 1979). One woman who had great difficulty grieving the loss of her mother said at the end of treatment, "Now I just miss her. Before it was anguish. I think mother would be happy with my progress. Her death revived a lot of childhood feelings of frustration and helplessness. I'm not that angry anymore. There are some days when I don't even think of mother and that surprises me."

Behavioral Changes

Without suggestions, many patients experience observable behavioral changes. Searching behavior stops, they begin to resocialize, they begin to form new relationships. Patients who have previously avoided religious activities begin to return to them. People who have avoided visiting the gravesite now visit without it being suggested. One woman, who had never changed her dead son's room, came to the last session of grief therapy and said, "I'm going to dismantle my son's room and store his things in the basement. I don't think it will dishonor his memory to do this and to make a den out of his bedroom." I had never suggested this to her, but these kinds of behavioral changes are very common in somebody who has passed through a grief therapy sequence to the other side. A widow came on her own to the point where she removed her wedding rings, saying, "I'm not a married woman anymore." In still another case a woman who previously would not fly the flag which draped her son's casket would now fly it on appropriate holidays.

Symptom Relief

There are also measurable signs of symptom relief when somebody has completed a sequence of grief therapy. Patients report fewer body aches and abatement of the symptom which originally brought them in for treatment. One patient exhibited gagging symptoms, which were giving her great difficulty. They turned out to be very similar to the symptoms her father exhibited during the last two days of his life and that she had observed as a young person. These symptoms abated naturally after she had completed the grief therapy sequence and had taken care of the unfinished business with her dead father.

The point I am making here is that grief therapy works. Unlike some other psychotherapies, in which one may not be certain about the effectiveness and efficacy of the treatment, grief therapy can be very effective. The subjective experiences and observable behavioral changes lend credence to the value of such targeted therapeutic intervention.

References

Hodgkinson, P. E. (1982). Abnormal grief: The problem of therapy. *British Journal of Medical Psychology, 55*, 29–34.

Lazare, A. (1979). Unresolved grief. In: A. Lazare (Ed.), *Outpatient psychiatry: Diagnosis and treatment*. Baltimore: Williams & Wilkens.

Melges, F. T., & Demaso, D. R. (1980). Grief-resolution therapy: Relieving, revising, and revisiting. *American Journal of Psychotherapy, 34*, 51–61.

Parkes, C. M. (1972). *Bereavement: Studies of grief in adult life*. New York: International Universities Press.

Pincus, L. (1974). *Death and the family*. New York: Pantheon.

Simos, B. G. (1979). *A time to grieve*. New York: Family Service Association.

Volkan, V. (1972). The linking objects of pathological mourners. *Archives of General Psychiatry, 27*, 215–221.

death of her younger brother. She felt some of the normal responsibility for this but her burden was increased when her grandparents told her outright that she was responsible for his death. She was young and her inability to reality test the guilt led her to a long and bizarre sequence of self-destructive behavior.

Guilt can sometimes be manifested as blame. Some people handle their own sense of culpability by projecting their guilt onto others and blaming them for the death. Finding someone to blame can be an attempt to affirm control and to find a sense of meaning in a difficult to understand situation.

People who survive a death by suicide usually experience intense feelings of *anger*. They perceive the death as a rejection; when they ask, "Why, why, why?" they usually mean, "Why did he do this to me?" The intensity of their rage often makes them feel guilty. A middle-aged woman whose husband killed himself paced through her house for nearly six months shouting, "Damn it, if you hadn't killed yourself I would kill you for what you're putting me through." She needed to get the rage out of her system and in a recent follow-up, she seems to be doing very well.

A correlate of this anger is low self-esteem. Erich Lindemann emphasized this when he said, "To be bereft by self-imposed death is to be rejected" (Lindemann & Greer, 1953). Survivors often speculate that the deceased did not think enough of them or they would not have committed suicide. This "rejection" is an indictment of the survivors' self-worth. In these cases, counseling can be especially helpful.

Fear is a common response after a suicide. Farberow and colleagues found higher levels of anxiety among suicide survivors than among survivors of natural deaths (Farberow et al., 1987).

A common primary fear among survivors of suicide is of their own self-destructive impulses. Many seem to carry with them a sense of fate or doom. This is especially true of sons of suicide victims:

> Characteristically they find life lacking a certain zing. They tend to feel more rootless than most, even in a notoriously rootless society. They are squeamish-ly incurious about the past, numbly certain about the future, to this grisly extent—they suspect that they too will probably kill themselves. [Cain, 1972, p. 7]

I have been following a series of young men whose fathers killed themselves when these sons were in early adolescence. Each of these young men, now in their twenties and thirties, believe that suicide will be his own fate. It is not unusual for suicide survivors to develop this preoccupation with suicide. But while some scare themselves with this, others cope by working as volunteers for suicide prevention groups such as the Samaritans.

In cases where there have been several suicides in one family there may be anxiety concerning genetic transmission of the tendency. One young woman came for counseling, prior to her marriage, because of this fear. Two of her siblings had killed themselves and she wondered if her offspring would have a tendency to suicide or if she would fail as a parent as she felt her parents had failed her brothers.

Distorted thinking is another feature found among suicide survivors. Very often survivors, especially children, need to see the victim's behavior not as a suicide but as an accidental death. What develops is a type of "distorted communication" in families. The family creates a myth about what really happened to the victim and if anyone challenges this myth by calling the death by its real name, they reap the anger of the others, who need to see it as an accidental death or some other type of more natural phenomenon. This kind of distorted thinking may prove helpful on a short-term basis, but it is definitely not productive in the long run.

It is important to keep in mind that suicide victims often come from families in which there are difficult social problems such as alcoholism or child abuse. Within this context ambivalent feelings may already exist among family members and the suicide only serves to exacerbate these feelings and problems. In order to maximize the effectiveness of grief counseling, the counselor must take into consideration the social and family difficulties that may exist as correlates to the suicide itself.

Counseling Suicide Survivors

When counseling the survivors following a suicidal death, it is important to remember that death by suicide is one of those unspeakable losses mentioned earlier. Both the survivors and others are hesitant to talk about such a death. A counselor or therapist can move in and help fill the gap caused by this loss of communication with others. Intervention with such survivors can include the following.

Reality Test the Guilt and Blame

This procedure, described in Chapter 3, may take more time in the case of a suicide survivor. Again, much of the guilt may be unrealistic and will yield itself to reality testing, giving the person some sense of relief. One young woman who felt guilt over her brother's death was helped when she read a letter she had sent to him shortly before his suicide. The letter was among his effects and it helped her see that she *had* reached out to him. There are some instances, however, in which the person really is culpable, and the counselor is challenged to help the person deal with these valid feelings of guilt. When blame is the predominant feature, the counselor can also promote reality testing. If the blame takes the form of scapegoating, family meetings can be an effective way to resolve this.

Help Correct Denial and Distortions

Survivors need to face the reality of the suicide in order to be able to work through it. Using "tough" words with them such as "killed himself" or "hanged himself" can facilitate this. People who witnessed the suicide are sometimes plagued by intrusive images of the scene. For people who were not present, the imagined scene can sometimes be worse than the actual one. Exploring graphic images can be difficult, but discussing them can help with reality testing. These images usually fade with time, but if not, special intervention may be required.

Another task is to help correct distortions and redefine the image of the deceased, bringing it closer to reality. Many survivors tend to see the victim as being either all good or all bad, an illusion that needs to be challenged. I worked with one young woman whose father committed suicide. During her therapy it was important for her to redefine his image from that of a "Superdad" to that of a "Superdad who suffered deep clinical depression, saw no way out and, in desperation, took his own life."

Explore Fantasies of the Future

Explore the fantasies survivors have as to how the death will affect them in the future by reality testing. If there is a reality involved, explore ways to cope with that reality.

Work with Anger

Working with the anger and rage such a death can engender allows for its expression while reinforcing personal controls the survivor has over these feelings. A woman whose husband killed himself said at the final counseling session, "I've gotten through the hard part. It is a relief to be angry and you've given me permission to do this. There is still grief, but I feel it's OK."

Reality Test the Sense of Abandonment

Feeling abandoned is perhaps one of the most devastating results of a suicide. People who lose loved ones through natural death feel abandoned, even though the death was neither desired nor caused by the deceased. However, in the case of death by choice, the sense of abandonment is extreme. There may be some reality in this feeling, but the level of reality can be assessed through counseling.

Here are some additional intervention suggestions:

1. Contact the person or family right away, before distortions set in. Family myths begin early.

2. Watch for acting-out potential in counseling. The clients may try to get the counselor to reject them in order to fulfill their own negative self-image.
3. If there are sufficient people grieving this type of loss, consider starting a group for suicide survivors in your community. We have such a group in the Greater Boston area that has proven to be very helpful to its members, as have groups in other parts of the country (Wrobleski, 1984).
4. Don't assume that all families will fall apart. Some families grow closer together through this type of crisis (McNiel, 1988).

Sudden Death

Sudden deaths are those that occur without warning and require special understanding and intervention. Although suicidal deaths fall into this category, there are other types of sudden deaths such as accidental deaths, heart attacks, and homicides that need to be discussed. Several studies have followed people for a number of months subsequent to such a loss to assess the resolution of bereavement. In most of these studies, the conclusions are similar—sudden deaths are more difficult to grieve than other deaths in which there is some prior warning that death is imminent (Parkes, 1975).

There are certain special features which should be considered when working with the survivors of a sudden death. A sudden death will usually leave the survivor with a sense of unreality about the loss. Whenever the phone rings and one learns that a loved one has died unexpectedly, it creates this sense of unreality which may last a long time. It is not unusual for the survivor to feel numb and to walk around in a daze following such a loss. It is not unusual for the survivor to experience nightmares and intrusive images after a sudden loss, even though they were not present at the time of the death. Appropriate counseling intervention can help the survivor deal with this manifestation of sudden death and heighten the reality of the event.

A second feature that is often found in cases of sudden death has to do with the exacerbation of guilt feelings. Guilt feelings are common following any kind of death. However, in the case of a sudden death, there is often a strong sense of guilt expressed in "if only . . ." statements such as, "If only I hadn't let them go to the party," or "If only I had been with him." One of the main issues of counseling intervention is to focus on this sense of culpability and help the survivor reality test the issues of responsibility. A common manifestation found in children after a sudden death is that of guilt associated with the fulfillment of a hostile wish. It is not uncommon for children to wish that their parents were dead or that their siblings were dead and the sudden death of that person or persons toward whom the hostile wish was directed can leave the child with a very difficult load of guilt.

Related to the guilt is the need to blame, and in the case of a sudden death, the need to blame someone for what happened is extremely strong. Because of this, it is not unusual for someone within the family to become the scapegoat and, unfortunately, children often become easy targets for such reactions.

A fourth feature of sudden death is the frequent involvement of medical and legal authorities, especially in cases of accidents or homicide. For those whose loved one was the victim of homicide, getting on with the tasks of mourning is difficult if not impossible until the legal aspects of the case are resolved. For one family, whose young adult daughter was murdered, the legal process has gone on for six years after the death, with no end in sight. Her father recently said, "Usually, when you have a death in the family, you have the death, you have the mourning, and slowly but surely, you get on with your lives. But as long as this goes on, there is no end to the mourning, no time to put what happened behind" (*New York Times*, March 2, 1989). Some feel they have been victimized yet again by the systems that should be assisting them. These cases may need to be investigated and because there is often some strong hint of culpability, this may lead to an inquest and to a trial. As everyone knows, the judicial system moves slowly and these procedures often take a long time to reach completion. The delays can serve one of two functions: they can delay the grieving process; that is, people who are grieving may be so distracted by the details of the trial that they are kept from dealing with their own grief on a firsthand basis. However, there are times when these legal interruptions can play a positive role. When there is some adjudication of a case and the case is closed, this can help people put some closure on their grief.

A fifth special feature of sudden death is the sense of helplessness that it elicits on the part of the survivor. This type of death is an assault on our sense of power and on our sense of orderliness. Often this helplessness is linked with an incredible sense of rage, and it is not unusual for the survivor to want to vent his or her anger on someone. Occasionally, hospital personnel become the targets of violence or the survivor expresses a wish to kill certain people for having been involved in the death of a loved one. It is not uncommon to hear litiginous statements coming from survivors of a sudden death. This expression of their rage may help to counter the helpless feelings they are experiencing. The counselor should also be aware that the desire for retribution may be a defense against both the reality and the pain of the death (Rynearson, 1984).

A survivor can also exhibit manifest agitation. The stress of sudden death can trigger off a "flight or fight" response in a person and lead to a very agitated depression. A sudden increase in levels of adrenalin usually is associated with this agitation.

Unfinished business is another special concern of survivors of sudden deaths. The death leaves them with many regrets for things they did not say and things they never got around to doing with the deceased. Counseling intervention can help the survivor to focus on this unfinished business and find some way to closure.

A final special feature of sudden death is an increased need to understand. In any death, people are interested in why it happened, but in the case of sudden death, there seems to be an especially strong interest. This search for meaning can be related to the need for mastery when a death has been traumatic. Along with this, of course, is the need to ascribe not only the cause but the blame. At this point, some people find that God is the only available target for their recriminations and it is not infrequent to hear someone say, "I hate God," when they are trying to put together the pieces following the death.

Now let's look at some interventions that can be helpful to people after a sudden death.* Intervention in these cases really becomes "crisis intervention" and the principles of crisis intervention are appropriate here. It is of interest historically that the writing on crisis intervention actually began after Lindemann's publication of his work (1944) on the survivors of the Coconut Grove fire when he worked with a bereaved population.

The counselor should try to begin intervention at the scene of the crisis—in many cases this will be the hospital—and offer help aggressively. People in a state of numbness cannot always ask for help and if the intervener asks, "Do you need any help?," he or she may get a negative reply. It is more productive for the intervener to say to those involved, "I see all people who have experienced such a loss and I'm here to talk with you and to work with you."

Help the survivors actualize the loss. There are several ways that this can be done. One is viewing the body of the deceased to facilitate grief and actualization. Give them the choice to see the body. I have seen this to be a salutory experience on many occasions and advocate allowing people to see the body tastefully displayed, even in the case of death by automobile or other violent accidents. If the body is mutilated, the family should be informed of this before seeing the deceased. Being able to see the body, or part of the body, can help bring home the reality of the loss—Grief Task I. I have spoken to people who didn't see the body after an accidental death and who years later tell me that they wish they had. Another way to help actualize the loss is to keep them focused on the death (the loss), not on the circumstances of the accident or the blame.

Another intervention that the counselor can use to help the person come to the reality of the loss is to use the word "dead." For example, "Jenny

---

*I am indebted to Chaplain Jim Gibbons, my colleague in the grief counseling program at the University of Chicago, for many of these ideas on sudden death.

is dead. Whom do you want to notify about her death?" Using this word helps bring home the reality of death as well as giving assistance with regard to arrangements that need to be made.

The counselor should also be familiar with the hospital and direct the physical comfort of the family members, making it possible for them to be with each other, if at all possible, in a place away from the hustle and bustle of the emergency care service. Everything possible should be done to make them physically comfortable.

As a caregiver, be careful not to handle your own sense of helplessness through the dispensation of platitudes. Occasionally we still hear comments at the hospital like, "You've still got your husband" or "You've still got your kids" as an attempt to be helpful. Most survivors report that these comments are not comforting. For the caregiver to say, "It's going to be all right," is really to hold out false promise. However, for the caregiver to say, "You will survive," is not a platitude but a matter of truth, and occasionally this comment can bring some comfort to a person in that type of crisis.

Finally, offer follow-up care, either from yourself or from community or religious resources. For example, there are specialized groups who meet, such as support groups for parents of murdered children. Be aware of these kinds of resources and make referrals to these specialized groups as part of the ongoing care for people who have sustained a sudden death.

Sudden Infant Death (SIDS)

One type of sudden death that should be considered separately is sudden infant death. Over 7000 babies die this way each year in the United States alone. SIDS occurs in infants under one year of age and is most frequently found in infants aged two to six months. The causes of this phenomenon are not fully known and the pathogenesis of SIDS has not been firmly established. Parents who lose children to SIDS often conceptualize that the baby died of suffocation or choking or that the baby had some previously unsuspected illness.

There are several fctors that complicate grieving this type of loss. First, the death occurs without warning in babies that appear healthy. Coming as a surprise, there is no opportunity to prepare for the loss as there is in the case of infants or children who die of some progressive disease. Second, there is the absence of a definite cause, which gives rise to considerable guilt and blame. Other family members and friends are always wondering, "Why did the baby die?" The absence of definitive information always casts the pall of suspicion that there was some type of neglect on the part of the parents. This lack of cause may also trigger a relentless search by the parents for the reason for the death.

A third difficulty comes from the involvement of the legal system. As mentioned earlier, in the case of a sudden death, there is need for an investigation; very often the police investigate cases of SIDS. Many parents who have gone through this experience report that they had to endure insensitive interrogation and, in a few cases, even incarceration. With the increasing awareness of child abuse and child neglect, parents whose children have died of SIDS are now open to suspicion and legal investigation, which only adds to the stress of an already stressful situation.

Another issue in this type of loss is the meaning of the deceased child in the life of the family. It is not unusual for older siblings to have some resentment for the arrival of a new baby into the household, and then when the baby dies a few months after birth and there is no definite cause, it can create tremendous guilt reactions.

The break-up rate for partners suffering such a loss is high. Tensions build up after the death, and couples may not have sexual relations because of the fear of pregnancy and repeat of the experience. The wife may feel that her husband does not care enough about the death because he does not cry when she does. But what some wives do not realize is that the husband often does not cry because he does not want to upset her or he may be uncomfortable crying. Nevertheless, this type of misconception can place great strain on a relationship, and is a good example of the communication breakdown that can occur between parents under such pressure. Not only is there sadness, but there is also much anger. One father whose child died of SIDS at two months of age said to me, "I let him into my life for two months and he left me." At first he felt guilty about these feelings, but through counseling, he was helped to understand that they were normal.

There are certain things we can do to help people better manage this type of loss. The first has to do with how the parents are treated in the hospital. Generally, after this type of death, the infant is rushed to the hospital, where death is pronounced. How this information is passed on to the parents is important in terms of helping them to adjust to the loss. At the hospital, a sensitive intervention on the part of the hospital staff is to allow the parents the option of spending time with the dead baby. This can be extremely important because often the parents want to be near the child, to hold the child, or to talk to their dead child. There is a difference of opinion among hospital personnel as to the value of this type of procedure. But in my opinion, it is very important to let the parents have this option. A number of parents who have spent time with their dead babies have later reported how this helped them get through this very difficult experience.

Second, autopsy permission is also important in this type of death and cannot be overemphasized. It provides the parents with some reality as to what really did or did not happen. Morgan and Goering, writing on this subject, have suggested that "post-mortem examination" is more acceptable to the lay person than "autopsy" (Morgan & Goering, 1978). Permission for autopsy is sometimes denied in the case where the parent feels some guilt about the loss. However, the person asking permission can mention a number of important reasons for doing the autopsy: it is the last chance to learn all the facts about the illness and cause of death; it is easier to accept death when we know that it was inevitable; the knowledge of the exact cause of death is often necessary for settling insurance or legal matters. If the person requesting the autopsy is convinced of its importance, he or she is much more likely to obtain permission. Family members should not be bullied into giving this permission but should be tactfully encouraged to do so.

It is very important for the physician to provide information to the family about sudden infant death syndrome. It is also important to give parents some information about the grief process so that they do not feel like they are going crazy or that grief will never end. And the therapist should not overlook the siblings and their thoughts and feelings about the loss. This can be done within the context of family therapy as well as by monitoring their behavior following the death. Often trouble sleeping or problems in school will arise for these children.

Finally, parents can be counseled about subsequent pregnancies. Very often they are afraid of having another child because of the circumstances of SIDS. Counselors should also be cognizant of the high probability of denial in this type of death due to the circumstances, the age of the child, and the suddenness of the death. Many parents feel a need to keep the room intact, to draw daily baths, and to keep on with the routine for a long time until they can gradually come to the completion of Grief Task I—the awareness that the child is gone and is never coming back.

Counseling should take place over time because it is very difficult for the parents to absorb all the information at once. I think that an important part of counseling is to encourage patients to talk to other couples or families involved in similar trauma. Such sharing helps them develop a growing awareness that it was not their fault that their baby died, that there was nothing more they could do. One comment often heard from parents whose infant died during the night is, "I wish that I had been awake when she died." Referring parents to a local chapter of the national SIDS organization can be very helpful so they can share these feelings with others. The National SIDS Foundation operates a toll-free information service at 1-800-638-7437. They will provide information about SIDS or assist any organization of local parent support groups.

Miscarriages

Parents who have experienced miscarriages generally receive considerable support from family and friends. However, there are certain common experiences that people go through and these sometimes make grieving more difficult.

Generally, when a woman has a miscarriage, everyone's first concern is for her health. It is only later that people begin to come to the full recognition of what has been lost. There are a number of concerns that come to the fore at such a time. For a woman who miscarries at her first pregnancy, there is her concern as to whether she will ever be able to have more children. Physicians are usually fairly good at handling this concern, but the doctor's posture basically is one of focusing on statistics and probability levels of having a future successful pregnancy for someone of her age and physical condition. Although this information can be helpful to the woman, it is also important that the doctor recognize that she has sustained a significant loss and not try to mask or minimize this loss by focusing on the possibility of future pregnancies. Future pregnancies are certainly a concern of the woman, but many physicians, in their discomfort over a miscarriage, may deal with this by focusing on this issue alone.

Self-blame is another major concern of the woman who has experienced a miscarriage. She generally needs to blame someone and often the first focus of her recrimination is inward—was it caused by jogging, dancing, or some other physical activity? Women today may delay a first pregnancy, choosing instead to concentrate on career goals, and saving childbearing for later, when their careers are established. Losing a pregnancy under these circumstances can add to the degree of self-blame and the impact of the loss. Women also focus some of their blame on their husbands. "If only my husband hadn't been so eager for sexual relations, this wouldn't have happened," said one woman patient shortly after she had miscarried. Husbands are often the target of their wife's anger. This happens because the woman blames him for not having the same feelings that she has, or at least she perceives that they are not the same. Generally, in the circumstances surrounding a miscarriage, the husband feels powerless and his need to act strong and to be supportive may be misinterpreted by the woman as not caring.

Out of this sense of helplessness, many husbands find an ally in the physician, who is often male and who focuses on the fact that the couple can conceive and have another child soon. Although this may make him feel less helpless and may be realistic in the situation, it may not be what the woman wants to hear at that particular time. Here, as in other losses, it is very important that people be able to talk openly and honestly regarding their feelings.

Because a miscarriage involves the loss of a person, it is important that grief work be done. There is mixed opinion as to whether or not the parents should see the fetus as part of the grieving process. I have spoken to several parents who have asked to see the fetus and they have said that this was a helpful procedure—it helped them focus on the reality of the loss, then enabling them to move forward and deal with their feelings about such a loss. "It helped me see this experience as a death," one woman said after she had asked the physician to let her see her unborn baby. She was then able to say goodbye to the child and she later told me that it helped her through her mourning.

As in other losses, there is an important need to be able to talk about the loss, but in the case of miscarriages, as in the case of abortions, friends and family members are often unaware of the pregnancy or uncomfortable talking about such an experience. Their discomfort does nothing to help the parents in the resolution of their grief.

If there are other children in the family, the problem may arise of how to tell them about the death. Generally, it is important to tell the older children about the experience and to allow them to talk about their thoughts and feelings regarding the loss and to help them to grieve for a lost sibling.

Still Births

For the most part, what is true for miscarriages also pertains to *still births*. If there is one thing that sums up the approach the health care professional should take to a husband and wife undergoing this kind of experience, it is to recognize that the parents have sustained a real loss, a death. Do not try to minimize the loss by an upbeat focus on the future and the possibility of other pregnancies and other children. Although it is not unusual for some couples to want to initiate a pregnancy immediately after experiencing a still birth, counsel with them regarding acting with haste. It is often best to wait a while, until grieving is done for the child who was lost.

It is important to work with both partners involved in the loss. Fathers need to grieve too—and they do grieve, despite occasional comments to the contrary in the professional literature. Studies show that the best adaptation to this type of loss comes when both parents have similar coping styles and more open communication (Feeley & Gottlieb, 1988). Work with the parents concerning their feelings about the loss, especially the feelings of fear and guilt. Fears of special importance are the fear of future pregnancy, the fear of the impact of the loss on the marriage, and the fear of being a failure as a parent. Guilt can lead to blame or self-blame. Explore these tendencies and their resulting impact on self-esteem.

Look with the parents at their fantasies about the child they have lost. This includes looking at the meaning of the pregnancy. For example, was it planned and wanted by both partners, or was there ambivalence surrounding the pregnancy; was it the result of infertility therapy, or a pregnancy late in their marriage. If the infant was deformed, the parents have two losses to grieve—the child they *thought* they had, and the child they actually lost.

Help families to make the loss real by encouraging them to share decisions about disposition of the body, to name the baby, and to participate in rituals such as a funeral or memorial service. A meaningful collection of articles related to the baby, such as pictures of the baby, the birth certificate, a footprint, lock of hair, nursery bracelet, and cards received from friends can help make the loss real. Use the autopsy report to reality test the cause of death and to provide an opportunity for questions to be addressed.

Don't overlook the siblings. Perinatal death can be an invisible loss for the children at home. Not seeing the lost infant makes the death less real, a reality that is diminished even further if the loss is not acknowledged by the parents. A child's understanding of the loss will, of course, be influenced by his or her cognitive and emotional development. An inadequate understanding of the loss, coupled with magical thinking, can lead to a belief of personal culpability for the loss or lead to blaming the loss on the lethality of the parents. The latter can increase the child's anxiety and personal vulnerability resulting in a concern for his own safety and well-being.

With this type of death, the family grieves as much for what they might have had as for what they've lost. Consider referral to an existing support group with parents who have shared similar losses. If there are none in your area, you might want to help establish such a group. Do ongoing follow-up with the couple and with family members.

Abortion

Many people take a casual attitude regarding the experience of abortion—at times this seems to border on the cavalier. When I worked at a university health service, I counseled many women who had had abortions, and frequently they did not recognize that the unresolved grief from a previous abortion lay behind what was currently troubling them. Abortion is one of those unspeakable losses that people would rather forget. The surface experience after an abortion is generally one of relief; however, a woman who does not mourn the loss may experience the grief in some subsequent loss.

The experience of Maria, a 27-year-old woman who was in a weekly therapy group, provides an example of this type of delayed grieving. One day she came to the group sad and upset because a friend and co-worker had just lost a baby six months *in utero*. She was very distressed, and the group rallied to her support. At the next week's meeting she brought up the same issue and, again, the group extended its support. However, after five or six weeks of bringing up the same issue, it seemed to me that she was possibly more concerned over this loss than the real mother herself. Her behavior seemed overreactive to the situation, and my hunch was that there might be an unmourned pregnancy in this woman's life. When I tactfully inquired, I found that this was the case. Several years earlier, when she was 24, Maria had become pregnant and had had an abortion and quickly put it out of her mind. Because of the casual relationship she had with the man, she did not tell him and because of her Catholic upbringing, she did not tell her parents. She thought that the best way to cope, without any other emotional support, was to forget it as quickly as possible. However, by doing that, she robbed herself of the necessary grieving process. She was not aware of the necessity to grieve the loss, an awareness that only surfaced because of her friend's miscarriage. With help, she was able to work through her loss as part of her experience in the therapy group.

One of the ways to handle the issue of grief around abortion is to do more complete counseling before the abortion itself so that the person involved can explore ambivalent feelings, discuss various options, and receive emotional support. Most women seeking abortions tend to do so in haste and, because of the stigma and shame associated with abortion, they may make the decision without the emotional support of friends and family.

Post-abortion counseling can be effective, but women do not tend to seek it. Abortion in our society is often viewed as a socially negated loss. To view it as a death, and thus appropriate to grieve, could bring up profound guilt feelings. Grief may appear at the due date or years later when the woman reaches menopause or if she discovers herself infertile (Joy, 1985). The grief often manifests itself as anger or guilt, which results in self-punishing depression.

Adolescents are less likely to come in for post-abortion counseling, even though they find it more difficult to get emotional support. The adolescent's parents are usually angry at her because she got pregnant and sometimes siblings are angry because they see their sister as having killed her baby. She often cannot turn to her peers because of the particular stigma attached to pregnancy at such an early age. In one study done in the Chicago area (Horowitz, 1978), Horowitz found that after the abortion experience, many of the teenagers she approached did not want to talk about the experience or about their feelings. Most of the young women in her study were black and were from the south and west sides of Chicago, but I believe that the same would hold true for any group that age.

One of the ways that grief is managed by some teenagers is through a subsequent pregnancy. A common interpretation of a subsequent pregnancy would be as unconscious acting-out behavior. However, Horowitz and colleagues found that many young women *consciously* got pregnant a second or third time as one way to handle their feelings about the first abortion (Horowitz, 1978). To put the experience of abortion "out of mind" is to minimize its importance, but I do not believe that it can be minimized and adequate grieving is definitely necessary.

Anticipatory Grief

The term *anticipatory grief* refers to grieving that occurs prior to the actual loss. It is distinguished from "normal survivor grief," which we have been discussing up to this point. Many deaths occur with some forewarning and it is during this period of anticipation that the potential survivor begins the task of mourning and begins to experience the various responses of grief. Problems can arise which are specific to this situation and which may need specific types of intervention. While sudden death is exceedingly traumatic, prolonged grieving can produce resentment, which then leads to guilt.

The term anticipatory grief was coined some years ago by Lindemann (1944) to refer to the absence of overt manifestations of grief at the actual time of death in survivors who had already experienced the phases of normal grief and who had freed themselves from their emotional ties with the deceased. The term was further developed by psychiatrist Knight Aldrich in an important paper of his entitled, "The Dying Patient's Grief" (1963).

One of the first questions that comes to mind when one thinks about anticipatory grief is, "Does it help post-death bereavement?" That is, do people who have sustained a period of pre-death bereavement handle their grief better and do they grieve for less time than those who do not begin grieving before the death? There does seem to be some evidence, particularly from the studies of Parkes, that people who had some advance warning of a pending death did better when assessed at 13 months post-death than did people who did not have this advance warning (Parkes, 1975). However, not all studies draw the same conclusions and the evidence is not all in. One should keep in mind that grief behavior is multi-determined and, as outlined in Chapter 2, there are many determinants of this behavior, all contributing to its strength and to its outcome. Having some advance warning of death, some opportunity for pre-death bereavement, is one of these determinants. However, there are many more determinants and it is too simplistic to look at this one variable alone.

It is important from a clinical standpoint for the practitioner who works with patients and families prior to an anticipated death to have an understanding of anticipatory grief in order to be helpful to both patients and family members.

In this type of situation the mourning process begins early and involves the various tasks of mourning already discussed. With regard to Task I, there is an awareness and acceptance of the fact that the person is going to die and hence the working through of this task begins early. However, in most cases the awareness of the inevitability of death will alternate with experiences of denial that the event is really going to happen. Of all the tasks of mourning, perhaps Task I is most facilitated by a period of anticipation, particularly when the person is dying of some deteriorating illness. As one sees the person go downhill, it brings the reality and inevitability of death closer. I have, however, seen some people hold out hope and reinforce denial when faced with extremes of visual evidence.

With regard to Task II, there may be a whole variety of feelings associated with the anticipated loss, feelings that we generally associate with post-death bereavement. One feeling frequently observed during this period is an increase in anxiety. In Chapter 1 we have looked at separation anxiety—where it comes from and what it means. For many people anxiety increases and accelerates the longer the period of anticipatory grief and the closer the person comes to death. Aldrich likens this to a mother who is insecure about her child going to school for the first time and who feels more upset about it on Labor Day than she did on the Fourth of July (Aldrich, 1963).

In addition to the issue of separation anxiety, under these circumstances existential anxiety is exacerbated through an increase in personal death awareness (Worden, 1976). As you watch someone deteriorate during a progressive illness, you cannot help but identify with the process, having some awareness that this too may be your own fate. Also, the case of watching your parents deteriorate and decline gives rise to the awareness that one is now moving up a generational step and will be the next one to face death in the overall order of things.

There is an interesting phenomenon which occurs too with regard to Task III—the task of accommodating oneself to an environment where the deceased is missing. When there is some anticipation of death, it is common for survivors to do "role rehearsal" in their minds, that is, to run over the issues of "What will I do with the children?" "Where will I live?" "How will I manage without him?" This is what Janis, in his study of surgical patients, has called the "work of worry." He found that those who do the work of worry in advance of surgery do better in post-surgical responses (Janis, 1958). This type of role rehearsal is normal and plays an important part in overall coping. However, it can be viewed by others as socially unacceptable behavior. The person who talks in detail about what they will do after the death may be perceived as insensitive, and their comments may seem premature and in bad taste. One of the things that the counselor can do is to help interpret this, both to the people exhibiting such behavior and to their friends and family members. Statements from well-meaning people such as, "Oh, don't worry, things will work out," may cut off this very important process of the work of worry.

One of the difficulties in too long a time period of anticipatory grief is that someone may withdraw emotionally too soon, long before the person has died, and this can make for an awkward relationship. Michael's elderly mother was dying of a progressively deteriorating disease. He anticipated her death, as did the other family members, and they had said the necessary goodbyes and made preparations. But the mother lived on and on, although in a seriously deteriorated stage. He came to the session one day expressing much turmoil and guilt over the fact that he wanted to make reservations to take his family away for a winter vacation, something they had done every year around the same time, yet he felt like he could not go ahead and make the plans as long as she was still living. Under these circumstances Michael very much wished that she were dead and he felt very guilty for having these feelings. This is not an unusual situation, particularly if the dying person is requiring much care and is in a seriously deteriorated condition. Weisman and Hackett (1961) talk about this withdrawal by family members and comment that such actions as drawing the shades, speaking in hushed voices and presenting unnatural attitudes may communicate to the patient capitulation, abandonment, and premortem burial.

The opposite type of behavior can also occur; rather than moving too far away in terms of emotional detachment, the family members move too close to the dying patient. They move close to obviate feelings of guilt and loss and in such cases they may want to *overmanage* the patient's medical care. This is particularly true when someone is trying to handle ambivalent feelings toward the dying person and the guilt that goes with such feelings. They may move in to be overly caring of the patient or seek nontraditional treatments, and this can be a problem not only for the patient but also for the medical staff.

I observed one woman whose husband was a patient in the hospital's private service. She wanted to keep her husband alive and went to the most extreme means, extreme even to the most conservative of medical opinion. On the surface it looked to the nurses and other people caring for the patient like she cared so much for her husband that she wanted to keep him alive against all odds. But you only had to scratch the surface slightly to see that this woman had an extremely ambivalent relationship with her husband and she was expressing her ambivalence through this oversolicitation.

The time preceding a death can be used very effectively and can have an important impact on subsequent grief if the survivor is encouraged to take care of unfinished business. Unfinished business does not simply mean wills and other matters of estate, but being able to express both appreciations and disappointments, things that need to be said before the person dies. If the counselor can encourage family members and patients to have this kind of communication, this pre-death period can have a very salutary effect on all concerned. When these things are expressed, the survivor does not have to spend time in grief counseling later on where they might have to deal with regrets over things that were not ever said when they had the opportunity. So if you have access to patients and families in a situation prior to death, help them to see that even though this is a pending tragedy, it can also be an opportunity for them to take care of the things they want to deal with before the person dies. Often people need encouragement or permission to do this, but I think it is more often the exception than the rule that they will go ahead without the encouragement of the caregiving staff.

So far we have primarily considered anticipatory grief of the survivor. But people who are dying can also experience this anticipatory grief, although they may feel it in ways that are somewhat different from survivors'. The survivors are only losing one loved one. The person who is dying often has many attachments in his own life and, to that extent, will be losing many significant others all at once. The anticipation of loss can be overwhelming and very often the patient will withdraw and turn his face to the wall in order to cope with the impact of this. A counselor can help to interpret this kind of behavior both to the patient, who may be having trouble with it, and to the family and friends.

One more thing should be considered before concluding this section on anticipatory grief. It concerns the use of support groups. There is one population that has a particularly difficult time with anticipatory grief and needs a lot of support—parents who are losing young children because of terminal illness. When one loses a child there is the sense of untimeliness about the death. Children are not supposed to die before their parents—it is not in the order of things. This, and a myriad of other kinds of experiences, which usually include a long series of medical treatments, put great stresses on family members, not only the parents but the children as well.

There are support groups such as the Candlelighters available for parents whose children are very sick or dying. In these groups the parents can deal with some of their anticipatory grief in a social setting. Many parents who have participated in these groups have said that it was helpful to them because it gave them the opportunity to share their feelings with other parents who were going through the same thing. It also enabled them to better cope with some of the stresses that were occurring in their marriages as well as some of the difficulties they were having with regard to the management of other children, especially the very common feeling that they were neglecting others of their offspring because of the attention they were giving to the dying child.

The headquarters of one of these groups, The Candlelighters Foundation, is located at 2025 I Street, N.W., Washington, DC, 20006. Another support group, The Society of Compassionate Friends, helps families after the death of a child. For information about this organization and its local chapters write: Society of Compassionate Friends, P.O. Box 1347, Oak Brook, IL 60521.

AIDS

Over the past decade an ever increasing number of people have become afflicted with and died from Acquired Immune Deficiency Syndrome

(AIDS). It is estimated that by the year 2000 a half million people in the United States will have died from AIDS-related disorders. Each of those who die will leave family and friends to face the consequences particular to this type of loss. Survivors of those who die from AIDS constitute a population of mourners with few existing guidelines for care. The fact that the syndrome is caused by an infectious virus, that it currently lacks a cure, that it carries a social stigma, and that it often leads to protracted illness can influence the mourning behavior of those who have sustained such a loss. Let us look at some features associated with AIDS that could affect the bereavement process.

Contagion. Because AIDS is transmitted through bodily fluids, the deceased's sexual partners may be anxious about their own health. Physical symptoms usually considered a normal part of the grieving process, such as fatigue, insomnia, and headaches, can be interpreted as symptoms associated with AIDS-related illnesses. The counselor needs to educate survivors regarding these physical aspects of bereavement so that these are not construed as AIDS and so that anxiety due to these physical symptoms can be diminished.

The feeling of vulnerability and the fear of developing the disease can lead survivors to feel angry at the deceased. One survivor said, "I feel like a walking time-bomb." Some of this vulnerability is real and not neurotic. One can only wonder what the stress of bereavement may do to the survivor's immune system, which may already be compromised by the virus (Schleifer, 1983).

Another aspect associated with the contagion factor is guilt. Some survivors feel guilty for transmitting the virus to their partner or for participating in activities or in a lifestyle in which the possibility of transmission was heightened. These feelings of guilt need to be addressed and evaluated. Contagion factors can also play a role when a survivor sets about to establish a new relationship. Some people reject relationships with AIDS survivors while in other cases survivors themselves may have doubts about forming new relationships.

Stigma. An AIDS-related death can be one of those unspeakable losses discussed earlier. Because of this stigma, some people fear they will be rejected and judged harshly if the cause of death becomes known. So they may lie and attribute the death to cancer or something other than AIDS. This may get them "off the AIDS hook" but it takes another type of emotional toll in the form of fear of discovery, and anger and guilt over what they have done. Helping survivors deal with the reality of the stigma and assisting them to find appropriate ways to share the circumstances of the loss can help to attenuate these feelings of anxiety and fear.

Lack of Social Support.   Because of the stigma of AIDS, and because in our society kinship legitimizes grief, many survivors who had a non-traditional relationship with the deceased have difficulty finding the level of understanding and support they need after the death. The mother of one of my clients, who did not know of her son's relationship with his lover, said after the death, "Why are you so sad? He was only your roommate." If a relationship is not socially sanctioned, it is less likely to be recognized as important by people or by the law. The family may exclude the deceased's partners and friends from participation in funeral planning and activities. Significant others in the deceased's life may also be prevented from inheriting property or otherwise benefitting from the settlement of the estate.

Folta and Deck make an important point about grief and non-traditional relationships:

> While all of these studies tell us that grief is a normal phenomenon, the intensity of which corresponds to the closeness of the relationship with the deceased, they fail to take friendship into account. The underlying assumption is that "closeness of relationship" exists only among spouses and/or immediate kin. [Folta & Deck, 1976, p. 239]

Groups for families and friends of AIDS patients can be an excellent means of providing emotional support before and after the death.

Untimely Deaths.   Many of those who have succumbed to AIDS-related illnesses are young, between the ages of 20 and 35. Their deaths evoke the reactions that any untimely deaths evoke when parents outlive their children. Among friends and contemporaries there can be an increase in the awareness of personal mortality and its attendant anxiety (Worden, 1976). Many survivors are faced with these issues at an age when people are not usually confronted with mortality.

Multiple Losses.   In the gay community many people have lost a number of friends and significant others to AIDS. As noted earlier, multiple losses can lead to bereavement overload and may cause the grieving process to shut down or to manifest itself in various somatic symptoms. A recent study in New York City found that the number of distress symptoms varied with the number of personal friends the bereaved had lost to AIDS (Martin, 1988). Those providing bereavement services need to be aware of this association and reach out to those with multiple losses.

This is also a problem for those caregivers who are working with large groups of AIDS patients. One counselor working with AIDS patients in San Francisco said, "I reached a saturation point in my personal and professional life where I could not fit in another death. The cumulative deaths have an effect" (Bell, 1988). Those caring for people with AIDS need to be able to release their grief and sorrow and to stay connected with life-affirming activities in order to avoid burnout.

Protracted Illness and Disfigurement. The HIV virus compromises the immune system so that a number of opportunistic infections can invade the body. Many of these infections lead to progressive physical and mental deterioration. People with AIDS-related illness often experience wasting of their physical and mental capacities. Formerly youthful and attractive, they can be transformed into the visage of death camp victims. Because of this deterioration, some people find it difficult to be around those with AIDS whose illness is progressing. I have worked with a few survivors who felt intense guilt after a loss because they were not present when the person was dying. Others who are present through the dying process find it difficult to relinquish memories of a friend or family member in such an impaired condition. These people can be helped by realizing that such a phenomenon is normal and that gradually they will be able to recapture a more balanced set of memories.

Neurological Complications. Another feature of AIDS that affects loss are the neurological complications often associated with the illness. Several studies have found that when autopsies were done, up to 80 percent of AIDS patients suffered some kind of damage to the central nervous system. Sometimes the damage makes for subtle changes in behavior but more often one sees a higher level of impairment depending on the area of the brain that is under attack by the virus. These deteriorations of mental function can look like the impairments suffered by the Alzheimer's patient. Once dementia progresses, family and friends begin to lose the person they once had and these losses, as in the case of Alzheimer's disease, can precipitate an early grieving response.

The AIDS virus will continue to affect a broader segment of society than we have seen to date and those working with grief issues can expect to see more AIDS-related bereavement in the coming years.

References

Aldrich, C. K. (1963). The dying patient's grief. *Journal of the American Medical Association, 184,* 329–331

Bell, J. P. (1988). AIDS and the hidden epidemic of grief. A personal experience. *American Journal of Hospice Care, 5,* 25–31.

Cain, A. C. (Ed.) (1972). *Survivors of suicide.* Springfield, IL: Thomas.

Farberow, N. L., et al. (1987). An examination of the early impact of bereavement on psychological distress in survivors of suicide. *Gerontologist, 27,* 592–598.

Feely, N., & Gottlieb, L. N. (1988–89). Parent's coping and communication following their infant's death. *Omega, 19,* 51–67.

Folta, J., & Deck, E. (1986). Grief, the funeral, and the friend. In V. Pine et al. (Eds), *Acute grief and the funeral*. Springfield, IL: Thomas.

Horowitz, M. H. (1978). Adolescent mourning reactions to infant and fetal loss. *Social Casework*, 551–559.

Janis, I. L. (1958). *Psychological stress*. New York: Wiley.

Joy, S. S. (1985). Abortion: An issue to grieve? *Journal of Counseling and Development, 63*, 375–376.

Lindemann, E. (1944). Symptomatolgy and management of acute grief. *American Journal of Psychiatry, 101*, 141–148.

Lindemann, E., & Greer, I. M. (1953). A study of grief: Emotional responses to suicide. *Pastoral Psychology, 4*, 9.

Martin, J. L. (1988). Psychological consequences of AIDS—related bereavement among gay men. *Journal of Consulting and Clinical Psychology, 56*, 856–862.

McNiel, D. E., Hatcher, C., & Reubin, R. (1988). Family survivors of suicide and accidental death: Consequences for widows. *Suicide and Life-Threatening Behavior, 18*, 137–148.

Morgan, J. H., & Goering, R. (1978). Caring for parents who have lost an infant. *Journal of Religion and Health, 17*, 290–298.

Parkes, C. M. (1975). Determinants of outcome following bereavement. *Omega, 6*, 303–323.

Rynearson, E. (1984). Bereavement after homicide: A descriptive study. *American Journal of Psychiatry, 141*, 1452–1454.

Schleifer, S. J., et al. (1983). Suppression of lymphocyte stimulation following bereavement. *Journal of the American Medical Association, 250*, 374–377.

Weisman, A. D., & Hackett, T. P. (1961). Predilection to death. *Psychosomatic Medicine, 23*, 232–255.

Worden, J. W. (1976). *Personal death awareness*. Englewood Cliffs, NJ: Prentice-Hall.

Wrobleski, A. (1984). The suicide survivors grief group. *Omega, 15*, 173–184.

Chapter 7

Grief and Family Systems

Up to this point, our primary focus has been on the grief reactions of an individual and how this relates to his relationship with the deceased. However, most significant losses occur within the context of a family unit, and it is important to consider the impact of a death on the entire family system.

Most families exist in some type of homeostatic balance and the loss of a significant person in that family group can unbalance this homeostasis and cause the family to feel pain and to seek help. A well-known family therapist, Murray Bowen, says that "Knowledge of the total family configuration, the functioning position of the dying person in the family, and the overall level of life adaptation are important for anyone who attempts to help a family before, during or after a death" (Bowen, 1978, p. 328).

Specific factors that affect the grieving process and influence the degree of family disruption have been identified. These include: stages in the family life cycle; roles played by the deceased; power, affection, and communication patterns; and sociocultural factors (Vess et al., 1985; Davies et al., 1986).

My purpose here is to discuss how family dynamics can hinder adequate grieving. This chapter is not intended to be a treatise on family therapy. I will assume that the reader has some understanding and skill in the administration of this type of therapy. For those less familiar with this area who want an overview, I suggest *An Introduction to Family Therapy* by Vincent D. Foley (1986).

The concept of family therapy is based on the belief that the family is an interactional unit in which all members influence each other. Therefore, it is not sufficient to treat each individual in relationship to the deceased and to deal with his or her grief without relating it to the total family network. The characteristics of individual family members help determine the character of the family system, but this family system is more than the sum of its individuals' characteristics. The grief reactions of a family bear assessment apart from those of its individual members (Davies et al., 1986). One reason it is necessary to look at family grief as well as individual grief is because of the impact of family myths. These myths work in a similar fashion as defenses do for the individual and they give the family group definition and identity (Greaves, 1983). In addition, each change that occurs following the death of a family member is symbolic of the death of the family itself, leaving the primary task of establishing a new family from the old (Greaves, 1983).

Families vary in their ability to express and to tolerate feelings. If openly expressed feelings are not tolerated, this may lead to various types of acting-out behavior which serve as grief equivalents. Families who cope most effectively are open in their discussion about the deceased whereas closed families not only lack this freedom, but provide excuses and make comments that allow other family members to remain quiet. Functional families are also more likely to process feelings about the death, including admitting and accepting feelings of vulnerability (Davies et al., 1986).

One important reason for looking at a family systems approach is that unresolved grief may not only serve as a key factor in family pathology but may contribute to pathological relationships across the generations. Spark and Browdy have noted that postponed mourning related to one's family of origin impedes experiencing emotional loss and separation within the current family (Spark & Browdy, 1972). Reilly, who has looked at this phenomenon in relationship to drug abuse, believes that parents of youthful drug abusers have never fully mourned or resolved their ambivalent ties to their own parents. Therefore, they tend to project their conflicts over loss and abandonment onto their present-day families (Reilly, 1978). In order to assess the impact of intergenerational conflict, Bowen encourages taking an extensive family history, which should cover at least two generations, as part of the intake procedure (Bowen, 1978).

When assessing grief and family systems, at least three main areas need to be considered. The first is the functional position or role the deceased played in the family. There are various roles played by family members, such as the sickly one, the value setter, the scapegoat, the nurturer, the clan head, etc. To the extent that the deceased had a significant functional position, his death is going to create a corresponding disturbance of functional equilibrium. Bowen sees the family unit as having stasis and calm when each member is functioning at reasonable efficiency. But the addition or loss of a family member can result in disequilibrium. Through death the family can be deprived of an important role and another member might be sought out to fill the role vacancy (Bowen, 1978).

Children also play important roles in the family, and their deaths upset family balance. I saw an adolescent, the youngest of three children, before he died of leukemia. He had required numerous hospitalizations and subsequent care. This boy was resented by his brother, the oldest child, and after the death, the brother would not let his parents dismantle the room or store or give away his dead brother's belongings. He would become very angry when this was mentioned by his family because to do so would mean he would have to face the finality of the loss and his unresolved ambivalence for his brother.

The mother suffered because she had an unusually close relationship with the dead child. In a reversal of dependency, she leaned on him to bolster up her sagging self-esteem, placing him in a role more appropriate for her husband. The husband gave his wife even less attention after the death and refused to talk about his feelings. He spent increasingly long periods away from home. The middle child, a girl who lived away from home, was the only one who seemed to be doing well at all. Individual counseling for the members of this family could be done with some success, but it is my belief that three or four individual counselors would not be as effective as family therapy, where these various conflicts and issues could be worked out within the purview of each other. In fact, psychiatrist Norman Paul believes that grief work, confined to an individual and therapist, may deaden the relational possibilities for the individual and his or her family (Paul, 1986).

The death of either parent when the family is young can have long-range effects. "This not only disturbs the emotional equilibrium, but it removes the function of the breadwinner or the mother at a time when these functions are most important" (Bowen, 1978, p. 328). Another important death with widespread ramifications is the death of a patriarchal clan head who has been serving the decision-making function in family affairs for a long time. One woman had a grandfather who ran the family with an iron fist. Within two years of his death, her parents had divorced, the family business crumbled, and the family members had scattered to different parts of the country. But it is also important to realize that many people play only peripheral roles in family affairs. One might consider such a person as being somewhat neutral; therefore, deaths of these more neutral figures are not as likely to affect current or future family functioning with quite the same intensity.

A second area to assess is the emotional integration of the family. A well-integrated family will be better able to help each other cope with the death, even that of a significant family member, with little outside help. A less integrated family may show minimal grief reaction at the time of death, but members may respond later with various physical or emotional symptoms or some type of social misbehavior. It is important that the counselor understand this because merely to get the family to express feelings after a death does not necessarily increase the level of emotional integration (Bowen, 1978).

Since affective expression is so important in the mourning process, a third area to assess is how families facilitate or hinder emotional expression. In order to see this, one needs to understand the value families place on emotions and the kinds of communication patterns that give a person permission to express feelings or not express feelings. Davies found that in some less functional families, sadness is equated with craziness and manifest in comments such as, "I've seen enough tears." She also found that in more functional families the father was able to express grief openly instead of hiding his feelings or praising his son for not crying at the funeral. The latter reinforces gender related role rigidity and is a characteristic of less functional families (Davies et al., 1986). Because a death can trigger varied and intense feelings, a context in which these feelings can be experienced, identified, and brought to completion is important. Families that conspire to keep feelings down or at a distance may ultimately keep the individual from an adequate resolution of grief.

For example, Karen was the youngest of five children when her father, a ne'er-do-well alcoholic, was found dead in a local hotel. Because he had been a long-term embarrassment to the family, they opted for immediate cremation and his ashes were disposed of unceremoniously. Karen wanted to provide some kind of marker for her father, but no one in the family agreed with her and, being the youngest, she had little clout. She thought this was a "crummy way to die" and she was unable to detach herself from her father. She kept him with her through a type of pathological identification which developed over the years, and her family would often say, "You're just like your father." As a young woman Karen developed a serious drinking problem which turned out to be related in part to this pathological identification with her father. Through grief therapy she was able to see the connection, to say a final good-bye to her father, to deal with the other family members concerning his death, and, over time, to see her problem with alcohol resolved.

This family would probably not have seen the need for family therapy, believing, or wanting to believe, that the father's death had little impact on them or on the family system. But this case also suggests why those who have access to families after a death would be wise to assess the fantasies and feelings of all family members, including the younger ones.

Death of a Child

One very difficult loss, which impinges heavily on family equilibrium and can sometimes cause pathological reactions, is the death of a child and its effect on siblings. Surviving siblings frequently become the focus for unconscious manuevers designed to alleviate the guilt feelings of the parents and are used as a way to better control fate. One of the most difficult positions parents put the surviving siblings in is to be the substitute for the lost child. This often involves endowing the survivor-child with qualities of the deceased. In some cases it may even result in the subsequent child being named with a similar or identical name as that of the dead child. Davies and her colleagues found that healthy families were able to acknowledge the loss of a child without expecting other children to fill the empty space (Davies et al., 1986). The ability of the parents to help the siblings communicate within the family unit and the opportunity to directly express feelings lead to the healthy negotiation of grieving tasks (Schumacher, 1984).

Some families cope with their feelings about the death of a child by suppressing the facts surrounding the loss so that the subsequent children may not know anything about their predecessors and in some cases not even know there were predecessors at all. This happened to Judy. Her parent's first child was a boy who died in early infancy. They subsequently had another child, a girl, and then a third child, Judy, who was supposed to be the replacement for the dead son. This was never directly verbalized and obviously not communicated to her. But over the years, even though the parents did not talk about the dead brother, an awareness of him always hung in the background of her mind. Subconsciously she attempted to make up for all of the things that he might have been, which included a lot of "masculine" interests, activities, and hobbies.

But many years later, as her mother lay dying of cancer, Judy insisted that her parents discuss the dead brother—their disappointments in him and their expectations for her. This was not an easy thing for her to do, but she persisted until her parents could more consciously admit to their disappointments and expectations. Even though this took a great deal of effort and she met with considerable resistance, she felt it was important for her to clear things up before her mother's death. Fortunately, she was successful in this effort and was then able to move beyond this legacy and start being more her own person.

It is not uncommon for siblings of the lost child to be overlooked during the time immediately following the death. Sometimes it is assumed that the child is simply too young to comprehend the loss or that they need protection from what is perceived as a morbid situation. More often, children are not given the attention they need because their primary caregivers are in a state of trauma and are simply not able to extend themselves to help. This is when support networks can be helpful in alleviating some of the common reactions and feelings a child experiences when a sibling dies.

Children have a difficult time trying to sort out what their friends should be told and how to deal with the discomfort of other people in relation to the death. Many times, as a result of this discomfort, they are afraid to play or be happy because they don't want others to think they didn't care about their lost sibling (Schumacher, 1984).

Without open and honest communication children seek their own answers to questions that are often beyond their ability to understand. It is particularly important for parents to dispel magical and erroneous thinking regarding death in order to establish an emotional link between the remaining siblings and the parents. This is a crucial time that may affect their personality development and their ability to form and maintain future relationships (Schumacher, 1984).

The experience of the bereaved parents is central to the loss of a child and its impact on the family. Losing a child of whatever age can be one of life's most devastating losses and its impact lingers for years. Parental bonds are strong. They reflect aspects of the parent's personality as well as historical and social dimensions. Klass writes:

> The child represents to the parent both the parent's best self and the parent's worst self. Difficulties and ambivalences in the parent's life are manifest in the bond with the child. The child is born into a world of hopes and expectations, into a world of intricate psychological bonds, into a world that has a history. The parent-child bond can also be a recapitulation of the bond between the parent and the parent's parent, so the child can be experienced as praising or judging the parent's self. From the day the child is born, those hopes and expectations, bonds, and history are played out in the parent's relationship with the child. [Klass & Marwit, 1988, p. 178]

The grief determinants discussed earlier will affect the experience of this type of loss. Such deaths are often sudden and untimely—parents are supposed to outlive their children. Many children die in accidents, which heightens the challenge to the parent's sense of competency, as part of the parental role is to keep the child safe. This may also lead to strong feelings of guilt.

Friends and family may not know how to respond to such a loss and to be supportive. This can be especially true the further in time one is from the loss. I have worked with several bereaved mothers whose friends comment that they should be getting over the loss, since it has been over a year since their child died.

Both parents have sustained a loss, but the grief experience may be different for each due to their varied relationship with the child and their own different coping styles. These differences can put a strain on a marital relationship, and this in turn can cause tensions and alliances among family members.

Parents are often surprised at their own needs and responses when a child dies. The severity of the loss elicits a longing for closeness and intimacy, but some parents are surprised or feel guilty when they find themselves attempting to meet these needs sexually. It is important for the parents to recognize and understand these needs and feelings as part of the normal life process.

Grieving the loss of a child may become even more complicated when the parents of that child are divorced. Parents are often brought together in this time of crisis and this coming together can evoke strong emotions and extreme behaviors, from empathetic and caring behaviors to an all out struggle for power and control. But in this situation it is impossible to gain the type of control that is really desired—the recovery of a lost life (Burns, 1980).

The various tasks of mourning need to be worked through. For many parents who have lost children the reality of the loss is a struggle of belief and non-belief. On the one hand they know that the child is gone and on the other hand they don't want to believe it. Dealing with the possessions of their lost children is often a reflection of this struggle. Parents will sometimes keep a child's room intact for many years after the death.

Strong feelings, including anger, guilt, and blame, are frequently present. These are often processed best in groups like the Society of Compassionate Friends, where empathic listening is available from those with similar experiences. Many who have not undergone this type of loss believe that the last thing a grieving parent wants to do is to talk about their child, but this is exactly what most want to do.

Working through Task IV issues can be very difficult for bereaved parents. "The same ambivalences and multiple representations that were part of the living relationships with the child are part of the search for equilibrium when the child dies" (Klass & Marwit, 1988, p. 73). However, it is possible and, for some, this struggle with repositioning the lost child can lead to important self-awareness and possible personal growth coming out of this very difficult experience (Klass & Marwit, 1988).

Children Whose Parents Die

Another significant area that needs to be addressed is that of children who lose a parent. When this occurs in childhood or adolescence, the child may fail to adequately mourn and later in life may often present with symptoms of depression or the inability to form close relationships during adult years. As described in the chapter on grief therapy, the intervention focuses on the reactivation of the mourning process with the result that the patients improve symptomatically and are able to resume life tasks that were previously arrested.

There has been considerable controversy over the years, particularly stemming from psychoanalytic schools, as to whether or not children are capable of mourning. On the one side you find people like Martha Wolfenstein who say that children cannot mourn until there is a complete identity formation, which occurs at the end of adolescence when the person is fully differentiated (Wolfenstein, 1966).

On the other hand, people like Erna Furman and associates take the opposite position and say that children can mourn as early as three years of age when object constancy is achieved (Furman, 1974) and Bowlby, who pushes the age to six months (Bowlby, 1960).

Part of the controversy focuses around the definition of mourning. If mourning involves the task of detaching from the attachment object and recognizing oneself as a separate entity, then according to Wolfenstein, young children cannot mourn because of their limitation in terms of reality testing, object constancy, and the fact that they use regressive coping mechanisms to deal with loss and readily find substitute objects.

There are those, like myself, who take a third position—that children do mourn and what is needed is to find a model of mourning that fits children rather than imposing an adult model. Although young children show grief-like behavior when attachments are broken, the main issue centers around the cognitive development of the child. People need a certain level of cognitive development to understand death because they cannot integrate something that they do not understand. Some of the cognitive concepts that are necessary in order to fully understand death are: (1) time, including forever; (2) transformation; (3) irreversibility; (4) causality; and (5) concrete operation (Polombo, 1978). In his studies, Piaget suggests that concrete operations are developed only in children beyond the ages seven or eight (Piaget & Inhelder, 1969).

In our current understanding of child development, the child who is under 18 to 24 months of age does not fully understand that a physical object has an existence separate from his sensory perception and manipulation (Flavell, 1977). Between the ages of two and five years, this object constancy is achieved and the child has a better, although still incomplete, understanding of death. Children this age also reflect more of the adult feeling states following a loss, but the risk is that they may perceive the loss as due to their own responsibility and/or their own sense of badness. At this age children also exhibit a strong tendency to idealize the adult who was lost.

Between the ages of five and seven years, the child has a better understanding of death from a cognitive perspective but still lacks ego skills to deal with the intensity of the feelings. From the age of seven to adolescence, the child approaches mourning more like an adult, with more sufficient understanding and better coping skills. All this is to say that loss through death is experienced and expressed in different ways at different developmental phases.

The mental health practitioner needs to be aware of several things when dealing with children who have lost parents (Polombo, 1978):

1. Children do mourn, but differences in mourning are determined by both the cognitive and emotional development of a child.
2. The loss of a parent through death is obviously a trauma but does not in and of itself necessarily lead to arrested development.
3. Children between the ages of five and seven years are a particularly vulnerable group. They have developed cognitively enough to understand some of the permanent ramifications of death but they have very little coping capacity; that is, their ego skills and social skills are insufficiently developed to enable them to defend themselves. This particular group should be singled out for special concern by the counselor.
4. It is important also to recognize that the work of mourning may not end in quite the same way for a child as it does for an adult. Mourning for a childhood loss can be revived at many points in an adult's life when it is reactivated during important life events. One of the most obvious examples is when the child reaches the same age as the parent who died. When this mourning is reactivated, it does not necessarily portend pathology but is simply a further example of "working through."
5. It is important for the mental health worker to develop preventive approaches for children who have lost parents. The same tasks of grieving that apply to the adult obviously apply to the child, but these tasks have to be understood and modified in terms of the child's cognitive, personal, social, and emotional development.

Intervention Approaches

After a death, ask to meet with survivors both as individuals and as a family unit. The focus of such family meetings is not only to facilitate grief Tasks I and II, with the special focus on Task II being the expression of both positive and negative affects about the deceased, but also to try and identify some of the roles the deceased played and the ways these roles are being taken up or rejected by current family members—Task III. In the case of the death of the father, some of these roles may be assigned to the eldest son. The eldest son has either taken up the cudgel and suppressed a lot of himself and his own feelings, or has backed away from this demand, much to the frustration of the surviving parent or other relatives who are passing this role along.

Identifying the restructured roles within the family is particularly helpful when there are teenaged children involved. Their fears and their willingness to pick up various tasks can often be negotiated. However, it is often very difficult for surviving parents to negotiate these on their own after the death. Frequently the family ends up in a situation of bickering and conflict or with various family members withdrawing emotionally. Helping them sort out the real issues and the peripheral issues is a very important aspect of this kind of family therapy.

Role assignments are usually made subtly and nonverbally, but there are times when there is a direct verbal assignment. Jerry arrived home from school at age 15 to find the house full of neighbors and family surrounding his mother, who was trying very hard not to cry. His uncle told him that his father had died suddenly and also told him that he was going to be "the man in the family" because he was the oldest male. This was due in part to Jewish family tradition. Because he was now designated the "man" of the house, this overwhelmed boy was asked to make funeral decisions such as whether or not to have an open casket. He was able to make these decisions but what the family did not know was how responsible and burdened he felt because of his brother, who was four years his junior. These fears were aggravated because his mother offered little support during the time of death. It was only as an adult of 30 that Jerry became aware of how destructive this situation had been over the years in his relationship with his brother and he was able to verbalize how much of a burden this had been.

When Jerry finally confessed this to his mother, she told him that he was not responsible and freed him from this encumbrance. Shortly thereafter, through therapy, he was able to see how this sense of overresponsibility for his brother had colored all his relationships with women over the years in terms of limited commitment. If this had not been broken, he doubts that he could have the satisfying relationship he enjoys at present. No one, including the patient, blames the uncle for having bad intentions, but it is a difficult legacy to carry for 15 years and it points up the need to talk with children about their feelings and fantasies when there is a death in the family.

Related to roles is the issue of alliances. In any family situation there are various dyadic alliances formed. Usually these serve the various needs for power that individuals experience. They can also serve the need to reinforce self-esteem. Anyone who is studying families from a sociometric point of view can diagram these very important alliances. When a significant family member dies, upsetting the equilibrium of the family unit, new alliances need to be formed. The maneuvering for these new alliances may cause considerable tension and distress in the family.

Bowen suggests that many dyadic relationships become triangulated in order to remove some of the anxiety or the pressure of a dyadic relationship (Bowen, 1978). After someone dies, there is a need for shifting and re-equilibrating family triangles. Various alliances that have formed need to be altered. However, if no substitute is found, then the deprived member may seek homeostasis through various social, physical, or emotional illnesses (Kuhn, 1977).

Another problem that can arise in families after a death is that of scapegoating. Throughout this book we have looked at the issue of anger and the importance of the ways in which it is handled by the bereaved. One way that anger is handled ineffectively is through displacement; likewise, one of the least effective ways of handling anger vis-à-vis displacement in the family is through scapegoating—one of the family members becomes the target for the wrath and the blame and the anger for the death. Sometimes this scapegoating role is imposed on one of the younger and more vulnerable members of the family. I recently saw a 6-year-old girl whose mother blamed her for the death of her infant brother and sent her off to live with relatives.

Finally, family therapy can address the impact of incomplete mourning on subsequent family life and interaction. Incomplete mourning is a pervasive defense against further losses and disappointments and can be transmitted unwittingly to other family members, especially to offspring. To overcome this, psychiatrist Norman Paul and his colleagues have developed what he calls "operational mourning" and used it in conjoint family therapy (Paul & Crosser, 1965; Paul, 1986).

Operational mourning consists of inducing the mourning response by directly asking one family member about reactions to actual losses they have sustained. Then the other family members who are present are asked to talk about their feelings, which have been stimulated by directly witnessing the grief reaction of the first person. In this way children, often for the first time, observe their parents expressing intense emotions. This gives the therapist an opportunity to assure them of the normality of these feelings. It also gives the therapist the opportunity to review the episodic threats of abandonment by a parent or other family member which have been an important influence in current family life. During these periods of activated mourning, family members are encouraged to share their affective experiences and to react empathetically to affects expressed by each other. In using this procedure, Paul finds an enormous amount of resistance and denial on the part of the family, but if this resistance is overcome, the intervention is very beneficial.

Grief and the Elderly

One issue that affects the family system is the increase in the elderly bereaved population. While the maximum age for human beings has not increased significantly in recent time, the number of people living into their seventies and eighties has grown and will continue to grow. With this increase comes a larger number of elderly who have experienced bereavement, especially the loss of a spouse. Widowhood affects three out of four women. In 1984 there were 7.8 million widowed women aged 65 and older in the United States and 1.5 million widowed elderly men. Although the experience of grief is shaped by determinants discussed previously, several features of grief in the elderly deserve to be noted.

Interdependence.   Many elderly widows and widowers had been married for a long time, leading to deep attachments and to the entrenchment of family roles. There is interdependence in any marriage. However, in these lengthy marriages it's possible that the spouses were highly dependent upon one another. To the extent that the bereaved were highly dependent on their spouses for certain roles or activities, this will make for a more difficult adjustment after the loss.

Multiple Losses.   With age, the number of deaths of friends and family members increases. This increased number of losses in a brief period can cause a person to be overwhelmed and not to grieve. Concurrent with the losses of friends, relatives, and family members, are other losses the aging person may experience. These can include the loss of occupation, loss of environment, loss of family constellations, loss of physical vigor, including physical disabilities, the diminishing of one's senses, and for some, the loss of cerebral functioning. All of these changes, added to losses through death, need to be grieved. But the ability one has to grieve may be lessened because of many losses in an abbreviated time period.

Personal Death Awareness.   Experiencing loss of contemporaries such as a spouse, friends, or siblings, may heighten one's personal death awareness. This increase in the awareness of personal mortality can lead to existential anxiety. Counselors need to be comfortable discussing the bereaved's personal sense of mortality and to be aware of the extent this death awareness might be troublesome.

Loneliness.   Many bereaved elderly live alone. A study done by Lopatta showed that younger widows and widowers were more likely to move after the loss, whereas older ones were more likely to remain in the home they lived in at the time of the death (Lopatta, 1979). Living alone can lead to intense feelings of loneliness, particularly intensified by living alone in the same physical surroundings shared with the spouse. Some elderly cannot continue to live alone after the death of a spouse and may require institutional care. There's anecdotal evidence to support the fact that elderly people who are forced to move out of their homes after losing a spouse may be at higher risk for mortality.

Role Adjustment.   For elderly men, the loss of a spouse and its effect on day-to-day living may be more disruptive than for women. Many men face new roles, particularly homemaking, and may need help adjusting to these roles. When a woman loses her husband, there often is not the same level of disruption in terms of her ability to keep house and her self-reliance as a homemaker. There are certain counseling interventions that can be useful when working with the elderly bereaved.

Support Groups.   Support groups for the bereaved can be useful at any age, but it's particularly important for the elderly, whose network of support is often diminished and whose isolation is often pronounced. Support groups can offer important human contact to those who are experiencing high levels of loneliness. In a recent study, Lund discovered that both elderly men and women would be willing to participate in support groups. The most eager to participate in a support group were those whose confidant was less available than previously, those with more depression and less life satisfaction, and those who perceived that they were not coping well. There was also more willingness on the part of elderly in the age group 50 to 69 to participate in groups than for those of more advanced age (Lund, Diamond, & Juretich, 1985).

Touch.   Another useful intervention is touch. Many men and women, but particularly men, who've been married for a long time and then lose their spouse, have a strong need to be touched. Without their spouse they may find it difficult to get this need met. A counselor who is comfortable with physical contact can include touching in working with the elderly bereaved. However, anytime touch is used therapeutically, the counselor must be clear as to its suitability and must also attend to whether or not the person is willing or ready to be touched.

Reminiscing.   Another intervention technique is reminiscing, something that is common among the elderly and can be stimulated therapeutically in an elderly bereaved population. Reminiscing is sometimes called life review. It is a naturally occurring process that brings the person to a progressive return to consciousness of past experiences and in particular to the resurgence of unresolved conflicts. It is generally assumed that reminiscing serves an adaptational function for the aging person and that it is not a sign of intellectual decline.

Reminiscing contributes to the maintenance of identity. Even though a person may have lost loved ones, the mental representations of these people endure. Through the process of reminiscing, the past can be reworked. The counselor can encourage the client to reminisce and in doing so, this can have a salutory effect, particularly with conjugal bereavement. The elderly never truly lose the deceased, since so much of what the deceased represented is internalized and significant in the present (Moss & Moss, 1984).

Discussing Relocation.   The counselor can help the elderly person decide whether they should move from their home. This decision, of course, depends on the ability of the person to take care of him or herself. However, one should never underestimate the importance of a home, where the bereaved may have lived for a long time and which may represent a whole scrapbook of meanings for the older person. To move from the house may reduce a person's sense of self as well as dilute the tie with the deceased spouse. Being able to remain in their home gives elderly people a sense of personal control and offers an arena in which they can recall the cherished past.

Skill Building.   It's possible for some of the bereaved elderly to become too dependent on their adult children. Though bereaved, these people have the capacity to develop new skills and, in doing so, can reap the sense of self-esteem that comes through mastery. One bereaved elderly woman called her adult children continually and wanted them to come to her home to fix things, for example the furnace, even when these repairs were needed in the middle of the night. The children were happy to do this for a while, but it became clear to them that their mother needed to learn to call the plumber and to take care of those things that, prior to the death, her husband would have handled. She was very resistant to the suggestion and felt like her children were rejecting her. However, reason finally prevailed and when she did learn how to handle some of these day-by-day activities, she felt good that she had developed some of these skills. The counselor needs to keep in mind that mastery and self-esteem go together, and this is true for the elderly and the elderly bereaved.

In any discussion of the bereaved elderly it is important to keep in mind that research has shown that stresses experienced by these bereaved may be stronger prior to the death than afterward. This is particularly the case when one has been the primary caretaker of a sick spouse. If this be true, then one might want to begin interventions early and not wait until after the death has occurred.

Family versus Individual Needs

Before concluding this chapter on grief and the family system, there are two points I want to emphasize. First, it is important to recognize that not everyone in a family will be working on the same tasks at the same time. Individual family members will process tasks at their own rate and in their own way. For example, it may be that bereavement in the elderly takes a long time, and to some extent, it may not have an end point. Families need to be encouraged not to rush a person through the grief experience. I spoke recently with a woman whose father had died four months earlier. She was very upset with her mother for continuing to have long crying spells. I tried to help her see that this was a very natural thing and that, in time, her mother would probably cry less.

An important second point is that individual members of a family will sometimes be reluctant to come in for counseling with the entire group. But, even when met with resistance, it is important for the counselor to try and include the entire family in the sessions. The family interacts as a unit with each individual influencing the others. When the counselor can assess the feelings of all the family members, the probability is greater that the grief counseling will be effective and that equilibrium will be restored to the family unit.

References

Bowen, M. (1978). *Family therapy in clinical practice*. New York: Aaronson.

Bowlby, J. (1960). Grief and mourning in infancy and early childhood. *Psychoanalytic Study of Child, 15*, 9–52.

Burns, D. (1980). *Feeling good: The new mood therapy*. New York: Signet.

Davies, B., Spinetta, J., Martinson, I., & Kulenkamp, E. (1986). Manifestations of levels of functioning in grieving families. *Journal of Family Issues, 7*, 297–313.

Flavell, J. H. (1977). *Cognitive development*. Englewood Cliffs, NJ: Prentice-Hall.

Foley, U. D. (1986). *An introduction to family therapy* (2nd Ed.). New York: Grune & Stratton.

Furman, E. (1974). *A child's parent dies: Studies in childhood bereavement*. New Haven: Yale University Press.

Greaves, C. C. (1983). Death in the family: A multifamily therapy approach. *International Journal of Family Psychiatry, 4*, 247–259.

Klass, D. (1988). *Parental grief: Solace and resolution*. New York: Springer Publishing Company.

Klass, D., & Marwit, S. J. (1988–89). Toward a model of parental grief. *Omega, 19*, 31–50.

Kuhn, J. S. (1977). Realignment of emotional forces following loss. *Family, 5*, 19–24.

Lopata, H. Z. (1979). *Women as widows*. New York: Elsevier.

Lund, D. A., Diamond, M. F., & Juretich, M. (1985). Bereavement support groups for the elderly: Characteristics of potential participants. *Death Studies, 9*, 309–321.

Moss, M. Z., & Moss, S. Z. (1984). Some aspects of the elderly widow's persistant tie with the deceased spouse. *Omega, 15*, 195–206.

Paul, N., & Crosser, G. H. (1965). Operational mourning and its role in conjoint family therapy. *Community Mental Health Journal, 1*, 339–345.

Paul, N. L. (1986). The paradoxical nature of the grief experience. *Contemporary Family Therapy, 8*, 5–19.

Piaget, J., & Inhelder, B. (1969). *The psychology of the child*. New York: Basic Books.

Polombo, J. (1978). *Parent loss and childhood bereavement*. Conference on Children & Death, University of Chicago.

Reilly, D. M. (1978). Death propensity, dying, and bereavement: A family systems perspective. *Family Therapy, 5*, 35–55.

Schumacher, J. D. (1983). Helping children cope with a sibling's death. In J. C. Hansen (Ed.), *Death and grief in the family*. Rockville, MD: Aspen.

Spark, G. M., & Browdy, E. M. (1972). The aged are family members. In C. Sager &

H. Kaplan (Eds.), *Progress in group and family therapy*. New York: Brunner/Mazel.

Vess, J., et al. (1985–86). Understanding family role reallocation following a death: A theoretical framework. *Omega, 16,* 115–128.

Wolfenstein, M. (1966). How is mourning possible? *Psychoanalytic Study of the Child, 21,* 93–123.

Chapter **8**

The Counselor's Own Grief

Grief counseling presents a special challenge to the mental health worker. Most of us go into this profession in order to benefit the people who come to us for help, but there is something about the experience of grief which precludes our ability to help. Bowlby touches on this when he says:

> The loss of a loved person is one of the most intensely painful experiences any human being can suffer, and not only is it painful to experience, but also painful to witness, if only because we're so impotent to help. [Bowlby, 1980, p. 7]

Parkes echoes this sentiment when he says:

> Pain is inevitable in such a case and cannot be avoided. It stems from the awareness of both parties that neither can give the other what he wants. The helper cannot bring back the person who's dead, and the bereaved person cannot gratify the helper by seeming helped. [Parkes, 1972, p. 163]

Because the experience of grief makes it difficult for us to be or feel helpful to the person experiencing bereavement, the counselor can easily feel frustration and anger. Or the counselor may be so uncomfortable witnessing the pain in the other person that this discomfort causes him or her to cut the relationship short.

In addition to challenging our need to be helpful, the experience of bereavement in others also touches the counselor personally in at least three more ways. First, working with the bereaved may make us aware, sometimes painfully so, of our own losses. This is particularly true if the loss experienced by the bereaved is similar to losses that we have sustained in our own lives. If this loss is not adequately resolved in the counselor's life, it can be an impediment to a meaningful and helpful intervention. If it has been adequately integrated, the counselor's experience with a similar loss can be beneficial and useful when working with the client. The counselor who has lost a spouse, through death or divorce, and for whom the loss is very recent, will find it difficult, if not impossible, to work with a person who has sustained a similar loss. However, if this counselor has moved through his or her own bereavement and found resolution at the other side of the loss, this can be useful and helpful in the counseling intervention. "Treatment of the bereaved needs to emerge from a compassion based on recognition of the common vulnerability of all human beings in the face of loss" (Simos, 1979, p. 177).

A second area where grief may get in the way is in terms of the counselor's own *feared* losses. All of us who work in this area have sustained various losses in our lifetimes, but we also come to the counseling situation with apprehension over pending losses—for example, our parents, our children, our partners. Usually this apprehension is at a low level of awareness. However, if the loss our client is experiencing is similar to the one we most fear, our apprehension can get in the way of an effective counseling relationship.

For example, if a counselor is overanxious about the possible death of his children and if this anxiety is translated into an overprotective relationship, this counselor may have a great deal of difficulty working with someone whose child has died. This is especially true if the counselor has not adequately brought his anxiety into consciousness and addressed the problem.

A third area in which grief counseling presents a special challenge to the mental health worker has to do with existential anxiety and one's own personal death awareness. In an earlier book, I addressed this issue and how this type of awareness can make a person more effective or less effective as a human being (Worden, 1976). When a client comes for grief counseling, the counselor is put in touch with the inevitability of death and with the extent to which he or she is uncomfortable with this inevitability in his or her own life. This situation is especially difficult when the person who's being grieved is similar to the counselor in terms of age, sex, or professional status, all of which can greatly increase the anxiety of the counselor. All of us are anxious to one degree or another about our own mortality, but it is possible to come to terms with this reality and not have it as a closet issue, making us uncomfortable and hindering our effectiveness.

Because grief counseling presents a special challenge to the mental health worker, we encourage the counselors in our training programs to explore their own history of losses. We believe that this can make them more effective counselors. In the first place it can help the counselor to better understand the process of mourning, what it is like to go through the experience of grief, and how the curative process of mourning takes place. There is nothing like looking at a significant loss in one's own life to bring home the reality of the grief process. It also gives the counselor an understanding of coping methods and an idea of how long the process can go on before it comes to an adequate resolution.

Second, by exploring a personal history of losses, the counselor can get a clear sense of the kinds of resources available to the bereaved. This includes not only what was helpful to oneself when undergoing a specific loss, but also what was *not* helpful. An exploration of this can make for more creative intervention on the counselor's part, not only knowing *what* to say, but also what *not* to say. When looking at personal losses, the counselor can identify his or her own coping style and how this personal coping style affects behavior in a counseling intervention.

The counselor can also identify any irresolution that is still present from prior losses. The Zeignerik psychological principle suggests that an incompleted task will be remembered until completed. The counselor who has a grasp on his or her own life will know about and be able to face honestly and squarely those losses that have not been adequately grieved at this particular time, and what he or she still needs to do to resolve these particular losses. Not only is it important to identify currently unresolved losses but it is also important to identify the conflict that that loss portends for the counselor and the way that that conflict can be identified and dealt with.

Finally, looking at one's own grief will help the counselor or therapist know his or her limitations with respect to the kinds of clients and the kinds of grief situations that one is able to deal with. A few years ago Elisabeth Kübler-Ross and I surveyed 5000 health professionals on issues of terminal care (Worden & Kübler-Ross, 1977). One of the areas we were interested in concerned difficulties caregivers had with dying patients. Of the respondents to our inquiry, 92 percent reported that there were one or more types of dying patients with whom they had special difficulty. The types of patients varied widely, although there was a certain clustering among the various professional groups. Because not everyone can work adequately with all types of dying patients, it is important for the caregiver to recognize personal limitations and make referrals to other colleagues who can handle certain cases more effectively.

Similar limitations hold true for the grief counselor. It is important for the grief counselor to know the kind of grieving person with whom he or she cannot work effectively and to be able to make a referral or share the support when faced with such a client. One of the subtle seductions in the mental health professions is the notion that one is capable of handling all situations.

This obviously is not so, and the mature counselor knows his or her own limitations and knows when to refer. The type of client the grief counselor has personal difficulty with is usually related to the counselor's own area of unresolved conflict.

At this point, let me suggest that you look at your own history of losses. Below you will find a series of questions. Write your answers either in the book or on a separate paper, and spend some time reflecting on your answers. If possible, talk this over with a friend or colleague. This reflection on your own life can pay dividends later on in helping to make you more effective in your own work.

1. The first death I can remember was the death of:

2. I was age:

3. The feelings I remember I had at the time were:

4. The first funeral (wake or other ritual service) I ever attended was for:

5. I was age:

6. The thing I most remember about that experience is:

7. My most recent loss by death was (person, time, circumstances):

8. I coped with this loss by:

9. The most difficult death for me was the death of:

10. It was difficult because:

11. Of the important people in my life who are now living, the most difficult death for me would be the death of:

12. It would be the most difficult because:

13. My primary style of coping with loss is:

14. I know my own grief is resolved when:

15. It is appropriate for me to share my own experiences of grief with a client when:

Stress and Burnout

There is much current interest in the problem of burnout and stress management among health care providers. One focus for this interest has been the health care providers who work with terminally ill patients and their families. Many bereavement counselors also work with the terminally ill and have had contact with the deceased as well as the family prior to the actual death. Mary Vachon has compared staff stress among those working in a hospice setting and those working with the seriously ill in a general hospital. She finds stress in both settings and concludes that the best care can be given if caregivers are cognizant that they too have needs (Vachon, 1979).

Since much of my work at the Massachusetts General Hospital has been with terminal patients as well as with the family's bereavement issues, I have also been interested in this issue of staff stress. There are three guidelines that I would like to suggest to the counselor who may be working with dying patients. The first is to know your own personal limitations in terms of the number of patients with whom you can work intimately and be attached to at any given point in time. One can work with a number of patients and do an adequate job, but there is a definite limit to the number of dying patients with whom one can work and have any kind of in-depth, attached relationship. This number, of course, varies from person to person, but it is extremely important for the counselor to recognize personal limitations and not be overly involved and attached to too many dying people. To the extent that there is an attachment, there is going to be a loss which the counselor will need to grieve.

In the second place, a counselor can avoid burnout by practicing active grieving. When a patient dies, it is important for the counselor to go through this period of active grieving. One thing I find personally helpful and recommend to our staff is that they attend the funeral services of the person with whom they have been working. It is also important that they allow themselves to experience the sadness and other feelings after someone dies, and not feel guilty if they do not grieve the same way for each death.

Third, the counselor should know how to reach out for help and know where his or her own support comes from. Sometimes this can be a very difficult thing for health care people to do. After lecturing to a group of funeral directors in the Midwest, I was approached by a funeral director's wife who was very concerned about her husband. He had sustained an important loss and was not doing well. He was able to help others with their grief, but found it very difficult to reach out for help himself. This man's experience is similar to that of many counselors. Counselors are well known for their inability to negotiate their own help and support systems. Therefore, those of you doing grief counseling and grief therapy need to know (1) where you get emotional support, (2) what your limitations are, and (3) how to reach out for help when you need it.

For those working in institutional settings such as hospitals, nursing homes, and hospices, support often comes from others on the caregiving team and a team leader can be responsible for facilitating this support. Regular staff meetings where participants are encouraged to talk about problems that arise in the care of the dying and their families, and their own feelings, can help prevent excessive stress and can facilitate the feelings associated with grief and loss. Mental health professionals who are not a part of the management team can also be available to others for private consultation or to the team should it need help. I provided such consultation to the Gynecologic Service Staff at the hospital for several years. Parkes, in speaking of support for staff who work in settings where there are numbers of deaths, says, "With proper training and support we shall find that repeated griefs, far from undermining our humanity and our care, enable us to cope more confidently and more sensitively with each succeeding loss" (Parkes, 1986, p. 7). I believe this is true.

Vachon, in a recent book, outlined a procedure that could be useful in some institutional settings. After a patient dies, the attending nurse tape records the circumstances of the death, who was present, their reactions, and an informal assessment of which family members might be at risk following the loss. The nurse also dictates personal feelings that he or she may be having at the time. Later in the week others on the team listen to the tape during rounds set up for the entire caregiving team to discuss deaths on the unit. The tape is used not only to provide information to those not present at the death, but also to stimulate a discussion about the loss, to share feelings that have been engendered by the death, and to assess how treatment could have been different or improved. Each of the staff signs a sympathy card that is sent to the survivors about a month after the death (Vachon, 1987).

As part of this consideration of the counselor's own grief, I want to comment on the use of volunteers as lay counselors. Personal bereavement has often motivated people to serve as volunteers in the various bereavement outreach programs that have proliferated in the past decade. Most hospice programs both here and abroad use volunteers in some capacity to work with the dying and their families. The same holds true for the many Widow-to-Widow programs, stemming from the early work of Phyllis R. Silverman, that have been so effective (Silverman, 1986). These use widows as volunteers to befriend and offer counsel to those more recently bereaved.

Volunteers can be effective, but it is my strong conviction that lay counselors should be people who have worked through their own grief and have experienced some degree of resolution. I have noticed that some of the people attending the various training workshops I have conducted across the country are experiencing acute grief, and their interest in further training in grief counseling comes from a need to work through their own grief. I do not believe that grief counseling is the place for a counselor to work through a recent bereavement—there are too many blind spots that hinder effective counseling. However, a person who has gone through a grief experience and come to some resolution has the potential for doing more significant intervention than someone who has never experienced loss and grief.

Garfield and his colleagues at the Shanti program in the San Francisco Bay area have found that the volunteers who do the most effective work are those who have a history of mutually satisfying interpersonal relationships and whose motivations for work are personally relevant. They recommend that programs that use volunteers be set up to offer training, supervision, support, and the opportunity to explore one's style of coping and its effectiveness. The same would be advisable for professionals working in this field (Garfield & Jenkins, 1981–82).

References

Bowlby, J. (1980). *Attachment and loss: Loss, sadness, and depression* (vol III). New York: Basic Books.

Garfield, C. A., & Jenkins, G. J. (1981–82). Stress and coping of volunteers counseling the dying and the bereaved. *Omega, 12,* 1–13.

Parkes, C. M. (1972). *Bereavement: Studies of grief in adult life.* New York: International Universities Press.

Parkes, C. M. (1986). Orienterring the caregiver's grief. *Journal of Palliative Care, 1,* 5–7.

Silverman, P. R. (1986). *Widow to widow.* New York: Springer Publishing Company.

Simos, B. G. (1979). *A time to grieve.* New York: Family Service Association.

Vachon, M. L. S. (1979). Staff stress in the care of the terminally ill. *Quality Review Bulletin, 251,* 13–17.

Vachon, M. L. S. (1987). *Occupational stress in the care of the critically ill, the dying & the bereaved.* Washington: Hemisphere.

Worden, J. W. (1976). *Personal death awareness.* Englewood Cliffs, NJ: Prentice-Hall.

Worden, J. W., & Kübler-Ross, E. (1977–78). Attitudes and experiences of death workshop attendees. *Omega, 8,* 91–106.

Chapter 9

Training for Grief Counseling

In 1976 Mary Conrad, who was then Director for Programming for the University of Chicago Center for Continuing Education, and I decided to offer a two-day grief counseling program for health professionals. We had previously presented workshops geared to help health professionals deal with various aspects of terminal illness care, but we shared the belief that our efforts to help train people in this type of care would not be complete until we addressed the issues of grief counseling and grief therapy.

We decided on a two-day format so that we could make the program as comprehensive as possible not only to present didactic material but also to help the participants increase their skills when dealing with bereaved individuals. It was necessary to address a wide variety of issues related to the general area of bereavement. Not only did we want to present information about the theory of mourning and why it was necessary, but we also wanted to address issues of differential diagnosis of normal and pathological grief and to look at some of the special interventions surrounding grief such as grief from sudden death or from partial losses such as amputations.

One aspect was unique to our program and proved to be a very successful training technique. At the beginning of the two-day program we divided the attendees into groups of ten which met throughout the program. At their first meeting, after introductions, they shared aspects of their own grief history. Each member was encouraged to do this and although, on the surface, their experiences of grief were different, there was an underlying awareness that each had experienced the pain of loss and bereavement. This awareness of similar experiences contributed to group dynamics and brought the group close together in a relatively short period of time.

On the second day a great deal of time was given over to role-playing various grief-related situations. To facilitate this, I had developed a series of vignettes, based on cases in my files, which represented a variety of situations and grief-related issues. They are included at the end of this chapter and can be used in training. The role-playing was set up in a format similar to one we used at Harvard Medical School to train medical students in their counseling skills, particularly with dying patients and bereaved families.

The procedure requires that members of the group volunteer to play the various roles, which may include family and friends but which always include a counselor in some capacity. The roles are assigned and the volunteers are asked to read their part carefully and adhere to the script. They are also asked not to discuss their parts among themselves. *It is very important that the individual know only his part and not the whole vignette* because it stimulates creativity and adds considerably to the vitality and realism of the role-playing situation. While the volunteers are out of the room, the group leader reads only the counselor's part to the remaining members of the group. The players are called back into the room and the session is ready to begin.

The group leader allows the role-playing to go on as long as it seems productive and then rotates the part of the counselor to another member of the group. This is done several times so that at least two or three people are able to try their skills as a counselor. Then the whole process is critiqued and evaluated. The various people playing the counselors are asked to explain the direction they took and what they had in mind, and the people who played the bereaved talk about which interventions were helpful and which were not. The observing group members share their observations and the group leader can add his or her own suggestions. After the critique, the same situation can be role-played again, or the group can go on to a different one. The participants in the role-playing, particularly those playing the counselors, are reminded that they are not expected to be perfect and that they are there because they wanted to further their skills development.

Although two days is obviously not enough time to develop experienced grief counselors, this did seem to be a favorable format and we have repeated the program for various health professionals across the country. The basic assumption behind such a workshop is that the participants already have certain understandings and skills as mental health practitioners. The purpose of the workshop is to give them further information about the special aspects related to bereavement as well as to give them some hands-on experience on doing counseling and having it critiqued in front of a peer group.

Most of the vignettes are set up to address the issue of grief counseling and not the issue of grief therapy. Grief therapy is a much more complicated procedure and cannot be addressed in such an abbreviated manner. Again, as I have emphasized throughout this book, people should not attempt grief therapy unless they have the necessary education and training. This includes a thorough knowledge of psychodynamics, including the ability to assess the decompensating potential of the patient or client. There are many people who attempt psychotherapy without adequate background and training. One of the most valuable qualities of a good therapist is knowing one's own limitations and knowing when to refer or to consult with a more experienced professional.

Grief Sketch 1

Woman: Twelve weeks ago your husband of 33 years left to drive to an appointment several hundred miles from your home. He was to stay overnight and return home the next day but he never returned. Several days later his dead body was found in his car on a remote road where he apparently died of a heart attack. Decomposition was rapid because of the heat and you were advised not to see his body. You attended the funeral and burial in his home state a great distance from your home. Even now you cannot believe he is dead and you wait for him to come home. You cry all the time and don't know what to do so you seek counseling.

Counselor: A 58-year-old woman lost her husband to a heart attack while he was away on a business trip. She never saw his body and is having difficulty believing he is really dead. Assist her with this first task of mourning and in any other way she may need your help.

From *Grief Counseling and Grief Therapy,* 2nd Edition, by J. William Worden, Ph.D. Copyright © 1991 by Springer Publishing Company.

Grief Sketch 2

Father: Your 17-year-old son was killed in a car accident while riding as a passenger with other teenagers. You are extremely angry with the doctors and the hospital for doing an autopsy on your boy. You have nightmares of the way he was cut up "needlessly" since it was obvious that he died as the result of injuries sustained in a car accident. Sometimes you feel angry at everyone around you. Your wife has suggested you talk with a professional about this.

Counselor: You are asked to see a father whose 17-year-old son was killed in an automobile accident. This father is extremely angry. Your role is to help him sort out the sources of his anger and to help him target the anger in a way that will bring him a sense of closure.

From *Grief Counseling and Grief Therapy*, 2nd Edition, by J. William Worden, Ph.D. Copyright © 1991 by Springer Publishing Company.

Grief Sketch 3

Woman: You are 38 and single. Three months ago your alcoholic stepfather died suddenly of a heart attack. He had come into your life when you were age three and over the years he had been physically and sexually abusive to you until you left home at age 17. You were happy to hear of his death, are glad that he is finally out of your life, and can only remember negative things about him. Since his death, you have had several dreams of him with his arms outstretched to you. You are not sure of the meaning of the dreams but you awaken from them upset and are unable to go back to sleep. Your disturbed sleep is beginning to affect your work performance so you have decided to seek counseling.

Counselor: A 38-year-old single woman has been experiencing sleep difficulties over the past three months since her stepfather died suddenly of a heart attack. Explore her symptoms in light of her recent loss. If there is grief work to be done, help her to identify and facilitate it.

From *Grief Counseling and Grief Therapy*, 2nd Edition, by J. William Worden, Ph.D. Copyright © 1991 by Springer Publishing Company.

Grief Sketch 4

Woman: You are a 51-year-old single woman whose mother died. The two of you always lived together and had a close but ambivalent relationship. You cared for your mother during her lengthy illness, which involved several hospitalizations. Your mother was not an easy person to get along with and several times during her final years you told her in anger that if she didn't shape up, you would send her off to a nursing home. You really wouldn't have, but now that she is dead, you miss her terribly and you're feeling very guilty about having said these things.

Counselor: A 51-year-old single woman has approached you for help with the guilt she feels since her mother's death. Your task is to help her reality test her guilt and to find a way to better cope with it.

From *Grief Counseling and Grief Therapy*, 2nd Edition, by J. William Worden, Ph.D. Copyright © 1991 by Springer Publishing Company.

Grief Sketch 5

Widower: You are 29 and your wife of six years died of cancer four months ago leaving you with a son 3 and a daughter 5. You had a good marriage and are hurting a great deal and want to find something to help you cut the pain you are now feeling. You believe if you can only get remarried, all of this will be over and behind you. You have dated several women but each one has left you feeling more depressed than before. Nevertheless, you still believe if you can get remarried soon, your kids will have a new mother, you will feel better about yourself, and your pain will be gone. You will see the bereavement counselor from the hospice that took care of your wife.

Counselor: You have been asked to see a 29-year-old man whose wife died of cancer in your hospice program four months ago. You did not work with the family before the death but will now see the husband as part of your bereavement follow-up.

From *Grief Counseling and Grief Therapy*, 2nd Edition, by J. William Worden, Ph.D. Copyright © 1991 by Springer Publishing Company.

Grief Sketch 6

Woman: Over the past three years you have lost your mother, your father, a brother, and a close friend. All of these losses have left you feeling numb. When you do feel, you are more aware of feelings of anxiety than you are of sadness. The anxiety has been increasing in recent months and you have seen your physician several times to check out heart palpitations. The physician says you are alright physically but your symptoms are associated with stress and anxiety. She has sent you to see a counselor to help you better manage your stress.

Counselor: A physician colleague has referred a woman to you to help this patient better manage her stress. She has lost several family members and friends to death during the recent past. Evaluate the relationship of these losses to her stress and intervene appropriately with her around these issues.

From *Grief Counseling and Grief Therapy,* 2nd Edition, by J. William Worden, Ph.D. Copyright © 1991 by Springer Publishing Company.

Grief Sketch 7

Wife: Your 8-year-old child died from leukemia two years ago. You are adjusting to the loss but have fear that over time you might forget some of the important details of your child's life and your time together. In order to keep this from happening you have kept your child's room intact, just as it was when he died. Your husband is upset with this. He feels that after two years the room should be dismantled, a few things kept, and the room put to other uses. Every time you and he discuss this, you end up in a fight and feel estranged from him.

Husband: After your 8-year-old child died of leukemia two years ago, nothing was changed in his room. This presented no problems for you then, but now, since two years have passed, you are pushing your wife to dismantle the room, save a few important memorabilia, and rearrange the room to serve another purpose. To you, keeping the room as is just adds to your painful memories. Your wife will not listen to "reason" and will not change the room.

Counselor: A couple has approached you to help them arbitrate a dispute they have regarding their dead child's room and possessions. The husband wants to dismantle this room and the wife doesn't. Help them to resolve this problem and to be in touch with their underlying fears and feelings engendered by this situation.

From *Grief Counseling and Grief Therapy,* 2nd Edition, by J. William Worden, Ph.D. Copyright © 1991 by Springer Publishing Company.

Grief Sketch 8

Wife: Seven months ago your father, age 78, committed suicide by shooting himself in the head. This came as a complete shock to you and he left no note explaining his action. Your mother had died the previous year and though your father lived at a distance, you spoke often with him by phone and believed that he was making an adequate adjustment to his loss. Since the death you have been irritable and short with everyone, especially with your husband. He is losing patience with you and has threatened to move out. You reluctantly agree to go with your husband to see a counselor.

Husband: Your father-in-law shot himself recently, within a year of losing his wife. This came as a shock to both you and your wife, and he left no note to help explain his suicide. Since his death your wife has been unbearable to live with. She is irritated with every little thing you do. You are so fed up with this behavior that you have threatened to leave. Before you do, you want to give counseling a chance, but you are not too hopeful.

Counselor: You will see a couple on the verge of splitting up. You know from the initial phone contact with the husband that his wife's father recently died. In your evaluation, see to what extent grief issues may or may not be contributing to their marital disharmony.

From *Grief Counseling and Grief Therapy*, 2nd Edition, by J. William Worden, Ph.D. Copyright © 1991 by Springer Publishing Company.

Grief Sketch 9

Mother: Your child died in the hospital after living for three months. It has been 15 months since the death and you are still feeling very depressed. You attended one group session for bereaved parents but left saying, "Story swapping is not what I need." You feel a lot of anger toward your husband for not being there when the baby died and for paying more attention to your two living children than he does to you. Your own father abandoned you and the family when you were five years old. Recently you have been dreaming of your dead child who says in the dream, "You didn't give me a chance." A friend suggested you see a counselor.

Father: After living only three months your newborn died in the hospital from congenital complications. You feel some guilt over this death and now you give your two living children more attention than you gave them before the death. Your wife has been depressed for the past 15 months since the loss. Her sadness bothers you and gives you a sense of helplessness. The only way you know how to help her is to appear strong and confident. This hasn't helped. She is going to see a counselor and wants you to go with her. You feel that you are okay but agree to go if it will help her.

Counselor: A couple lost their baby three months after birth. The wife has been depressed for the past 15 months since this happened. The couple has two other children. Both the husband and wife will attend the first counseling session. Your task is to see where they are in their grief and decide whether to work with them individually, as a couple, or as an entire family.

From *Grief Counseling and Grief Therapy*, 2nd Edition, by J. William Worden, Ph.D. Copyright © 1991 by Springer Publishing Company.

Grief Sketch 10

Father: Your wife died of cancer 10 months ago leaving you with three children, a daughter 14 and sons 11 and 6. You are doing your best to manage as a single parent but your work requires long hours and a lengthy commute. You thought that your children would pull together after the death but they seem to be going separate ways. You are especially annoyed at your daughter, who resents taking on household chores, something you feel she should do because she is a girl and the oldest child. When the school counselor called to report her truancy, you agreed to see a family counselor.

Sister: You are 14 and lost your mother to cancer 10 months ago. You miss her and find your father has become a first class pain since she died. He expects you to fix breakfast and dinner, to shop, and to babysit your 6-year-old brother. You resent this, are doing poorly in school since your mother died, and prefer hanging around the mall with your friends instead of going to class. You see this as your only private time, since your household responsibilities don't leave you any other time just for yourself. You reluctantly agree to go see the family counselor.

Brother: Ten months ago, when you just turned 11, your mother died of cancer. Since then things have been chaotic at home and you prefer to be out of the house. You spend most of your time with your friends hanging out and playing hacky sack down at the park. Your older sister is bossy and you resent her telling you what to do. You like your 6-year-old brother but do not share many activities in common with him.

Brother: You are 6 years old. Since your mother died of cancer 10 months ago, you have felt abandoned. You don't really understand what happened to your mother or where she is now. You were not included in the funeral service. At night you have dreams of her and find these somewhat comforting. You have few friends to play with and after school and on weekends you spend most of your time watching TV.

Counselor: The school has referred a family to you for family counseling that may include family grief counseling. The mother died of cancer 10 months ago leaving her husband and three children—a daughter 14, a son 11, and a son 6. The daughter has been truant and is not doing well in school. The boys are not having difficulty in school but, according to his teacher, the 6-year-old seems "lost" and she is not sure what to do with him. Evaluate this family and develop an intervention strategy.

From *Grief Counseling and Grief Therapy*, 2nd Edition, by J. William Worden, Ph.D. Copyright © 1991 by Springer Publishing Company.

Grief Sketch 11

Young man: Your lover of eight years died six months ago of AIDS. You shared a house together and cared for him until he died at home. You feel that you did a lot of grieving during his 18-month illness. His older sister calls you frequently for emotional support. Although you like her and would like to help, her calls make you feel sad, and you prefer that she not call so often. Her brother was an important chapter in your life and you miss him, but you now want to move on with your life. You reluctantly agree to a single visit with her counselor in the hope that she will back off.

Sister: Your brother, who was seven years younger than yourself, died six months ago from AIDS. You helped his lover of eight years care for him during the 18-month-long illness. You are familiar with this caring role as your mother died when you were 12, leaving you, the oldest, to care for the rest of the family. You feel unsupported and alone in your grief. You are angry at your brother's lover and at your husband for wanting to put this difficult death behind and to move forward with life.

Husband: Your wife lost her brother to AIDS six months ago. You liked her brother and were sympathetic and supportive to your wife during the 18-month illness, but you felt real relief after he died. To you that meant the ordeal was over and you could get back to normal living. However, your wife cries a lot, refuses to return to work, and you are feeling frustrated, angry, and helpless. You reluctantly agree to go visit a counselor with the hope that it will bring an end to all of this.

Counselor: You have an appointment with a woman whose younger brother died of AIDS six months ago. She is bringing along her husband and her brother's lover. Your task is to bring the grief issues to light and to facilitate them within this family context.

From *Grief Counseling and Grief Therapy*, 2nd Edition, by J. William Worden, Ph.D. Copyright © 1991 by Springer Publishing Company.

Grief Sketch 12

Mother: Your son, age 15, was killed suddenly one evening a year ago. He was a passenger in a car driven by his 16-year-old friend and the car went out of control. Since that time you have been inconsolable. This boy was your firstborn, talented, and clearly your favorite. You cannot understand why your husband and two other children are not as grief stricken as you are. You have moments of deep rage that is targeted either to your husband, the boy who drove the car, or to your younger son who won't talk about his dead brother.

Father: You lost your 15-year-old boy in a car accident a year ago. For the first couple of months you felt devastated and cried a lot when you were alone. Although you still miss him, you believe that you, your wife, and two remaining children need to move on with your lives. Your wife cries much of the time and you feel tension in the family. Because of this you have contacted a family counselor to straighten all this out.

Brother: You are 13 and your 15-year-old brother died in a car accident a year ago while riding with a friend. You always felt inferior to your brother and you felt somewhat relieved when he died. Now you feel guilty about these feelings. His memory and presence linger around the house but when people talk about him, you get up and leave the room. This behavior upsets the rest of the family, but you don't care.

Sister: You are the 9-year-old sister of a boy, 15, who was killed when the car he was riding in went out of control. You feel sad and miss your brother. Your sadness is even worse because your mother is not as close to you as before and you feel you have lost her too. You are not sure what to do to get your mother back.

Counselor: You have been contacted to do family grief counseling by the father of a 15-year-old boy who was killed a year ago in a car accident. Your role is to see them, assess the issues, and to suggest an appropriate mode of intervention.

(This scenario could be played out over several therapy sessions)

From *Grief Counseling and Grief Therapy*, 2nd Edition, by J. William Worden, Ph.D. Copyright © 1991 by Springer Publishing Company.

Bibliography

Abraham, K. (1927). *Selected papers on psychoanalysis*. London: Hogarth.

Adams-Greenly, M., & Moynihan, R. T. (1983). Helping the children of fatally ill parents. *American Journal of Orthopsychiatry, 53*, 219–229.

Agee, J. (1957). *A death in the family*. New York: Bantam.

Akiyama, H., Holtzman, J. M., & Britz, W. E. (1986–87). Pet ownership and health status during bereavement. *Omega, 17*, 187–193.

Alarcon, R. D. (1984). Single case study: Personality disorder as a pathogenic factor in bereavement. *Journal of Nervous and Mental Disease, 172*, 45–47.

Aldrich, C. K. (1963). The dying patient's grief. *Journal of the American Medical Association, 184*, 329–331.

Alexander, D. A. (1988). Bereavement and the management of grief. *British Journal of Psychiatry, 153*, 860–864.

Alexander, J., & Kiely, J. (1986). Working with the bereaved. *Geriatric Nursing, 7*, 85–86.

Alexy, W. D. (1980). Coping with loss: The principal theme postulate. *Rehabilitation Literature, 41*, 66–71.

Alexy, W. D. (1982). Dimensions of psychological counseling that facilitate the growing process of bereaved parents. *Journal of Counseling Psychology, 29*, 498–507.

Amir, Y. & Sharon, I. (1982). Factors in the adjustment of war widows in Israel. In C. D. Spielberger et al. (Eds.), *Stress and Anxiety*, Vol. 8 (pp. 225–234). Washington DC: Hemisphere.

Averill, J. R. (1968). Grief: Its nature and significance. *Psychological Bulletin, 70*, 721–748.

Bailey, B. J., & Gregg, C. H. (1986). Grief, pathological grief, and rehabilitation counseling. *Journal of Applied Rehabilitation Counseling, 17*, 19–23.

Balkwell, C. (1981). Transition to widowhood: A review of the literature. *Family Relations, 30,* 117–127.

Bankoff, E. A. (1983). Aged parents and their widowed daughters. *Journal of Gerontology, 38,* 226–230.

Bankoff, E. A. (1983). Social support and adaptation to widowhood. *Journal of Marriage and Family, 45,* 827–839.

Barnes, G. E., & Prosen, H. (1985). Parental death and depression. *Journal of Abnormal Psychology, 94,* 64–69.

Barrett, C. J. (1978). Effectiveness of widows' groups in facilitating change. *Journal of Consulting Clinical Psychology, 46,* 20–31.

Barry, M. J., Jr. (1973). The prolonged grief reaction. *Mayo Clinic Proceedings, 48,* 329–335.

Barry, M. J., Jr. (1981). Therapeutic experience with patients referred for 'prolonged grief reaction'—some second thoughts. *Mayo Clinic Proceedings, 56,* 744–748.

Bartrop, R. W., (1977). Depressed lymphocyte function after bereavement. *Lancet, 16,* 834–836.

Belitsky, R., & Jacobs, S. (1986). Bereavement, attachment theory, and mental disorder. *Psychiatric Annals, 16,* 276–280.

Bendiksen, R., & Fulton, R. (1975). Childhood bereavement and later behavioral disorders. *Omega, 6,* 45–60.

Bengesser, G. (1988). Postvention for bereaved family members: Some therapeutic possibilities. *Crisis, 9,* 45–48.

Benoliel, J. Q. (1985). Loss and adaptation: Circumstances, contingencies, and consequences. *Death Studies, 9,* 217–233.

Berman, H., Cragg, C. E., & Kuenzig, L. (1988). Having a parent die of cancer: Adolescents' grief reactions. *Oncology Nursing Forum, 15,* 159–163.

Bifulco, A. T., Brown, G. W., & Harris, T. O. (1987). Childhood loss of parent, lack of adequate parental care and adult depression: A replication. *Journal of Affective Disorders, 12,* 115–128.

Birtchnell, J. (1970). Depression in relation to early and recent parent death. *British Journal of Psychiatry, 116,* 299–305.

Birtchnell, J. (1975). Psychiatric breakdown following recent parent death. *British Journal of Medical Psychology, 48,* 379–390.

Birtchnell, J. (1980). Women whose mothers died in childhood: An outcome study. *Psychological Medicine, 10,* 699–713.

Birthnell, J. (1981). In search of correspondences between age at psychiatric breakdown and age at death: Anniversary reactions. *British Journal of Medical Psychology, 54,* 111–121.

Black, D. (1974). What happens to bereaved children? *Proceedings of the Royal Society of Medicine, 69,* 38–40.

Black, D., & Urbanowicz, M. A. (1987). Family intervention with bereaved children. *Journal of Child Psychology and Psychiatry and Allied Disciplines, 28,* 467–476.

Blankfield, A. (1982–83). Grief and alcohol. *American Journal of Drug and Alcohol Abuse, 9,* 435–436.

Blazer, D. G. (1982). Social support and mortality in an elderly community population. *American Journal of Epidemiology, 115,* 684–694.

Bolton, C., & Camp, D. J. (1986–87). Funeral rituals and the facilitation of grief work. *Omega, 17,* 343–352.

Bolton, I. (1984). Families coping with suicide. *Family Therapy Collections, 8,* 35–47.

Bornstein, P. E., & Clayton, P. J. (1972). The anniversary reaction. *Diseases of the Nervous System, 33,* 470–472.

Bourke, M. P. (1984). The continuum of pre- and post-bereavement grieving. *British Journal of Medical Psychology, 57,* 121–125.

Bowlby, J. (1963). Pathological mourning and childhood mourning. *Journal of the American Psychoanalytic Association, 11,* 500–541.

Bowlby, J. (1969). *Attachment and loss: Attachment.* Vol. I. New York: Basic.

Bowlby, J. (1975). *Attachment and loss: Loss.* Vol. II. Harmondsworth: Penguin.

Bowlby, J. (1977). The making and breaking of affectional bonds, I and II. *British Journal of Psychiatry, 130,* 201–210; 421–431.

Bowlby, J. (1980). *Attachment and loss: Loss, sadness, and depression.* Vol. III. New York: Basic Books.

Bowlby-West, L. (1983). The impact of death on the family system. *Journal of Family Therapy, 5,* 279–294.

Bowling A. (1987). Mortality after bereavement: A review of literature on survival periods and factors affecting survival. *Social Science and Medicine, 24,* 117–124.

Bowling, A. (1988–89). Who dies after widow(er)hood? A discriminant analysis. *Omega, 19,* 135–153.

Bowling, A., & Cartright, A. (1982). *Life after death: A study of the elderly widowed.* London: Tavistock.

Brasted, W. S., & Callahan, E. J. (1984). A behavioral analysis of the grief process. *Behavior Therapy, 15,* 529–543.

Breckenridge, J. N., et al. (1986). Characteristic depressive symptoms of bereaved elders. *Journal of Gerontology, 41,* 163–168.

Breier, A., et al. (1988). Early parental loss and development of adult psychopathology. *Archives of General Psychiatry, 45,* 987–993.

Brink, T. L. (1985). The grieving patient in later life. *Psychotherapy Patient, 2,* 117–127.

Briscoe, C. W., & Smith, J. B. (1975). Depression in bereavement and divorce. *Archives of General Psychiatry, 32,* 439–443.

Brown, G. W., & Copeland, J. R. (1977). Depression and loss. *British Journal of Psychiatry, 130,* 1–18.

Brown, J. T., & Stoudemire, G. A. (1983). Normal and pathological grief. *Journal of the American Medical Association, 250,* 378–382.

Brubaker, E. (1985). Older parents' reactions to the death of adult children: Implications for practice. *Journal of Gerontological Social Work, 9,* 35–48.

Bugen, L. A. (1977). Human grief: A model for prediction and intervention. *American Journal of Orthopsychiatry, 47,* 196–206.

Burks, V. K., et al. (1980). Bereavement and remarriage for older adults. *Death Studies, 12,* 51–60.

Burnell, G. M., & Burnell, A. L. (1986). The compassionate friends: A support group for bereaved parents. *Journal of Family Practice, 22,* 295–296.

Cable, D. G. (1988). A comprehensive bereavement support program. An outline for development. *American Journal of Hospice Care, 5,* 32–35.

Cain, A. C. (Ed.) (1972). *Survivors of suicide.* Springfield, IL: Thomas.

Calabrese, J. R., Kling, M. A., & Gold, P. W. (1987). Alterations in immunocompetence during stress, bereavement, and depression: Focus on neuroendocrine regulation. *American Journal of Psychiatry, 144,* 1123–1134.

Cameron, J. & Parkes, C. M. (1983). Terminal care: Evaluation of effects on surviving family of care before and after bereavement. *Postgraduate Medical Journal, 59,* 73–78.

Carter, P. (1986). School nursing: Helping children to grieve. *Community Outlook, 13,* 16–17.

Carter, S. R. (1987). Use of puppets to treat traumatic grief: A case study. *Elementary School Guidance and Counseling, 21,* 210–215.

Cates, J. A. (1986). Grief therapy in residential treatment: A model for intervention. *Child Care Quarterly, 15,* 147–158.

Cerney, M. S. (1985). Imagery and grief work. *Psychotherapy Patient, 2,* 35–43.

Clayton, P. J. (1973). The clinical morbidity of the first year of bereavement: A review. *Comprehensive Psychiatry, 14,* 151–157.

Clayton, P. J. (1974). Mortality and morbidity in the first year of widowhood. *Archives of General Psychiatry, 30,* 747–750.

Clayton, P. J. (1979). The sequelae and nonsequelae of conjugal bereavement. *American Journal of Psychiatry, 136,* 1530–1534.

Clayton, P. J., Halikas, J. A., & Maurice, W. L. (1972). The depression of widowhood. *British Journal of Psychiatry, 120,* 71–78.

Clayton, P. J., Halikas, J. A., Maurice, W. L. & Robins, E. (1973). Anticipatory grief and widowhood. *British Journal of Psychiatry, 122,* 47–51.

Clayton, P. J., Herjanic, M., Murphy, G. E., & Woodruff, R. A. (1974). Mourning and depression: Their similarities and differences. *Canadian Psychiatric Association Journal, 19,* 309–312.

Condon, J. T. (1986). Management of established pathological grief reaction after stillbirth. *American Journal of Psychiatry, 143,* 987–992.

Conway, P. (1988). Losses and grief in old age. *Social Casework, 69,* 541–549.

Cooper, D. E. (1984). Group psychotherapy with the elderly: Dealing with loss and death. *American Journal of Psychotherapy, 38,* 203–214.

Corney, R. T. S., & Horton, F. J. (1974). Pathological grief following spontaneous abortion. *American Journal of Psychiatry, 131,* 825–827.

Cowan, M. E., & Murphy, S. A. (1985). Identification of post-disaster bereavement risk predictors. *Nursing Research, 34,* 71–75.

Crisp, A. H., & Priest, R. G. (1972). Psychoneurotic status during the year following bereavement. *Journal of Psychosomatic Research, 16,* 351–355.

Crook, T., & Eliot, J. (1980). Parental death during childhood and adult depression: A critical review of the literature. *Psychological Bulletin, 87,* 252–259.

Crook, T., & Raskin, A. (1975). Association of childhood parental loss with attempted suicide and depression. *Journal of Consulting and Clinical Psychology, 43,* 277.

Das, M., & Berrios, G. E. (1984). Dexamethasone suppression test in acute grief reaction. *ACTA Psychiatrica Scandinavica, 70,* 278–281.

David, C. J. (1975). Grief, mourning and pathological mourning. *Primary Care, 2,* 81–92.

Davidowitz, M., & Myrick, R. D. (1984). Responding to the bereaved: An analysis of "helping" statements. *Death Education, 8,* 1–10.

Davies, B. (1987). Family responses to the death of a child: The meaning of memories. *Journal of Palliative Care, 3,* 9–15.

Davies, B., Spinetta, J., Martinson, I., & Kulenkamp, E. (1986). Manifestations of levels of functioning in grieving families. *Journal of Family Issues, 7,* 297–313.

Demi, A. S., & Miles, M. S. (1987). Parameters of normal grief; A Delphi study. *Death Studies, 11,* 397–412.

Denny, G. M., & Lee, L. J. (1984). Grief work with substance abusers. *Journal of Substance Abuse Treatment,* 249–254.

Deutsch, H. (1937). Absence of grief. *Psychoanalytic Quarterly, 6,* 12–22.

Deutsch, H. (1985). Grief counseling with the mentally retarded clients. *Psychiatric Aspects of Mental Retardation Reviews, 4,* 17–20.

DeVaul, R., & Zisook, S. (1976). Unresolved grief: Clinical considerations. *Postgraduate Medicine, 59,* 267–270.

Dewey, D. (1988). When a congregation cares: Organizing ministry to the bereaved. *Death Education, 12,* 123–135.

Dimond, M. (1981). Bereavement and the elderly: A critical review with implications for nursing practice and research. *Journal of Advanced Nursing, 6,* 461–470.

Dobihal, E. F. (1984). *When a friend is dying: A guide to caring for the terminally ill and bereaved.* Nashville: Abingdon Press.

Doka, K. J. (1984–85). Expectation of death, participation in funeral arrangements, and grief adjustment. *Omega, 15,* 119–129.

Dopson, C. (1979). Unresolved grief presenting chronic lymphedema of the hand. *American Journal of Psychiatry, 136,* 1333–1334.

Dorpat, T. L. (1973). Suicide, loss, and mourning. *Life-Threatening Behavior, 3,* 213–224.

Dubin, W. R., & Sarnoff, J. R. (1986). Sudden unexpected death: Intervention with the survivors. *Annals of Emergency Medicine, 15,* 54–57.

Dush, D. M. (1988). Balance and boundaries in grief counseling: An intervention framework for volunteer training. *Hospice Journal, 4,* 79–93.

Elizur, E., & Kaffman, M. (1982). Children's bereavement reactions following death of the father: II. *Journal of the American Academy of Child Psychiatry, 21,* 474–480.

Elizur, E., & Kaffman, M. (1983). Factors influencing the severity of childhood bereavement reactions. *American Journal of Orthopsychiatry, 53,* 668–676.

Engel, G. L. (1961). Is grief a disease? A challenge for medical research. *Psychosomatic Medicine, 23,* 18–22.

Essa, M. (1986). Grief as a crisis: Psychotherapeutic interventions with elderly bereaved. *American Journal of Psychotherapy, 40,* 243–251.

Evans, D. L., Jeckel, L. L., & Slott, N. E. (1982). Erotomania: A variant of pathological mourning. *Bulletin of the Menninger Clinic, 46,* 507–520.

Farberow, N. L., et al. (1987). An examination of the early impact of bereavement on psychological distress in survivors of suicide. *Gerontologist, 27,* 592–598.

Faschingbauer, T. R., et al. (1977). Development of the Texas inventory of grief. *American Journal of Psychiatry, 134,* 696–698.

Feely, N., & Gottlieb, L. N. (1988–89). Parent's coping and communication following their infant's death. *Omega, 19,* 51–67.

Ferraro, K. F. (1985). The effect of widowhood on the health status of older persons. *International Journal of Aging and Human Development, 21,* 9–25.

Finkelstein, H. (1988). The long-term effects of early parent death: A review. *Journal of Clinical Psychology, 44,* 3–9.

Flatt, B. (1989). Grief counseling. *Pastoral Psychology, 36,* 133–145.

Fletcher, J. C. & Evans, M. I. (1983). Maternal bonding in early fetal ultrasound examinations. *New England Journal of Medicine, 308,* 392–393.

Fox, S. (1985). Children's anniversary reactions to the death of a family member. *Omega, 15,* 291–305.

Fraser, K. A. (1988). Bereavement in those who have killed. *Medicine, Science and the Law, 28,* 127–130.

Fredrick, J. F., & Fredrick, N. J. (1985). The hospice experience: Possible effects in altering the biochemistry of bereavement. *Hospice Journal, 1,* 81–90.

Freeman, E. M. (1984). Loss and grief in children: Implications for school social workers. *Social Work in Education, 6,* 241–258.

Freud, S. (1957). *Mourning and melancholia (1917),* standard edition, (vol. XIV) London: Hogarth.

Frost, N. R., & Clayton, P. J. (1977). Bereavement and psychiatric hospitalization. *Archives of General Psychiatry, 34,* 1172–1175.

Fulmer, R. H. (1983). A structural approach to unresolved mourning in single parent family systems. *Journal of Marital and Family Therapy, 9,* 259–269.

Fulton, R., & Fulton, J. (1971). A psychosocial aspect of terminal care: Anticipatory grief. *Omega, 2,* 91–100.

Fulton, R., & Gottesman, D. J. (1980). Anticipatory grief: A psychosocial concept reconsidered. *British Journal of Psychiatry, 137,* 45–54.

Furman, E. (1974). *A child's parent dies: Studies in childhood bereavement.* New Haven: Yale.

Furman, E. (1983). Studies in childhood bereavement. *Canadian Journal of Psychiatry, 28,* 241–247.

Furman, E. (1986). On trauma: When is the death of a parent traumatic? *Psychoanalytic Study of the Child, 41,* 191–208.

Gallagher, D. E., Thompson, L. W., & Peterson, J. A. (1982). Psychosocial factors affecting adaptation to bereavement in the elderly. *International Journal of Aging and Human Development, 14,* 79–95.

Garber, B. (1985). Mourning in adolescence: Normal and pathological. *Adolescent Psychology, 12,* 371–387.

Gardiner, A., & Pritchard, M. (1977). Mourning, mummification, and living with death. *British Journal of Psychiatry, 130,* 23–28.

Gardner, D. L., & Goldberg, R. L. (1982–83). Psychogenic seizures and loss. *International Journal of Psychiatric Medicine, 12,* 121–128.

Garfield, C. A., & Jenkins, G. J. (1981–82). Stress and coping of volunteers counseling the dying and the bereaved. *Omega, 12,* 1–13.

Garland, K. R. (1986). Unresolved grief. *Neonatal Network, 5,* 29–37.

Gauthier, Y., & Marshall, W. L. (1977). Grief: A cognitive behavioral analysis. *Cognitive Therapy and Research, 1,* 39–44.

Gauthier, Y., & Pye, C. (1979). Graduated self-exposure in the management of grief. *Behavioural Analysis and Modification, 3,* 202–208.

Geis, S. B., Fuller, R. L., & Rush, J. (1986). Lovers of AIDS victims: Psychosocial stresses and counseling needs. *Death Studies, 10,* 43–53.

Gelcer, E. (1983). Mourning is a family affair. *Family Process, 22,* 501–516.

Gelcer, E. (1986). Dealing with loss in the family context. *Journal of Family Issues, 7,* 315–335.

Geller, J. L. (1985). The long-term outcome of unresolved grief: An example. *Psychiatric Quarterly, 57,* 142–146.

Getzel, G. S., & Masters, R. (1984). Serving families who survive homicide victims. *Journal of Contemporary Social Work, 65,* 138–144.

Gill, H. S. (1986) Oedipal determinants in differential outcome of bereavement. *British Journal of Medical Psychology, 59,* 21–25.

Glick, I., Weiss, R., & Parkes, C. (1974). *The first year of bereavement.* New York: John Wiley & Sons.

Goalder, J. S. (1985). Morbid grief reaction: A social systems perspective. *Professional Psychology: Research and Practice, 16,* 833–842.

Goldberg, Rabbi J. (1980). Issues in pastoral bereavement counseling. *Journal of Pastoral Counseling, 2,* 5–18.

Goldney, R. D. (1981). Parental loss and reported childhood stress in young women who attempt suicide. *ACTA Psychiatrica Scandinavica, 64,* 34–47.

Goldney, R. D. (1985). Survivor-victims and crisis care. *Crisis, 6,* 1–19.

Gorer, G. D. (1965). *Death, grief, and mourning.* New York: Doubleday.

Gorkin, M. (1984). Narcissistic personality disorder and pathological mourning. *Contemporary Psychoanalysis, 20,* 480–420.

Gray, R. E. (1987). The role of the surviving parent in the adaptation of bereaved adolescents. *Journal of Palliative Care, 3,* 30–34.

Gray, R. E. (1988). The role of school counselors with bereaved teenagers. *School Counselor, 35,* 185–192.

Greaves, C. C. (1983). Death in the family: A multifamily therapy approach. *International Journal of Family Psychiatry, 4,* 247–259.

Green, S. A., & Goldberg, R. L. (1986). Management of acute grief. *American Family Physician, 33,* 185–190.

Hackett, T. P. (1974). Recognizing and treating abnormal grief. *Hospital Physician, 10,* 49–50, 56.

Hafner, R. J., & Roder, M. J. (1987). Agoraphobia and parental breavement. *Australian and New Zealand Journal of Psychiatry, 21,* 340–344.

Harrari, E. (1981). Pathological grief in doctor's wives. *British Medical Journal, 282,* 33–34.

Harris, T., Brown, G. W., & Bifulco, A. (1986). Loss of parent in childhood and adult psychiatric disorders: The role of lack of adequate parental care. *Psychological Medicine, 16,* 641–659.

Hartz, G. W. (1986). Adult grief and its interface with mood disorder: Proposal of a new diagnosis of complicated bereavement. *Comprehensive Psychiatry, 27,* 60–64.

Hatton, C. L., & Valente, S. M. (1981). Bereavement group for parents who suffered a suicidal loss of a child. *Suicide and Life-Threatening Behavior, 11,* 141–150.

Hauser, M. J., & Feinberg, D. R. (1976). An operational approach to the delayed grief and mourning process. *Journal of Psychiatric Nursing Mental Health Services, 14,* 29–35.

Helsing, K. J., & Szklo, M. (1981). Mortality after bereavement. *American Journal of Epidemiology, 114,* 41–52.

Helsing, K. J., Comstock, G. W., & Szklo, M. (1982). Causes of death in a widowed population. *American Journal of Epidemiology, 116,* 524–532.

Helsing, K. J., et al. (1981). Factors associated with mortality after widowhood. *American Journal of Public Health, 71,* 802–809.

Henley, S. H. (1984). Bereavement following suicide: A review of the literature. *Current Psychological Research and Reviews, 3,* 53–61.

Herrle, S. M., & Robinson, B. (1987). Helping staff cope with grief. *Nursing Management, 18,* 33–34.

Heymon, D., & Gianturco, D. (1973). Long term adaptation by the elderly to bereavement. *Journal of Gerontology, 28,* 359–362.

Hilgard, J. R., Newman, M., & Fisk, F. (1960). Strength of adult ego following childhood bereavement. *American Journal of Orthopsychiatry,* 788–798.

Hodkinson, P. E. (1982). Abnormal grief: The problem of therapy. *British Journal of Medical Psychology, 55,* 29–34.

Hofer, M. A. (1984). Relationships as regulators: A psychobiological perspective on bereavement. *Psychosomatic Medicine, 46,* 183–197.

Hofer, M. A., et al. (1972). A psychoendocrine study of bereavement (Parts I & II). *Psychosomatic Medicine, 34,* 481–504.

Hogan, N. S. (1988). The effects of time on the adolescent sibling bereavement process. *Pediatric Nursing, 14,* 333–335.

Horowitz, M. H. (1978). Adolescent mourning reactions to infant and fetal loss. *Social Casework,* 551–559.

Horowitz, M. J. et al. (1984). Brief psychotherapy of bereavement reactions. *Archives of General Psychiatry, 41,* 438–448.

Horowitz, M. J., et al. (1981). Initial psychological response to parental death. *Archives of General Psychiatry, 38,* 316–323.

Horowitz, M. J., Wilner, N., Marmar, C., & Krupnick, J. (1980). Pathological grief and the activation of latent self images. *American Journal of Psychiatry, 137,* 1157–1162.

Hunter, A. J. G. (1981). Brief psychotherapy for unresolved grief in an 82-year-old man. *Journal of Geriatric Psychiatry, 14,* 247–262.

Ingram, T. L., Hurley, E. C., & Riley, M. T. (1985). Grief-resolution therapy in a pastoral context. *Journal of Pastoral Care, 39,* 69–72.

Irwin, M., et al. (1987). Immune and neuroendocrine changes during bereavement. *Psychiatric Clinics of North America, 10,* 449–465.

Irwin, M., et al. (1988). Plasma cortisol and natural killer cell activity during bereavement. *Biological Psychiatry, 24,* 173–178.

Irwin, M. J., et al. (1987). Impaired natural killer cell activity during bereavement. *Brain, Behavior, and Immunity, 1,* 98–104

Jackson, E. N. (1957). *Understanding grief.* New York: Abingdon.

Jacobs, S. C. (1982). Brief guide to office counseling: Ethical management of grief following a spouse's death. *Medical Aspects of Human Sexuality, 16,* 69–70.

Jacobs, S. C., & Osterfield, A. (1977). An epidemiological review of the mortality of bereavement. *Psychosomatic Medicine, 39,* 344–357.

Jacobs, S. C., et al. (1985). Acute bereavement, threatened loss, ego defenses and adrenocortical function. *Psychotherapy and Psychosomatics, 44,* 151–159.

Jacobs, S. C., et al. (1986). Bereavement and catecholamines. *Journal of Psychosomatic Research, 30,* 489–496.

Jacobs, S. C., et al. (1987). Treating depression of bereavement with antidepressants: A pilot study. *Psychiatric Clinics of North America, 10,* 501–510.

Jacobs, S. C., et al. (1987). Urinary free cortisol and separation anxiety early in the course of bereavement and threatened loss. *Biological Psychiatry, 22,* 148–152.

Jacobs, S. C., et al. (1987–88). Attachment theory and multiple dimensions of grief. *Omega, 18,* 41–52.

Jacobsen, R. H. (1986). Unresolved grief of 25 years duration exacerbated by multiple subsequent losses. *Journal of Nervous and Mental Disease, 174,* 624–627.

Jansen, M. A. (1985). Psychotherapy and grieving: A clinical approach. *Psychotherapy Patient, 2,* 15–25.

Jansen, M. H. (1985). *The prescription to grieve. Hospice Journal, 1,* 103–109.

Jellinek, M. S., Goldenheim, P. D., & Jenike, M. A. (1985). The impact of grief on ventilatory control. *American Journal of Psychiatry, 142,* 121–123.

Jennings, L. E., & France, R. D. (1979). Management of grief in the hypochondriac. *Journal of Family Practice, 8,* 957–960.

Johnson, J. (1984–85). Sexual intimacy and replacement children after the death of a child. *Omega, 15,* 109–118.

Johnson, P. A., & Rosenblatt, P. C. (1981). Grief following childhood loss of a parent. *American Journal of Psychotherapy, 35,* 419–425.

Jones, D. R. (1987). Heart disease mortality following widowhood: Some results from the OPCS Longitudinal Study. *Journal of Psychosomatic Research, 31,* 325–333.

Jones, D. R., & Goldblatt, P. O. (1987). Cause of death in widow(er)s and spouses. *Journal of Biosocial Science, 19,* 107–121.

Jones, D. R., Goldblatt, P. O., and Leon, D. A. (1984). Bereavement and cancer. *British Medical Journal, 289,* 461–464.

Kaffman, M., & Elizur, E. (1979). Children's bereavement reactions following death of the father. *International Journal of Family Therapy, 1,* 203–229.

Kaffman, M., & Elizur, E. (1983). Bereavement responses of kibbutz and non-kubbutz children following the death of the father. *Journal of Child Psychology and Psychiatry and Allied Disciplines, 24,* 435–442.

Kaffman, M., Elizur, E., & Gluckson, L. (1987). Bereavement reactions in children: Therapeutic implications. *Israel Journal of Psychiatry and Related Sciences, 24,* 65–76.

Kaltreider, N. B., & Mendelson, S. (1985). Clinical evaluation of grief after parental death. *Psychotherapy, 22,* 224–230.

Kaltreider, N. B., Becker, J., & Horowitz, M. J. (1984). Relationship testing after the loss of a parent. *American Journal of Psychiatry, 141,* 243–246.

Kamm, J. A. (1985). Grief and therapy: Two processes in interaction. *Psychotherapy Patient, 2,* 59–64.

Kane, R. L., et al. (1986). The role of hospice in reducing the impact of bereavement. *Journal of Chronic Disease, 39,* 735–742.

Kansky, J. (1986). Sexuality of widows: A study of the sexual practices of widows during the first fourteen months of bereavement. *Journal of Sex and Marital Therapy, 12,* 307–321.

Kaprio, J., Koskenvuo, M., & Rita, H. (1987). Mortality after bereavement: A prospective study of 95,647 widowed persons. *American Journal of Public Health, 77,* 283–287.

Kastenbaum, R. (1987). Vicarious grief: An integrational phenomenon. *Death Studies, 11,* 447–453.

Katz, S., & Florian, V. (1986). A comprehensive theoretical model of psychological reaction to loss. *International Journal of Psychiatric Medicine, 16,* 325–345.

Kerner, J., Harvey, B., & Lewiston, N. (1979). The impact of grief: A retrospective study of family functioning following loss of a child with Cystic Fibrosis. *Journal of Chronic Disease, 32,* 221–225.

Kirkley-Best, E., & Kellner, K. (1982). The forgotten grief: A review of the psychology of stillbirth. *American Journal of Orthopsychiatry, 52,* 420–429.

Kirschling, J. M., & Akers, S. (1986). Group experience for the recently widowed: A bereavement follow-up study. *American Journal of Hospice Care, 3,* 24–27.

Klass, D. (1982–83). Professional roles in a self-help group for the bereaved. *Omega, 13,* 361–375.

Klass, D. (1987–88). John Bowlby's model of grief and the problem of identification. *Omega, 18,* 13–32.

Klass, D. (1987). The self-help process and the resolution of parental bereavement. *International Journal of Family Psychiatry, 8,* 9–24.

Klass, D. (1988). *Parental grief: Solace and resolution.* New York: Springer Publishing Company.

Kleber, R. J., & Brom, D. (1987). Psychotherapy and pathological grief controlled outcome study. *Israel Journal of Psychiatry and Related Sciences, 24,* 99–109.

Klein, M. (1940). Mourning and its relationship to manic-depressive states. *International Journal of Psychoanalysis, 21,* 125–153.

Klerman, G. L., & Izen, J. (1977). The effects of bereavement and grief on physical health and general well being. *Advances in Psychosomatic Medicine, 9,* 63–104.

Klingman, A. (1985). Responding to a bereaved classmate: Comparison of two strategies for death education in the classroom. *Death Studies, 9,* 449–454.

Koocher, G. P. (1986). Coping with a death from cancer. *Journal of Consulting and Clinical Psychology, 54,* 623–631.

Kosten, T. R., et al. (1984). The dexamethasone suppression test during bereavement. *Journal of Nervous and Mental Disease, 172,* 359–360.

Kotch, J. B. (1985). SIDS counselors' reports of own and parents' reactions to reviewing the autopsy report. *Omega, 16,* 129–139.

Krell, R., & Rabkin, L. (1979). The effects of sibling death on the surviving child: A family perspective. *Family Process, 18,* 471–477.

Krishman, K., et al. (1984). Funeral mania in recurrent bipolar affective disorders: Reports of three cases. *Journal of Clinical Psychology, 45,* 310–311.

Krueger, D. W. (1983). Childhood parent loss: Developmental impact and adult psychopathology. *American Journal of Psychotherapy, 37,* 582–592.

Krupnick, J. L., & Horowitz, M. J. (1985). Brief psychotherapy with vulnerable patients: An outcome assessment. *Psychiatry, 48,* 223–233.

Krupp, G., Genovese, F., & Krupp, T. (1986). To have and have not: Multiple identification in pathological bereavement. *Journal of the American Academy of Psychoanalysis, 14,* 337–348.

Krupp, G. R., & Kligfield, B. (1962). The bereavement reaction: A cross cultural evaluation. *Journal of Religion and Health, 1,* 222–246.

Lane, R. D., et al. (1987). Sex differences in prolactin change during mourning. *Journal of Psychosomatic Research, 31.* 375–383.

Lattanzi, M., & Coffelt, D. (1979). *Bereavement care manual.* Boulder, CO: Boulder County Hospice.

Lattanzi, M., & Hale, M. E. (1984–85). Giving grief words: Writing during bereavement. *Omega, 15,* 45–52.

Lattanzi, M. (1982). Hospice bereavement services: Creating networks of support. *Family and Community Health, 5,* 54–63.

Laudenslager, M. L. (1988). The psychobiology of loss: Lessons from human and nonhuman primates. *Journal of Social Issues, 44,* 19–36.

Laudenslager, M. L., & Reite, M. L. (1984). Losses and separations: Immunological consequences and health implications. *Review of Personality and Social Psychology, 5,* 285–312.

Lazare, A. (1979). Unresolved grief. In A Lazare (Ed.), *Outpatient psychiatry: Diagnosis and treatment* (pp. 498–512). Baltimore: Williams and Wilkens.

Lehman, D. R., Ellard, J. H., & Wortman, C. B. (1986). Social support for the bereaved: Recipients' and providers' perspectives on what is helpful. *Journal of Consulting and Clinical Psychology, 54,* 438–446.

Lehman, D. R., Wortman, C. B., & Williams, A. F. (1987). Long-term effects of losing a spouse or child in a motor vehicle crash. *Journal of Personality and Social Psychology, 52,* 218–231.

Leon, I. (1987). Short-term psychotherapy for perinatal loss. *Psychotherapy, 24,* 186–195.

LeShan, E. (1976). *Learning to say good-by: When a parent dies.* New York: Macmillan.

Lesher, E. L., & Bergey, K. J. (1988). Bereaved elderly mothers: Changes in health, functional activities, family cohesion, & psychological well-being. *International Journal of Aging and Human Development, 26,* 81–90.

Levav, I., et al. (1988). An epidemiologic study and mortality among bereaved parents. *New England Journal of Medicine, 319,* 457–461.

Lewis, C. S. (1961). *A grief observed.* London: Faber & Faber.

Lewis, E., & Casement, P. (1986). The inhibition of mourning by pregnancy: A case study. *Psychoanalytic psychotherapy, 2,* 45–52.

Lieberman, M. A., & Videka-Sherman, L. (1986). The impact of self-help groups in the mental health of widows and widowers. *American Journal of Orthopsychiatry, 56,* 435–449.

Lieberman, P. B., & Jacobs, S. C. (1987). Bereavement and its complications in medical patients: A guide for consultation-liaison psychiatrists. *International Journal of Psychiatric Medicine, 17,* 23–39.

Lieberman, S. (1978). Nineteen cases of morbid grief. *British Journal of Psychiatry, 132,* 159–163.

Lindemann, E. (1944). Symptomatology and management of acute grief. *American Journal of Psychiatry, 101,* 141–148.

Littlefield, C. H., & Rushton, J. P. (1986). When a child dies: The sociobiology of bereavement. *Journal of Personality and Social Psychology, 51,* 797–802.

Lopata, H. Z. (1979). *Women as widows.* New York: Elsevier.

Lopata, H. Z. (1981). Widowhood and husband sanctification. *Journal of Marriage and the Family, 43,* 439–450.

Lopez, R. E. (1984). Libido adhesiveness and working through during pathological mourning. *Scandinavian Psychoanalytic Review, 7,* 35–48.

Lowman, J. (1979). Grief intervention and sudden infant death syndrome. *American Journal of Community Psychology, 7,* 665–677.

Lund, D. A. (1987). *Older bereaved spouses.* New York: Hemisphere.

Lund, D. A., Diamond, M. F., & Juretich, M. (1985). Bereavement support groups for the elderly: Characteristics of potential participants. *Death Studies, 9,* 309–321.

Lund, D. A., et al (1985–86). Identifying elderly with coping difficulties after two years of bereavement. *Omega, 3,* 231–224.

Lundin, T. (1984). Long-term outcome of bereavement. *British Journal of Psychiatry, 145,* 424–428.

Lundin, T. (1984). Morbidity following sudden and unexpected bereavement. *British Journal of Psychiatry, 144,* 84–88.

Maddison, D. C., & Viola, A. (1968). The health of widows in the year following bereavement. *Journal of Psychosomatic Research, 12,* 297–306.

Maddison, D. C., & Walker, W. L. (1967). Factors affecting the outcome of conjugal bereavement. *British Journal of Psychiatry, 113,* 1057–1067.

Madonna, J. M., & Chandler, R. (1986). Aggressive play and bereavement in group therapy with latency-aged boys. *Journal of Child and Adolescent, 3,* 109–114.

Mahan, C. K., et al. (1983). Bibliotherapy: A tool to help parents mourn their infant's death. *Health & Social Work, 8,* 126–132.

Malmquist, C. P. (1986). Children who witness parental murder: Post-traumatic aspects. *Journal of the American Academy of Child Psychiatry, 25,* 320–325.

Margolis, O. S., et al. (Eds.) (1981). *Acute grief: Counseling the bereaved.* New York: Columbia University.

Markusen, E., & Fulton, R. (1971). Childhood bereavement and behavior disorders: A critical review. *Omega, 2,* 107–117.

Marmar, C. R., et al. (1988). A controlled trial of brief psychotherapy & mutual-help group treatment of conjugal bereavement. *American Journal of Psychiatry, 145,* 203–209.

Marris, P. (1974). *Loss and change.* London: Routledge & Kegan Paul.

Martin, J. L. (1988). Psychological consequences of AIDS-related bereavement among gay men. *Journal of Consulting and Clinical Psychology, 56,* 856–862.

Martinson, I. M., Davies, E. B., & McClowry, S. G. (1987). The long-term effects of sibling death on self-concept. *Journal of Pediatric Nursing, 2,* 227–235.

Masterman, S. H., & Reams, R. (1988). Support groups for bereaved preschool and school-age children. *American Journal of Orthopsychiatry, 58,* 562–570.

Matussek, P., & Neuner, R. (1981). Loss events preceding endogenous and neurotic depressions. *ACTA Psychiatrica Scandinavica, 64,* 340–350.

Mauritzen, J. (1988). Pastoral care for the dying and bereaved. *Death Education, 12,* 111–122.

Mawson, D., et al. (1981). Guided mourning for morbid grief: A controlled study. *British Journal of Psychiatry, 138,* 185–193.

May, H. J., & Breme, F. J. (1982–83). SIDS family adjustment scale. *Omega, 13,* 59–74.

McAll, K., & Wilson, W. P. (1987). Ritual mourning for unresolved grief after abortion. *Southern Medical Journal,. 80,* 817–821.

McAvoy, B. R. (1986). Death after bereavement. *British Medical Journal, 293,* 835–836.

McCaughey, B. G. (1984). Bereavement: Intervention following an accident involving multiple deaths and no survivors. *Military Medicine, 149,* 687–688.

McClowry, S. G., et al (1987). The empty space phenomenon: The process of grief in the bereaved family. *Death Studies, 11,* 361–374.

McGovern, T. F., & Peterson, A. V. (1986). Distinguishing between depression and grief in alcoholism: A pilot clinical study. *Alcohol Treatment Quarterly, 3,* 31–45.

McHorney, C. A., & Mor, V. (1988). Predictors of bereavement depression and its health services consequences. *Medical Care, 26,* 882–893.

McKinney, W. T. (1986). Primate separation studies: Relevance to bereavement. *Psychiatric Annals, 16,* 281–187.

McNiel, D. E., Hatcher, C., & Reubin, R. (1988). Family survivors of suicide and accidental death: Consequences for widows. *Suicide and Life-Threatening Behavior, 18,* 137–148.

Melges, F. T., & Bowlby, J. (1969). Types of hopelessness in psychopathological processes. *Archives of General Psychiatry, 20,* 690–699.

Melges, F. T., & Demaso, D. R. (1980). Grief-resolution therapy: Reliving, revising, and revisiting. *American Journal of Psychotherapy, 34,* 51–61.

Melson, S. J., & Rynearson, E. K. (1982). Unresolved bereavement: Medical reenactment of a loved one's terminal illness. *Postgraduate Medicine, 72,* 172–179.

Middleton, W., & Raphael, B. (1987). Bereavement: State of the art and state of the science. *Psychiatric Clinics of North America, 10,* 329–343.

Miles, M. S. (1985). Helping adults mourn the death of a child. *Issues in Comprehensive Pediatric Nursing, 8,* 219–241.

Miles, M. S., & Demi, A. S. (1984). Toward the development of a theory of bereavement guilt: Sources of guilt in bereaved parents. *Omega, 14,* 299–314.

Miller, K., Moore, N., & Lexius, C. (1985). A group for families of homicide victims: An evaluation. *Social Casework, 66,* 432–436.

Mor, V., McHorney, C., & Sherwood, S. (1986). Secondary morbidity among the recently bereaved. *American Journal of Psychiatry, 143,* 158–163.

Morgan, J. H., & Goering, R. (1978). Caring for parents who have lost an infant. *Journal of Religion and Health, 17,* 290–298.

Morgan, L. A. (1984). Changes in family interaction following widowhood. *Journal of Marriage and Family, 46,* 323–331.

Moseley, J. R., et al. (1988). Developing a bereavement program in a university hospital setting. *Oncology Nursing Forum, 15,* 151–155.

Moss, M. S. (1986). Death of an adult sibling. *International Journal of Family Psychiatry, 7,* 397–418.

Moss, M. S., & Moss, S. Z. (1983–84). The impact of parental death on middle aged children. *Omega, 14,* 65–75.

Moss, M. S., & Moss, S. Z. (1984). Some aspects of the elderly widow's persistent tie with the deceased spouse. *Omega, 15,* 195–206.

Mount, B. M. (1986). Dealing with our losses. *Journal of Clinical Oncology, 4,* 1127–1134.

Mulhern, R., Laurer, M., & Hoffman, R. (1983). Death of a child at home or in the hospital: Subsequent psychological adjustment of the family. *Pediatrics, 71,* 743–747.

Murphy, P., & Perry, K. (1988). Hidden grievers. *Death Studies, 12,* 451–462.

Murrell, S. A., Himmelfarb, S., & Phifer, J. F. (1988). Effects of bereavement/loss and pre-event status on subsequent health in older adults. *International Journal of Aging and Human Development, 27,* 87–107.

Norris, F. H., & Murrell, S. A. (1987). Older adult family stress and adaptation before and after bereavement. *Journal of Gerontology, 42,* 606–612.

O'Neil, M. K., Lancee, W. J., & Freeman, S. J. (1987). Loss and depression: A controversial link. *Journal of Nervous and Mental Disease, 175,* 354–357.

Osterweis, M. (1985). Bereavement and the elderly. *Aging, 348,* 8–13, 41.

Osterweis, M., Solomon, F., & Green, M. (1984). *Bereavement: Reactions, consequences and care.* Washington, DC: National Academy.

Owen, G., Fulton, R., & Markusen, E. (1982–83). Death at a distance: A study of family survivors. *Omega, 13,* 191–225.

Palombo, J. (1981). Parent loss and childhood bereavement: Some theoretical considerations. *Clinical Social Work, 9,* 3–33.

Parker, G., & Manicavasagar, V. (1986). Childhood bereavement circumstances associated with adult depression. *British Journal of Medical Psychology, 59,* 387–391.

Parkes, C. M. (1965). Bereavement and mental illness, part I: A clinical study of the grief of bereaved psychiatric patients. *British Journal of Medical Psychology, 38,* 1–26.

Parkes, C. M. (1965). Bereavement and mental illness, part II: A classification of bereavement reactions. *British Journal of Medical Psychology, 38,* 13–26.

Parkes, C. M. (1972). *Bereavement: Studies of grief in adult life.* New York: International Unversities Press.

Parkes, C. M. (1975). Determinants of outcome following bereavement. *Omega, 6,* 303–323.

Parkes, C. M. (1980). Bereavement counselling: Does it work? *British Medical Journal, 281,* 3–6.

Parkes, C. M. (1981). Evaluation of a bereavement service. *Journal of Preventive Psychiatry, 1,* 179–188.

Parkes, C. M. (1986). Care of the dying: The role of the psychiatrist. *British Journal of Hospital Medicine, 36,* 250–255.

Parkes, C. M. (1986). Orienteering the caregiver's grief. *Journal of Palliative Care, 1,* 5–7.

Parkes, C. M. (1987–88). Research: Bereavement. *Omega, 18,* 365–377.

Parkes, C. M. (1987). Models of bereavement care. *Death Studies, 11,* 257–261.

Parkes, C. M., & Brown, R. J. (1972). Health after bereavement: A controlled study of young Boston widows and widowers. *Psychosomatic Medicine, 34,* 449–461.

Parkes, C. M., & Stevenson-Hinde, J. (Eds.). (1982). *The place of attachment in human behavior.* New York: Basic.

Parkes, C. M., & Weiss, R. S. (1983). *Recovery from bereavement.* New York: Basic.

Parkes, C. M., Benjamin, B., & Fitzgerald, R. G. (1969). Broken heart: A statistical study of increased mortality among widowers. *British Journal of Medicine, 1,* 740–743.

Pasnau, R. O., Fawzy, F. I., Fawzy, N. (1987). Role of the physician in bereavement. *Psychiatric Clinics of North America, 10,* 109–120.

Paterson, G. W. (1987). Managing grief and bereavement. *Primary Care, 14,* 403–415.

Paul, N., & Grosser, G. H. (1965). Operational mourning and its role in conjoint family therapy. *Community Mental Health Journal, 1,* 339–345.

Paulley, J. W. (1983). Pathological mourning: A key factor in the psychopathogenesis of autoimmune disorders. *Psychotherapy and Psychosomatics, 40,* 181–190.

Payton, J. B., & Krocker-Tuskan, M. (1988). Children's reactions to loss of parent through violence. *Journal of the American Academy of Child and Adolescent Psychiatry, 27,* 563–566.

Peach, M. R., & Klass, D. (1987). Special issues in the grief of parents of murdered children. *Death Studies, 11,* 81–88.

Pedder, J. R. (1982). Failure to mourn and melancholia. *British Journal of Psychiatry, 141,* 329–337.

Pennebaker, J. W. (1984). Confiding in others and illness rates among spouses of suicide and accidental death victims. *Journal of Abnormal Psychology, 93,* 473–476.

Pfeifer, D. (1982). A new perspective on agitated grief reactions. *Journal of Contemporary Psychotherapy,, 13,* 61–69.

Pfohl, B., et al. (1983). The association between early parental loss and diagnosis in the Iowa 500. *Archives of General Psychiatry, 40,* 965–967.

Pheifer, W. G., & Houseman, C. (1988). Bereavement and AIDS: A framework for intervention. *Journal of Psychosocial Nursing and Mental Health Services, 26,* 21–26.

Pincus, L. (1972). *Death and the family.* New York: Pantheon.

Pine, V., et al. (1976). *Acute grief and the funeral.* Springfield, IL: Thomas.

Pollock, G. H. (1987). The mourning liberation process in health and disease. *Psychiatric Clinics of North America, 10,* 345–354.

Priest, R. G., & Crisp, A. H. (1973). Bereavement and psychiatric symptoms: An item analysis. *Psychotherapy Psychosomatics, 22,* 166–171.

Pynoos, R. S., et al. (1987). Grief reactions in school age children following a sniper attack at school. *Israel Journal of Psychiatry and Related Sciences, 24,* 53–63.

Rabkin, R., & Krell, L. (1979). The effects of sibling death on the surviving child: A family perspective. *Family Process, 18,* 471–477.

Ragan, P. V., & McGlashan, T. H. 91986). Childhood parental death and adult psychopathology. *American Journal of Psychiatry, 143,* 153–157.

Rait, P. E., & Ward, M. (1987). When a student dies: Helping teachers who grieve. *Education of the Visually Handicapped, 18,* 151–156.

Ramsay, R. W. (1977). Behavioral approaches to bereavement. *Behavior Research and Therapy, 15,* 131–135.

Ramsey, R. W., & Noorberger, R. (1981). *Living with loss.* New York: Morrow.

Rando, T. A. (1985). Creating therapeutic rituals in the psychotherapy of the bereaved. *Psychotherapy, 22,* 236–240.

Rando, T. A. (1986). *Parental loss of a child.* Champaign, IL: Research Press.

Rando, T. A. (1988). Anticipatory grief: The term is a misnomer but the phenomenon exists. *Journal of Palliative Care, 4,* 70–73.

Rando, T. A. (Ed.) (1986). *Loss and anticipatory grief.* Toronto: Lexington.

Raphael, B. (1975). The management of pathological grief. *Austrialian and New Zealand Journal of Psychiatry, 9,* 173–180.

Raphael, B. (1977). Preventive intervention with the recently bereaved. *Archives of General Psychiatry, 34,* 1450–1454.

Raphael, B. (1979). A primary prevention action program: Psychiatric involvement following major rail disaster. *Omega, 10,* 211–226.

Raphael, B. (1983). *The anatomy of bereavement.* New York: Basic.

Raphael, B. (1986). Grieving over the loss of a baby. *Medical Journal of Australia, 17,* 281–282.

Raphael, B., & Middleton, W. (1987). Current state of research in the field of bereavement. *Israel Journal of Psychiatry and Related Sciences, 24,* 5–32.

Rees, W. D., & Lutkins, S. G. (1967). Mortality of bereavement. *British Medical Journal, 4,* 363–368.

Reilly, D. M. (1978). Death propensity, dying, and bereavement: A family systems perspective. *Family Therapy, 5,* 35–55.

Remondet, J. H., & Hansson, R. O. (1987). Assessing a widow's grief: A short index. *Journal of Gerontological Nursing, 13,* 31–34.

Rickarby, G. A., Single, T., & Raphael, B. (1977). Four cases of mania associated with bereavement. *Journal of Nervous and Mental Disease, 165,* 255–261.

Rickgarn, R. L. (1987). The Death Response Team: Responding to the forgotten grievers. *Journal of Counseling and Development, 66,* 197–199.

Rogers, J., et al. (1980). A self-help program for widows as an independent community service. *Hospital and Community Psychiatry, 31,* 844–847.

Rogers, J., et al. (1982). Help for families of suicide survivors support program. *Canadian Journal of Psychiatry, 27,* 444–448.

Rogers, M. P., & Reich, P. (1988). On the health consequences of bereavement. *New England Journal of Medicine, 319,* 510–512.

Rosen, E. J. (1988–89). Family therapy in cases of interminable grief for the loss of a child. *Omega, 19,* 187–202.

Rosen, H. (1985). Prohibitions against mourning in childhoood sibling loss. *Omega, 15,* 307–316.

Rosen, H. (1986). When a sibling dies. *International Journal of Family Psychiatry, 7,* 389–396.

Rosenheim, E., & Reicher, R. (1986). Children in anticipatory grief: The lonely predicament. *Journal of Clinical Child Psychology, 15,* 115–119.

Rosenman, S. J., & Taylor, H. (1986). Mania following bereavement: A case report. *British Journal of Psychiatry, 148,* 468–470.

Rosenthal, P. A. (1980). Short-term family therapy and pathological grief resolution with children and adolescents. *Family Process, 19,* 151–159.

Roskin, M. (1984). Buffers for the bereaved: The impact of social factors on the emotional health of bereaved parents. *International Journal of Social Psychiatry, 30,* 311–319.

Roy, A. (1980). Early parental loss in depressive neurosis compared with other neurosis. *Canadian Journal of Psychiatry, 25,* 503–505.

Roy, A. (1981). Role of past loss in depression. *Archives of General Psychiatry, 38,* 301–302.

Roy, A. (1983). Early parental death and adult depression. *Psychological Medicine, 13,* 861–865.

Roy, A., et al. (1988). The CRH stimulation test in bereaved subjects with and without accompanying depression. *Psychiatric Research, 25,* 145–156.

Roy, P. F., & Sumpter, H. (1983). Group support for the recently bereaved. *Health & Social Work, 8,* 230–232.

Rubin, S. S. (1981). A two track model of bereavement: Theory and application in research. *American Journal of Orthopsychiatry, 5,* 101–109.

Rubin, S. S. (1984). Mourning distinct from melancholia: The resolution of bereavement. *British Journal of Medical Psychology, 57,* 339–345.

Rubin, S. S. (1985). The resolution of bereavement: A clinical focus on the relationship to the deceased. *Psychotherapy, 22,* 231–235.

Rubin, S. S. (1986). Child death and the family: Parents and children confronting loss. *International Journal of Family Psychiatry, 7,* 377–388.

Rynearson, E. K. (1984). Bereavement after homicide: A descriptive study. *American Journal of Psychiatry, 141,* 1452–1454.

Rynearson, E. K. (1987). Psychotherapy of pathologic grief. *Psychiatric Clinics of North America, 10,* 487–499.

Sabatini, L. (1985). The first step program: A bereavement service for widowed people. *Crisis Intervention, 14,* 72–83.

Sabatini, L. (1988–89). Evaluating a treatment program for newly widowed people. *Omega, 19,* 229–236.

Sanders, C. M. (1979–80). A comparison of adult bereavement in the death of a spouse, child, and parent. *Omega, 10,* 303–322.

Sanders, C. M. (1989). *Grief: The mourning after.* New York: Wiley.

Sanders, C. M., & Mauger, P. A. (1979). *A manual for the grief experience inventory.* Tampa: University of South Florida.

Schleifer, S. J., & Keller, S. E. (1987). Conjugal bereavement and immunity. *Israel Journal of Psychiatry and Related Sciences, 24,* 111–123.

Schmale, A. H. (1971). Psychic trauma during bereavement. *International Psychiatric Clinics, 8,* 147–168.

Schneider, J. M. (1980). Clinically significant differences between grief, pathological grief, and depression. *Patient Counseling and Health Education,* 161–169.

Schoenberg, B. M., et al. (Eds.) (1974). *Anticipatory grief.* New York: Columbia University.

Schoenberg, B. M., & Carr, A. (1970). *Loss and grief: Psychological management in medical practice*. New York: Columbia University.

Schwab, R. (1986). Support groups for the bereaved. *Journal for Specialists in Group Work, 11*, 100–106.

Schwartz-Borden, G. (1986). Grief work: Prevention and intervention. *Social casework*, 499–505.

Scully, E. J. (1985). Men and grieving. *Psychotherapy Patient, 2*, 95–100.

Segal, R. M. (1984). Helping children express grief through symbolic communication. *Social Casework, 65*, 590–599.

Sekaer, C. (1987). Toward a definition of "childhood mourning." *American Journal of Psychotherapy, 41*, 201–219.

Shackleton, C. H. (1984). The psychology of grief: A review. *Advances in Behavior Research and Therapy, 6*, 153–205.

Shanfield, S. B., & Swain, B. J. (1984). Death of adult children in traffic accidents. *Journal of Nervous and Mental Disease, 172*, 533–588.

Shanfield, S. B., et al. (1984). Parents' reactions to the death of an adult child from cancer. *American Journal of Psychiatry, 141*, 1092–1094.

Shanfield, S. B., et al. (1986–87). Parents' responses to the death of adult children from accidents and cancer: A comparison. *Omega, 17*, 289–297.

Sheldon, A. R., et al. (1981). A psychosocial analysis of risk of psychological impairment following bereavement. *Journal of Nervous and Mental Disease, 169*, 253–255.

Shields, V. (1988). Grief therapy and family systems. *Melita Theologica, 39*, 33–43.

Shorr, M., & Speed, M. N. (1963). Delinquency as a manifestation of the mourning process. *Psychiatric Quarterly, 37*, 540–558.

Shuchter, S. R. (1986). *Dimensions of grief: Adjusting to the death of a spouse*. San Francisco: Jossey-Bass.

Shuchter, S. R., & Zisook, S. (1986). Treatment of spousal bereavement: A multi-dimensional approach. *Psychiatric Annals, 16*, 295–305.

Shuchter, S. R., et al. (1986). The dexamethasone suppression test in acute grief. *American Journal of Psychiatry, 143*, 879–881.

Siegal, R. L., & Hoefer, D. D. (1981). Bereavement counseling for gay individuals. *American Journal of Psychotherapy, 35*, 517–525.

Siegel, K., Weinstein, L. (1983). Anticipatory grief reconsidered. *Journal of Psychosocial Oncology, 1*, 61–73.

Silverman, P. R. (1969). The widow-to-widow program: An experiment in preventive intervention. *Mental Hygiene, 53*, 333–337.

Silverman, P. R. (1981). *Helping women cope with grief*. Beverly Hills, CA: Sage.

Silverman, P. R. (1986). *Widow to widow*. New York: Springer Publishing Company.

Silverman, P. R. (1987). The impact of parental death on college-age women. *Psychiatric Clinics of North America, 10*, 387–404.

Silverman, P. R., & Cooperhand, A. (1975). On widowhood: Mutual help and the elderly widow. *Journal of Geriatric Psychiatry, 8*, 9–40.

Simon-Buller, S., et al. (1988–89). Correlates of sensing the presence of a deceased spouse. *Omega, 19*, 21–30.

Simos, B. G. (1977). Grief therapy to facilitate health restitution. *Social Casework*, 337–342.

Simos, B. G. (1979). *A time to grieve*. New York: Family Service Association.

Singh, B., & Raphael, B. (1981). Post-disaster morbidity of the bereaved. *Journal of Nervous and Mental Disease, 169*, 203–212.

Singh, I., Jawed, S. H., & Wilson, S. (1988). Mania following bereavement in a mentally handicapped man. *British Journal of Psychiatry, 152*, 866–867.

Skolnick, V. (1979). The addictions as pathological mourning: An attempt at restitution of early losses. *American Journal of Psychotherapy, 33*, 281–290.

Smith, E. W. (1985). A Gestalt therapist's perspective on grief. *Psychotherapy Patient, 2*, 65–78.

Snowdon, J., Solomons, R., & Druce, H. (1978). Feigned bereavement: Twelve cases. *British Journal of Psychiatry, 133*, 15–19.

Soricelli, B. A., & Utech, C. L. (1985). Mourning the death of a child: The family and group process. *Social Work, 30*, 429–434.

Spiegel, D. (1981). Vietnam grief work using hypnosis. *American Journal of Clinical Hypnosis, 24*, 33–40.

Spinetta, J., Swarner, J., & Sheposh, J. (1981). Effective parental coping following the death of a child from cancer. *Journal of Pediatric Psychology, 6*, 251–263.

Stack, J. 91984). The psychodynamics of spontaneous abortion. *American Journal of Orthopsychiatry, 54*, 162–167.

Stack, J. M. (1982). Grief reactions and depression in family practice: Differential diagnosis and treatment. *Journal of Family Practice, 14*, 271–275.

Steele, D. W. (1975). *The funeral director's guide to designing and implementing programs for the widowed*. Milwaukee: National Funeral Directors Association.

Stern, E. M. (1985). *Psychotherapy and the grieving patient*. New York: Haworth.

Stroebe, M. S., & Stroebe, W. (1983). Who suffers more? Sex differences in health risks of the widowed. *Psychological Bulletin, 93*, 279–301.

Stroebe, M. S., et al. (1981–82). The broken heart: Reality or myth? *Omega, 12*, 87–106.

Stroebe, W., & Stroebe, M. S. (1987). *Bereavement and health: The psychological and physical consequences of partner loss*. Cambridge: Cambridge University.

Tatelbaum, J. (1980). *The courage to grieve*. New York: Harper.

Tennant, C., & Bernardi, E. (1988). Childhood loss in alcoholics and narcotic addicts. *British Journal of Addiction, 83*, 695–703.

Tennant, C., et al. (1980). Parental death in childhood and risk of adult depressive disorders. *Psychological Medicine, 10*, 289–299.

Tennant, C., et al. (1981). Parental loss in childhood: Relationship to adult psychiatric impairment and contact with psychiatric services. *Archives of General Psychiatry, 38*, 309–314.

Thomas, L. E., & DiGiulio, R. C., & Sheehan, N. E. (1988). Identity loss and psychological crisis in widowhood: A reevaluation. *International Journal of Aging and Human Development, 26*, 225–239.

Thompson, L. W., et al. (1984). Effects of bereavement on self-perceptions of physical health in elderly widows and widowers. *Journal of Gerontology, 39*, 309–314.

Tick, E. (1985). Vietnam grief: Psychotherapeutic and psychohistorical implications. *Psychotherapy Patient, 2*, 101–115.

Tilley, S. (1985). Multiple phobias and grief: A case study. *Behavioral Psychotherapy, 13*, 59–68.

Toedter, L. J., et al. (1988). The Perinatal Grief Scale: Development and initial validation. *American Journal of Orthopsychiatry, 58*, 435–449.

Towse, M. S. (1986). "To be or not to be": Anxiety following bereavement. *British Journal of Medical Psychology, 59*, 149–156.

Trouy, M. B., & Ward-Larson, C. (1987). Sibling grief. *Neonatal Network, 5*, 35–40.

Turco, R. (1981). The treatment of unresolved grief following loss of an infant. *Journal of Obstetrics and Gynecology, 141*, 503–507.

Ulene, A., & Worden, J. W. (1987). *How to survive the death of a loved one.* New York: Random House.

Vachon, M. L. S. (1976). Grief and bereavement following the death of a spouse. *Canadian Psychiatric Association Journal, 21*, 35–44.

Vachon, M. L. S. (1987). *Occupational stress in the care of the critically ill, the dying & the bereaved.* Washington: Hemisphere.

Vachon, M. L. S. (1987). Unresolved grief in persons with cancer referred for psychotherapy. *Psychiatric Clinics of North America, 10*, 467–486.

Vachon, M. L. S., et al. (1977). Social support networks and the crises of bereavement. *Social Science and Medicine, 11*, 35–41.

Vachon, M. L. S., et al. (1980). A controlled study of self-help intervention for widows. *American Journal of Psychiatry, 137*, 1380–1384.

Vachon, M. L. S., et al. (1982). Predictors and correlates of adaption to conjugal bereavement. *American Journal of Psychiatry, 139*, 998–1002.

Valeriote, S., & Fine, M. (1987). Bereavement following the death of a child: Implications for family therapy. *Contemporary Family Therapy: An International Journal, 9*, 202–217.

Van Der Hart, O. (1988). An imaginary leave-taking ritual in mourning therapy: A brief communication. *International Journal of Clinical Experimental Hypnosis, 36*, 63–69.

Van Der Hart, O., & Goossens, F. A. (1987). Leave-taking rituals in mourning therapy. *Israel Journal of Psychiatry and Related Sciences, 24*, 87–98.

Van Eerdewegh, M., et al. (1982). The bereaved child. *British Journal of Psychiatry, 140*, 23–29.

Vess, J. et al. (1985–86). Understanding family role reallocation following a death: A theoretical framework. *Omega, 16*, 115–128.

Vedeka-Sherman, L. (1982). Coping with the death of a child: A study over time. *American Journal of Orthopsychiatry, 52*, 688–698.

Videka-Sherman, L., & Lieberman, M. (1985). The effects of self help and psychotherapy intervention on child loss: The limits of recovery. *American Journal of Orthopsychiatry, 55*, 70–82.

Vogelsang, J. (1983). A psychological and faith approach to grief counseling. *Journal of Pastoral Care, 37*, 22–27.

Volkan, V. (1970). Typical findings in pathological grief. *Psychiatric Quarterly, 44*, 231–250.

Volkan, V. (1971). A study of patient's "re-grief work" through dreams, psychological tests and psychoanalysis. *Psychiatric Quarterly, 45*, 255–273.

Volkan, V. (1972). The linking objects of pathological mourners. *Archives of General Psychiatry, 27*, 215–221.

Volkan, V. (November, 1973). More on "linking objects". Paper presented at the Symposium on Bereavement. Columbia-Presbyterian Medical Center, New York City.

Volkan, V., & Showalter, C. R. (1968). Known object loss, disturbance in reality testing and "re-grief" work as a method of brief psychotherapy. *Psychiatric Quarterly, 42*, 358–374.

Volkan, V. (1985). Complicated mourning. *Annual of Psychoanalysis, 12*, 323–348.

Wahl, C. W. (1970). The differential diagnosis of normal and neurotic grief following bereavement. *Psychosomatics, 11*, 104–106.

Walls, N., & Weyers, A. W. (1984–85). Outcome in group treatment for bereavement: Experimental results and recommendations for clinical practice. *International Journal of Mental Health, 13*, 126–147.

Warmbrod, M. E. T. (1986). Counseling bereaved children: Stages in the process. *Social Casework, 351–358.*

Warner, S. L. (1987). A comparative study of widows' and widowers' perceived social support during the first year of bereavement. *Archives of Psychiatric Nursing, 1*, 241–250.

Wass, H., & Corr, C. A. (1984). *Helping children cope with death: Guidelines and resources.* New York: Hemisphere.

Watt, N. F., & Nicholi, A. (1979). Early death of a parent as an etiological factor in schizophrenia. *American Journal of Orthopsychiatry, 49*, 465–473.

Weber, J. A., and Fournier, D. G. (1985). Family support and a child's adjustment to death. *Family Relations, 34*, 43–49.

Weber, J. A., & Fournier, D. G. (1986). Death in the family: Children's cognitive understanding and sculptures of family relationship patterns. *Journal of Family Issues, 7*, 277–296.

Weinbach, R. W. (1989). Sudden death and secret survivors: Helping those who grieve alone. *Social Work, 34*, 57–60.

Weisman, A. D. (1970). Partial grief and total bereavement. *Journal of Geriatric Psychiatry, 4*, 23.

Weisman, A. D. (1973). Coping with untimely death. *Psychiatry, 36*, 366–379.

Weisman, A. D., & Hackett, T. P. (1961). Predilection to death. *Psychosomatic Medicine, 23*, 232–255.

Weller, E. B., et al. (1988). Should children attend their parent's funeral? *Journal of the American Academy of Child and Adolescent Psychiatry, 27*, 559–562.

Whitaker, L. C. (1985). Visiting the parental grave in psychotherapy. *Psychotherapy, 22*, 241–247.

Widen, H. A. (1987). Phase-specific symptomatic response to sibling loss in late adolescence. *Adolescent Psychiatry, 14*, 218–229.

Williams, W. V., & Polack, P. R. (1979). Follow-up research in primary prevention: A model of adjustment in adult grief. *Journal of Clinical Psychology, 35*, 35–45.

Williams, W. V., & Polack, P., & Vollman, R. (1972). Crisis intervention in acute grief. *Omega, 3*, 67–70.

Williamson, D. S. (1978). New life at the graveyard: A method of therapy for individuation from a dead former parent. *Journal of Marriage and Family Counseling,* 93–101.

Windholz, M. J., Marmar, C. R., & Horowitz, M. J. (1985). A review of the research on conjugal bereavement: Impact on health and efficacy of intervention. *Comprehensive Psychiatry, 26,* 433–447.

Wolfenstein, M. (1966). How is mourning possible? *Psychoanalytic Study of the Child, 21,* 93–123.

Wood, B. (1987). Survival kit for the holidays: A grief workshop approach. *Family Relations, 36,* 237–241.

Woodfield, R. L., & Viney, L. L. (1984). A personal construct approach to conjugally bereaved women. *Omega, 15,* 1–13.

Worden, J. W. (1976). *Personal death awareness.* Englewood Cliffs, NJ: Prentice-Hall.

Worden, J. W. (1985). Bereavement. *Seminars in Oncology, 12,* 472–475.

Worden, J. W., & Kubler-Ross, E. (1977–78). Attitudes and experiences of death workshop attendees. *Omega, 8,* 91–106.

Wortman, C. B., & Silver, R. C. (1989). The myth of coping with loss *Journal of Clinical Consulting Psychology, 57,* 349–357.

Wrobleski, A. 91984). The suicide survivors grief group. *Omega, 15,* 173–184.

Yalom, I. D., & Vinogradov, S. (1988). Bereavement groups: Techniques and themes. *International Journal of Group Psychotherapy, 38,* 419–446.

York, J. B., & Weinstein, S. A. (1980–81). The effect of a videotape about death on bereaved children in family therapy. *Omega, 11,* 355–361.

Zaiger, N. (1985–86). Women and bereavement. *Women and Therapy, 4,* 33–43.

Zambelli, G. C., et al. (1988). An interdisciplinary approach to clinical intervention for childhood bereavement. *Death Studies, 12,* 41–50.

Zeanah, C. H. (1988). Atypical panic attacks and lack of resolution of mourning. *General Hospital Psychiatry, 10,* 373–377.

Zimmerman, M., et al. (1988). Past loss as a symptom formation factor in depression. *Journal of Affective Disorders, 14,* 235–237.

Zisook, S. (Ed.). (1987). Biopsychosocial aspects of grief and bereavement. Washington: American Psychiatric Association.

Zisook, S., & DeVaul, R. A. (1984). Measuring acute grief. *Psychiatric Medicine, 2,* 169–176.

Zisook, S., & DeVaul, R. A. (1985). Unresolved grief. *American Journal of Psychoanalysis, 45,* 370–379.

Zisook, S., & Devaul, R. A. (1976). Grief related facsimile illness. *International Journal of Psychiatric Medicine, 7,* 329–336.

Zisook, S., & DeVaul, R. A. (1983). Grief, unresolved grief, and depression. *Psychosomatics, 24,* 247–256.

Zisook, S., & Shuchter, S. (1986). The first four years of widowhood. *Psychiatric Annals, 16,* 288–294.

Zisook, S., et al. (1987). Predictors of psychological reactions during the early stages of widowhood. *Psychiatric clinics of North America, 10,* 355–368.

Zisook, S., Shuchter, S., & Schuckit, M. (1985). Factors in the persistence of unresolved grief among psychiatric outpatients. *Psychosomatics, 26,* 497–503.

Index

NATIONAL UNIVERSITY LIBRARY
SACRAMENTO
e|

NATIONAL UNIVERSITY
9320 TECH CENTER DRIVE
SACRAMENTO, CA 95826-2558